THE BUFFALO SOLDIERS

THE BUFFALO SOLDIERS

Their Epic Story and Major Campaigns

DEBRA J. SHEFFER

PRAEGER

AN IMPRINT OF ABC-CLIO, LLC
Santa Barbara, California • Denver, Colorado • Oxford, England

Library of Congress Cataloging-in-Publication Data

Sheffer, Debra J.
  The buffalo soldiers : their epic story and major campaigns / Debra J. Sheffer.
      pages cm
  Includes bibliographical references and index.
  ISBN 978-1-4408-2982-6 (print : alk. paper) — ISBN 978-1-4408-2983-3
(e-book)   1. African American soldiers—History.   2. United States—Army—
African American troops—History.   I. Title.
  E185.63.S47 2015
  355.0089'96073—dc23   2014044495

ISBN: 978-1-4408-2982-6
EISBN: 978-1-4408-2983-3

19 18 17 16 15   1 2 3 4 5

This book is also available on the World Wide Web as an eBook.
Visit www.abc-clio.com for details.

Praeger
An Imprint of ABC-CLIO, LLC

ABC-CLIO, LLC
130 Cremona Drive, P.O. Box 1911
Santa Barbara, California 93116-1911

This book is printed on acid-free paper ∞

Manufactured in the United States of America

This book is dedicated to my mother, Vera Creek.
Thank you, Mom.

Contents

List of Illustrations

Acknowledgments

I owe thanks to many people for completion of this work. I can never repay some of them, and this work is theirs as much as mine.

Theodore Wilson at the University of Kansas, without whom this book would not exist. I am so fortunate that he was my first and most important contact at KU. He was and still is my mentor.

Taylor Sheffer, for enduring my struggles and moments of madness. She sacrificed much of her time to the project.

John Jumara, for his unfailing confidence and support—and the occasional push to keep me working.

Park University provided a research grant which supported much of the research for the project.

My fellow B-Club members, John Curatola, Kevin Benson, and Candy Ruff. Your support helped me more than you know.

Dr. Ben Post, whose expertise guided and corrected my research and whose conversations informed my perceptions.

Mike Sheets for helping me understand the categories of discharge from the army.

Fellow members of the Society for Military History graciously spoke with me about various aspects of this project and steered me to valuable sources.

Steve Catalano at Praeger Press has been very helpful to me during this process.

Lastly, I, like many, owe the Buffalo Soldiers a debt. Getting to know them has been a pleasure and an honor.

Prologue

Many very good books have the words *Buffalo Soldiers* in the title. Many focus on one regiment or on only cavalry or infantry. Others examine one time period or one war. William H. Leckie's *The Buffalo Soldiers: A Narrative of the Negro Cavalry in the West* is still essential reading for anyone interested in these men. He tells much of the story of the Ninth and Tenth Cavalry Regiments. Arlen Fowler's *The Black Infantry in the West, 1869–1891* is a must read for information about the Twenty-Fourth and Twenty-Fifth Infantry Regiments. Fowler includes chapters examining regimental chaplains and education, as well as information about Lieutenant John Bullis and the Black Seminole Scouts. In *The Black Regulars, 1866–1898*, William A. Dobak and Thomas D. Philips examine the administrative and political aspects of the all-black regiments as part of the larger story of the lives and experiences of the soldiers from their enlistment after the Civil War to the Spanish-American War. Bruce A. Glasrud and Michael N. Searles edited *Buffalo Soldiers in the West: A Black Soldiers Anthology*, which provides a useful literature review and examination of a variety of topics, including the only known female buffalo soldier, who served in the Thirty-Eighth Infantry.

Regimental histories provide valuable information. Five helpful volumes include Edward L. N. Glass's *The History of the Tenth Cavalry*, William G. Muller's *The Twenty-Fourth Infantry*, Herschel V. Cashin's *Under Fire with the Tenth U.S. Cavalry*, John Henry Nankivell's *History of the Twenty-Fifth Regiment*, and L. Albert Scipio II's *Last of the Black Regulars: A History of the Twenty-Fourth Infantry Regiment*. Works examining individual officers, such as Paul H. Carlson's *Pecos Bill: A Military Biography of William R. Shafter* and Leckie's *Unlikely*

Warriors: General Benjamin H. Grierson and His Family, contain information about the Buffalo Soldiers. Government documents and records provide a wealth of information, and many of these are now available in digital format or as reproductions. Newspaper articles and archival records contain details for a more complete story. These also are readily available in digital and print format. Few, if any, of these sources tell the whole story of the Buffalo Soldiers. In fact, no single book can tell the entire story of these men and regiments.

So, why another book about the Buffalo Soldiers when so many good ones exist? The year 2016 marks the 150th anniversary of the formation of the first six all-black regiments in the peacetime regular army, a milestone we should note. This book strives to tell the stories of all the Buffalo regiments, from their organization in 1866 through President Harry S. Truman's desegregation of the military in 1948. It endeavors to do something else that few others have, by examining the connections between those warriors known as the Buffalo Soldiers and those who served and sacrificed both before and after them. Though their service was excruciatingly isolated, the Buffalo Soldiers of the Indian War years did not serve in a vacuum. They built on the unrealized dreams of those who served before them, and they paved the way for those who followed. A larger historical context provides a more meaningful picture of the service of the Buffalo Soldiers, telling their story as part of black military service from the American Revolution to the Korean War, when desegregation ended the story of all-black units and the story of the Buffalo Soldiers.

Several themes surface in the story of these men. A major theme is their honest and faithful service. While not perfect, these men consistently served both honestly and faithfully. Like all soldiers, they broke rules and committed acts outside accepted boundaries. While the words honest and faithful service apply to many regiments, both white and black, these qualities are remarkable in the Buffalo Soldiers because of the particular problems they encountered at every turn, problems they sometimes overcame by their own efforts. Many lacked basic education as a result of years in slavery or lack of opportunity. Illiteracy made it impossible for them to fully function in their new roles as soldiers, especially as clerks and noncommissioned officers. A chaplain with each regiment provided basic education, and many of the men took advantage of the opportunity. Other difficulties were out of their control, the most persistent and most significant being racism. Throughout their decades of service, they experienced discrimination and racism from their officers, their white counterparts, the civilians they protected, the military, and governmental institutions including the office of the president. That they remained faithful and honest under such trying conditions speaks to their character.

What they most hoped for in return for honest and faithful service was equality and full citizenship. But they served without either, only hoping that their service would earn them those cherished goals that other Americans enjoyed and took for granted. They were denied and disappointed through many wars, but they did not give up. At times, they fought for freedom and equality for people in other countries, people they did not even know, when they did not enjoy those same rights at home. Racism and discrimination were indeed their toughest and most persistent foes. They were also the hurdles most out of their control.

Historians sometimes have to choose between writing for other historians and writing for everyone else. This book enjoys a different opportunity and tries to reach both groups of readers, with respect for scholarship and historiography and writing that appeals to a wide audience. The book examines some of the personal stories and struggles of these men. Chapters highlight individuals as part of the larger story, men such as Colonel Tye, a runaway slave who joined the British and led his guerrilla band, the Black Brigade, on highly dangerous and successful raids. Andre Cailloux led men from the Louisiana Native Guards in the hopeless suicidal attack at Port Hudson during the Civil War. Henry Johnson became a hero on the World War I battlefields in France. When he died years after the war, he was estranged from his family and destitute. Tye, Cailloux, and Johnson did not fight Indians. They either paved the way for or followed those who did. Their names and service are important parts of the story of the Buffalo Soldiers.

One tragic part of their story is their inability to tell most of it themselves. Many were illiterate due to decades of human bondage, and they left little in the way of personal records, such as letters and diaries. Much of what we know about them comes from white observation, problematic in itself with the specter of racism ever present. White accounts carry with them the attitudes and beliefs of their owners. Even white officers and civilians who championed their goals and fought for fair treatment held prejudices of their day, as citizens of a culture that embraced racism. Regimental returns do not usually include individual stories of the black soldiers. Service records add to the story, as do newspaper accounts and other government documents. Piecing together information from these sources helps us to understand the soldiers, their service, and their experiences, but the story remains elusive in many ways.

One of the mysteries surrounding the Buffalo Soldiers is the name itself. Historians generally agree that Indians started referring to the men as Buffalo Soldiers as early as 1870. Historians do not agree about other parts of that story; for example, historians disagree whether the name came from the Cheyenne or the Comanche. They also disagree on why Indians called them Buffalo Soldiers. William Leckie, in *The Buffalo Soldiers*, argues that Indians valued and respected the buffalo and called them buffalo soldiers out of respect for their fighting tenacity. Others claim the soldiers' hair reminded the Indians of the coat of the great buffalo. The men did not refer to themselves as Buffalo Soldiers, but they did include the Buffalo as part of their regimental identification. The name came into widespread use and is now a familiar term to most Americans. The name, like their service, extended beyond the original Buffalo regiments. Black regiments in World War I, World War II, and the Korean War identified themselves with the Buffalo Soldiers, calling themselves the buffalos or using the buffalo image as part of their identity.

The following chapters tell good stories and bad stories, in an effort to show readers more than just black Americans in uniform chasing Indians across the plains of the American Frontier. As part of their service to their country, they did indeed play an important role in the subjugation of the Indian peoples, but their story encompasses much more than that. They made significant contributions to the development of the American West, economically and physically. Their labor built the forts and outposts around which towns grew. Their labor built the roads, bridges, and communications that made it possible for Americans to settle in the West. They protected others whose labor built the railroad. Their service at forts and outposts provided the economic foundation for other Americans to build lives, businesses, and communities. Their thousands of miles of scouting provided valuable geographic and resource information about the country, which they mapped extensively. Their sacrifices saved countless lives. They protected civilians from Indians and bandits; they fought fires; and they provided rescue and relief during natural disasters. Unfortunately, at times, racism and Jim Crow laws led to poor behavior from both whites and blacks, and this book tells some of those stories as well.

From the time the first black regiments organized in 1866, they received the worst and most thankless assignments. White Americans did not want black soldiers stationed near them, so their first assignments were in isolated and rundown forts and outposts in the West and Southwest. In 1870, the Twenty-Fourth and Twenty-Fifth Infantry regiments went to Texas, where they served for many years with no relief. The Ninth and Tenth Cavalry regiments served in Texas, Arizona, Colorado, Kansas, and New Mexico during those same years. While white regiments stationed at the same locations routinely rotated east of the Mississippi River to give them a break from the isolation, the black regiments remained in the West and Southwest for the duration of the Indian Wars and beyond. A number of their white officers resigned so that they could relocate to less desolate, less harsh, and less isolated areas.

In 1898, the Buffalo regiments stationed temporarily in the East while they awaited ships to take them to Cuba to fight the Spanish, but as soon as the Spanish-American War ended, they headed back to isolation in the West. During the years following the Spanish-American War, they left the West and fought Filipino insurgents in the Philippine Insurrection and then rotated to the Philippines for occupation duty. They also chased the Mexican rebel Pancho Villa in the Punitive Expedition in 1916, but they always returned to assignments to isolated regions. As the United States prepared to enter World War I in 1918, white Americans did not want their veteran black soldiers on the battlefields in Europe, so they sent the four regiments to Hawaii, the Philippines, and the American Southwest to patrol the border with Mexico. After pressure from the black community, some black Americans did see service in Europe, but they were federalized National Guard units and draftees, not the men of the Buffalo Regiments. Most of their service overseas was as labor for the Service of Supply and Pioneer Infantry Units. Two divisions actually saw combat. Between wars, they quelled civil disturbance, protected government property during labor strikes, and protected Indians from white Americans.

After each war, the equality for which they hoped remained elusive. During the American Revolution, blacks fought on the side they believed would reward them with freedom. Both the British and the Americans promised that freedom, but neither kept the promise. During the Civil War, again, black Americans fought with freedom and equality as goals, only to be disappointed. The Thirteenth Amendment ended slavery, but equality was beyond the grasp of black America.

They sacrificed for decades in the West. They contributed to the physical and economic development of the frontier and made it safe for settlers, but they were still not safe on their own streets. They experienced increased levels of racism and inequality, all too often in the form of violence. As the United States prepared to enter World War I in 1917, white America denied some of their most experienced soldiers the chance to serve in the war. After the war, racism and violence actually increased, with the summer of 1919 known as Red Summer because of murders and lynchings of black Americans, some of them still in uniforms. On the eve of World War II, black Americans were divided about black service.

Some believed that this could be the war through which their service finally gained them equality. Others had given up hope. Still others were just angry. Black Americans fought in World War II, under the symbol of the Double V—victory in Europe and victory at home. In 1948, President Harry S. Truman desegregated the military, but the United States entered the Korean War with segregated units, and black Americans were still not safe or treated equally at home. The following chapters strive to tell the experiences and service of these Americans with balance, noting their remarkable contributions and their struggles.

Chapter 1 tells the story of black service in the American Revolution. Approximately five thousand blacks fought on the American side, and many more fought for the British. They pledged their service to the side they believed would lead to freedom, since many of them were slaves. The British and the Americans used this valuable source of manpower for their own ends, with no consideration for the people they exploited. The United States established a pattern in this war that it would follow for decades. It denied blacks the opportunity to serve except in times of critical need. As soon as the need ended, black soldiers were mustered out as quickly as possible and barred from service during peacetime. Colonial forces needed black manpower on the battlefield, and they needed to deny that manpower to the British. After the war, black soldiers were mustered out immediately. Black Americans served in the War of 1812. They also participated in the Seminole Wars, against American forces. Their goal in every conflict was equality and citizenship.

Chapter 2 is the story of black service in the American Civil War. At the beginning of the war, 3.5 million black Americans were still enslaved in the South. Approximately half a million free blacks lived in the North. As in the Revolutionary War, black Americans offered to serve but were shunned. It would be a white man's fight, until white manpower reached dangerously low levels. Once again, when white manpower became insufficient, black Americans were promised freedom in exchange for service. Most served as laborers rather than as soldiers on the battlefield. A few did see combat and fought admirably. The end of the war brought the end of slavery, but their service did not gain them the equality and full citizenship they desired.

Chapter 3 tells of a new day. For the first time, black Americans served in the peacetime army. In 1866, Congress created and organized six all-black regiments, four infantry and two cavalry. White officers commanded all six regiments. Recruitment and enlistment posed special challenges, mostly because nearly all of the recruits were illiterate as a result of their years as slaves. Each regiment had a chaplain to instruct them in basic reading and writing. Many of the recruits were not physically fit to serve. Their biggest enemies were racism and boredom. They encountered racism at every turn, from some of their officers, their white counterparts, government officials, institutions, and the civilians they served to protect. Americans in the South and those living in urban areas in the North did not want the black regiments stationed nearby, so nearly all of their assignments were to isolated posts in the West and Southwest. Army reorganization in 1869 consolidated the four infantry regiments to two. Their assignments involved labor in the form of constructing their forts and posts, building roads and bridges, and erecting telegraph lines. They guarded railroad workers and stagecoach lines. They fought Indians. They fought whites who trespassed on Indian lands. They fought Mexican bandits and rustlers who crossed into the United States to raid and then disappeared back into Mexico. They endeavored on, despite their numbers being far from adequate for the duties they performed and the vast areas they protected. This chapter also looks at regimental bands and Medal of Honor recipients.

Chapter 4 examines the Ninth Cavalry from its organization in 1866 through its service in the Indian Wars. It tells the story of Victorio and his Mimbres Apaches and the months the Ninth spent trying to capture him and return him to the "hell's forty acres" that was the San Carlos reservation. The Ninth became embroiled in the Lincoln County War between civilians fighting over government contracts to provide beef, grains, food, and other supplies to the troops at Fort Stanton and to the Indians at the Mescalero Agency in New Mexico. They protected Indians against white trespassers known as Boomers who wanted to settle on Indian lands in Indian Territory in Oklahoma. They received the difficult task of returning starving Sioux and Cheyenne to the Pine Ridge Agency during the time of the Ghost Dance and Wounded Knee Massacre in South Dakota. They guarded the U.S. mail during the Pullman Strike. After the Indian Wars, they spent their time in drill and fort maintenance.

Chapter 5 tells of the service of the Tenth Cavalry from its organization through the Spanish-American War and the Punitive Expedition. Its commander, Colonel Benjamin H. Grierson, was famous for his 1863 cavalry raid through Mississippi during the Civil War. His raid played a significant role in General Ulysses S. Grant's success at Vicksburg. Grierson was not fond of horses when he enlisted in the Civil War. A horse kicked him in the head when he was eight, leaving a scar on his face and a dislike of horses. He accepted the cavalry assignment and became one of Grant's favorite cavalry commanders. Grant handpicked him to command the Tenth. The Tenth spent time on scouts and on patrol. They fought Indians, white rustlers, and Mexican bandits. They guarded stage depots and provided escorts for stagecoaches and other travelers. They guarded railroad workers, water holes, and mountain passes. They successfully denied Victorio access to water in 1880, sending him back into Mexico for the last time.

Chapter 6 presents the Twenty-Fourth Infantry from 1869 and their service beyond desegregation in 1948. The Thirty-Eighth and Forty-First Infantry Regiments, organized in 1866, combined as the Twenty-Fourth in 1869. The Thirty-Eighth had the only known female soldier of these six regiments. Their duties as infantry included mostly labor while the cavalry spent their time scouting. The infantry, however, did participate in campaigns, as mounted infantry. The Twenty-Fourth, under the command of Lieutenant Colonel William R. Shafter, extensively scouted the forbidding Staked Plains, locating and mapping water and other resources. These expeditions taxed the men and their horses to the breaking point. Their efforts made it possible for settlers to establish ranches and other businesses in an area previously known as the "Great American Desert." Like the other regiments, they battled racism more than any other enemy. In 1917, racist treatment from whites in Jim Crow Houston, Texas, resulted in what became known as the Houston Mutiny, forever a stain on their record. The legacy of this incident haunted the Twenty-Fourth and the other black regiments as well for the rest of their existence.

Chapter 7 details the experiences of the Twenty-Fifth Infantry from 1869 until all-black regiments were a part of the past. The Thirty-Ninth and Fortieth Infantry Regiments, organized in 1866, combined to form the Twenty-Fifth in 1869. They built an impressive record of honest and faithful service. Like the other black regiments, they served in the West, the Southwest, and the Northwest throughout the Indian War years. Like all infantry, much of their service involved labor of various sorts. When the regiments moved West after the Civil War, forts and outposts abandoned at the outbreak of the war were dilapidated and required much repair just to be livable. They built roads and established communications over the vast distances between forts and posts. Adequate and healthy water supplies were always problematic, so they had to dig wells and guard water sources. The Twenty-Fifth conducted an experiment using bicycles instead of horses or trains, with the idea that bicycles might be cheaper and more reliable than horses and would enable the soldiers to reach areas inaccessible via train. The regiment also worked closely with Lieutenant John Bullis and the Seminole Negro Indian Scouts. All the regiments suffered from racial abuse, but, like the Twenty-Fourth, the Twenty-Fifth experienced an event that forever changed the lives of many of the men and unfairly marred the regiment's record. In 1906, parts of the regiment were stationed at Fort Brown near Brownsville, Texas. On August 13, violence erupted, ending in the death of a town bartender and injury to a policeman. The citizens of Brownsville blamed the soldiers, on flimsy evidence. To make matters worse, the government and ultimately President Theodore Roosevelt came to the same conclusion. Many of the soldiers never recovered from this incident.

Chapter 8 brings the four regiments back together for the stories of their service in the Spanish-American War, the Philippine Insurrection, and the Punitive Expedition into Mexico. These regiments had served so long on the frontier that the local citizens in many areas had come to accept them, and the two groups had a mostly amiable relationship. As they left their western posts and headed east to staging areas for departure for Cuba, Americans along their journey expressed their disapproval of black men in blue uniforms, insulting them, denying them food and accommodations, and even resorting to violence against them. The men were dismayed and impatient with the increased levels of racism and were glad to finally board ships for Cuba. While in Cuba, they dispelled a long-standing myth that black troops were "immune troops," immune to tropical diseases. They served well in Cuba, receiving praise from their white counterparts and officers, but as soon as they returned home, racism once again surfaced. They resumed their duties on the frontier until they were needed in the Philippines to fight rebel guerrillas. As in Cuba, they served admirably and returned to their western posts. They served with General John J. Pershing in the Punitive Expedition into Mexico to capture Pancho Villa. In all three conflicts, they served as well as or better than their white counterparts, but racism denied them the credit they deserved. Equality remained elusive.

Chapter 9 examines the ongoing struggle of black Americans during World War I, the struggle to serve. Even though the black regulars served well on the frontier, in Cuba, the Philippines, and Mexico, events after those conflicts tainted their reputation in the eyes of white Americans. In 1906, the Twenty-Fourth was embroiled in what became known as the Houston Riot or Houston Mutiny. Racism and Jim Crow were the immediate causes, and the Twenty-Fourth paid a severe penalty, but no whites were charged with crimes. In 1917, the Twenty-Fifth was the target of racial violence at Fort Brown in Texas. As with the Twenty-Fourth, three companies of the regiment paid an extreme penalty. Again, no whites were charged with crimes. On the eve of American entry into

World War I in 1918, Americans were not willing to send the black regulars to Europe. They chose instead to send them to Hawaii, the Philippines, and to forts along the border with Mexico. This would keep them busy and out of public view. Black America, however, demanded combat service in Europe. Black National Guard units and black draftees headed to France. Most performed labor with the Service of Supply and the Pioneer Infantry. The Ninety-Second and Ninety-Third Infantry Divisions, however, did see combat. Again, they hoped for equality in exchange for service. That did not happen. After the war, violence against black Americans escalated.

Black Americans served admirably in World War II and Korea. In World War II, even though they were still slated for labor assignments, they built impressive service records as part of the Tuskegee Airmen, the Red Ball Express, and the 761st Tank Battalion. In 1948, President Harry S. Truman desegregated the U.S. military with Executive Order No. 9981. When white Americans and the military establishment dragged their feet on implementing the order, the president instructed Charles Fahy to form a committee, the Fahy Committee, to assist the military branches with implementation. The U.S. entered the war in Korea with segregated troops, but by the end of the war, implementation of Order No. 9981 was widespread. Desegregation of the military brought an end to all-black units and thus an end to the Buffalo Soldiers. Black equality no longer remains as elusive as in the past, and the Buffalo Soldiers paved the way for that progress.

The year 2016 is the 150th anniversary of the 1866 creation of the first six all-black regiments, marking the first peacetime service of black Americans in the nation's history. Historians have all too often told the story of America—and the West—with insufficient attention to important groups, especially black Americans and Indians. History portrays them as victims or savages. Neither is true. Recent historians, and this volume, are correcting the story with a more inclusive examination of their important history.

A brief note about terminology is necessary. Ideal and widely agreed upon terms for certain groups of people simply do not exist. Usage also changes over time, and shifting between terms or using past politically correct terms is cumbersome. As a result, selecting terms for use in this book was difficult. The terms finally settled upon are not ideal, but they were chosen after careful and thoughtful consideration.

CHAPTER 1

Thanks, but No Thanks: Black Service in the American Revolution, the War of 1812, and the Seminole Wars

Colonel Tye was dead, from gangrenous wounds received leading a raid on September 1, 1780. Five years earlier, on November 8, 1775, John Corlies posted an advertisement offering a three-pound reward for the return of a slave named Titus. Corlies owned a prosperous farm in Colts Neck, New Jersey, and Titus, one of his slaves, was born there in 1754. Corlies claimed Titus had run away to join Lord Dunmore's Ethiopian Regiment. Corlies did not recover Titus or discover news of his whereabouts. Lord Dunmore, Virginia's governor John Murray, was the Fourth Earl of Dunmore and a loyalist in the service of the Crown as governor in the colonies, first of New York in 1770, then of larger Virginia in 1771. He was a popular governor, but his popularity steadily diminished beginning in 1773, when he dissolved the Virginia House of Burgesses because they wanted to form a Committee of Correspondence and amidst rumors that he planned to arm his own slaves and any runaway slaves he could get to fight for the Crown against rebelling colonists. His popularity plummeted after November 1775, when he formally issued what came to be known as Dunmore's Proclamation.

He issued the proclamation on November 14, 1775, calling slaves to leave their masters and fight for the British in return for freedom. Rumors of his plan had circulated for weeks, and Titus might well have run away to enlist with Dunmore. Titus surfaced in 1777, leading members of the Black Brigade, a guerrilla group fighting with the British. Their motive was personal freedom, with the added opportunity for set-tling old scores, but the British benefitted from their efforts. Their raids resulted in resources for the British and blows to patriot militia forces. Their allegiance to the British also deprived the colonists of their man-power for the war effort. Local newspapers referred to Titus as "one of Dunmore's crew."[1] His effectiveness as a guerrilla leader earned him the sobriquet of Colonel Tye.

Dunmore's Proclamation and the exploits of men such as Tye changed American policy and practice regarding black service during the war. Many states, and the Continental Army, were reluctant to arm black Americans for a variety of reasons. Some whites did not think that blacks could fight well. Some believed that arming blacks placed whites in danger. Some thought the war would be of short duration and that white forces could and should do the fighting. Most worried about what to do with black Americans, both slave and free, after the war if they sac-rificed and served. Freedom and citizenship were cherished rights many whites did not wish to offer in exchange for military service.

Dunmore's Proclamation also pushed the South and those parts of the North previously still loyal to the Crown into the patriot camp and strengthened their objections to black service. Up to the time of the Proclamation, around a third of the colonists remained loyal to the Crown. In the weeks before he issued the proclamation, word spread, and slaves ran away and headed to his home in Williamsburg. Know-ing he would have difficulty defending his home, Dunmore moved his headquarters, his family, his troops, and his supplies to a British warship, the *Fowey*, in the harbor near Yorktown, on June 8, 1775. For the next few months, Dunmore's men, white and black, conducted guerrilla-style raids onshore for supplies. Tye led some of these raids. When Dunmore needed to reestablish a land base in November, his men defeated rebel militia at Kemp's Landing on the Elizabeth River, and runaway slaves arrived in increasing numbers to join the Ethiopian Regiment. Virginia rebels reacted quickly, with increased patrols to capture runaways and harsh reminders that all slaves caught taking up arms against their own-ers would be killed, unless they surrendered by December 24. The rebels wasted no time in sending Colonel William Woodford and two hun-dred militiamen from Virginia and North Carolina against Dunmore in early December. The two forces spent days building defenses on oppo-site sides of Great Bridge, a 120-foot wooden crossing on the Elizabeth River. Loss of this conflict sent Dunmore and his troops back to vessels on the river. Supplies ran perilously low, so once again, Tye led raids ashore for food and water. During the winter weeks aboard nearly one hundred vessels, smallpox reduced the black troops from around eight hundred to approximately one hundred and fifty, with Tye among the survivors. Surviving women and children brought the number to around three hundred. Half of these survivors accompanied Dunmore on his final retreat in August 1776, but Tye and others remained to continue the fight against the rebels.

Tye's reputation as an effective leader grew, and his raids continued through 1778, 1779, and 1780. His name sent terror throughout the area, and many viewed him as unstoppable. From his years as a slave on Corlies's farm, he knew every detail of the surrounding country. His base of operations, Refugeetown at Sandy Hook, was a secluded maroon community. He could strike with no warning and escape nearly undetected. The Black Brigade garnered valuable supplies, but some raids had the goal of reprisal, targeting enemy militia officers known for ordering executions of loyalists. During the June 28, 1778 Battle of Monmouth, he captured Captain Elisha Shepard, an officer in the Monmouth County Militia. On July 15, 1779, Tye conducted a raid into Shrewsbury, in the region where he had been a slave. Tye stole eighty cattle and twenty horses for the British, but his two white captives, William Brindley and Elisha Cook, were taken in reprisal for past harsh treatment of slaves. The winter of 1779–1780 was especially cold and snowy, and supplies ran dangerously low. The British needed to both protect New York City and procure supplies. The British used the Queen's Rangers to protect the city and Tye's Black Brigade to conduct raids throughout the countryside for food and fuel.[2] In 1780, the Black Brigade was operating in Monmouth County and Bergen County, New Jersey, both hotbeds of partisan activity and areas with lots of old scores to settle. On March 30, Tye and his men captured Captain James Green and Ensign John Morris of the enemy militia. They destroyed the home of patriot raider John Russell. In April, they captured enemy patriot leader Matthias Halstead and several head of cattle for the British. June of that year marked the beginning of a series of raids, giving Tye the reputation of being invincible. On June 9, he killed Private Joseph Murray, wanted for executing loyalists. On June 12, Tye and twenty men captured Monmouth militia leaders Captain Barns Smock, Gilbert Vanmater, and a dozen other patriots, spiked their cannon, and stole their horses. Governor William Livingston declared martial law, but the raids did not diminish. Two weeks later, on June 22, Tye led members of the Black Brigade, Queen's Rangers, and Tories to Conascung, where they captured militia leader Captain James Johnson and six of his men, stole stock, and made it back to Refugeetown undetected. In August, he and his men captured militia leaders Hendrick and John Smock. Tye and the Black Brigade had captured or killed a high percentage of the Monmouth militia officer corps, destroyed enemy property and cannon, carried off valuables and livestock, struck terror into patriots, and escaped relatively unscathed.

The next raid was one Tye anticipated with relish, for he was after a man notorious for murdering captured loyalists, a man who had too long eluded capture himself, patriot militia leader Captain Josiah Huddy. Tye gathered his forces for a September 1 raid on Huddy's home in Tom's River. As Tye and men from the Black Brigade and Queen's Rangers approached Huddy's house in the late afternoon, they came under gunfire from the residence, enough to lead Tye to believe a number of patriots were inside. After two hours, Tye set fire to the house, flushing out Huddy and a female friend named Lucretia Emmons, who had quickly reloaded weapons for Huddy to make it seem he had several men in his forces. As Tye led his forces and his captive back to Refugeetown, Huddy jumped overboard and escaped. During the fight, Tye was shot in the wrist, a seemingly minor wound, but not long after the raid, lockjaw set in, and Tye was dead in a matter of days, at age twenty-six.

Woodford's patriot forces in the defeat of Dunmore at Great Bridge included a number of blacks. Not surprisingly, black Americans fought for both the British and the Americans during the war—unknown numbers for the British and approximately five thousand for the Americans. They chose the side they thought offered the best chance for their personal freedom from slavery. Until Dunmore's Proclamation, the American government maintained a policy, not strictly enforced, of exclusion of blacks from combat service, even when manpower ran dangerously low. British use of this valuable source of manpower prompted American reevaluation of their policy on federal and state levels. The American military could use the manpower, and it would deny those numbers to the British. A formal policy allowing black enlistment ratified the current practice of enlisting blacks anyway and opened the door for increased numbers of blacks in American ranks. Left unanswered was the question of what to do with these soldiers after the war, whether to grant them the promised freedom or to force them back into slavery. Indeed, some did gain their freedom; most did not, no matter which side they chose. Also unclear is what the war's outcome would have been had blacks not stepped forward to fight.

Slaves and freemen served admirably in times of military conflict from the settlement years through the colonial period, when colonists needed every available man, white and black, in the face of Indian threats.

Traditionally, blacks served only in times of danger, and then mostly as laborers, but a few served in combat roles. The slaves were paid, but the payment nearly always went to the owners. Few slaves gained their freedom through this kind of arrangement. Even most of those promised freedom found themselves re-enslaved. Colonies differed in their approach. South Carolina, in the face of a Spanish threat in Florida, passed a law in 1707 that required militia captains to "enlist, train up and bring into the field for each white, one able slave armed with a gun or lance."[3] South Carolina also armed slaves in the Yamasee War of 1715, but these were extreme circumstances. In the spring of that year, a confederation of Indians, including the Yamasee, reacted to white pressure on resources with overwhelming attacks on homes and villages. Two events prevented white defeat: the Cherokees did not join the confederacy, and South Carolina enlisted portions of its black population to join the fight. Other colonies, such as Virginia, Massachusetts, and Connecticut, passed legislation excluding blacks from service as early as 1639, when increasing numbers of blacks in their midst made colonists shy from the idea of arming them for any reason. Fear of slave uprisings drove much of this legislation. Indeed, a number of slave revolts and uprisings resulted in all the colonies passing such legislation by the end of the seventeenth century. Blacks could still serve as laborers, cooks, and musicians, but not in combat roles. They could not carry arms. Colonies might temporarily rescind or ignore the legislation in times of dire threat. For instance, blacks fought in King William's War from 1688 to 1697 and Queen Anne's War from 1702 to 1713. During Queen Anne's War, South Carolina offered freedom to any slave that killed or captured an enemy, with compensation to the slave's owner. Most of the time, however, slaves who managed this task did not gain their freedom but continued in slavery. Blacks participated in the militia during the Seven Years' War from 1756 to 1763, mostly as laborers, with few gaining freedom as a result of service. The willingness of black Americans to serve and gain their freedom through that service and the reluctance and refusal of white Americans to grant them that opportunity established a pattern of behavior that would persist for more than a century.

By the time conflict broke out between Britain and her colonists, blacks had a strong record of service. In 1775, 20 percent of the colonists were black, a potentially large source of manpower. Some southern colonies, such as South Carolina, had a black population comprising 40 percent of the total. Many Southerners pushed for blacks' complete exclusion from military service, even if they were used only for labor. White fear of revolt and uprising sustained black exclusion from training or service except in emergency. South Carolina and Georgia adhered to this policy throughout the war, even when it appeared that such a policy meant losing the war; other colonies changed or ignored policies during the war according to changing manpower needs. Initially, both freemen and slaves served in some militias. Slaves were promised freedom, and their owner received compensation for the slave's value. Some owners sent a slave as a substitute for their own service, again promising freedom in exchange for service. Though blacks had performed military service throughout the settlement and colonial years, local, state, and national policies in the early years of the Revolution excluded blacks, both free and slave, from serving.

When patriots faced the British at Boston, a black man, Crispus Attucks, gave his life against the British. At Lexington and Concorde, black Americans, free and slave, were among the patriots. Black soldiers also stood against the British at Bunker Hill and at nearly every conflict early in the war. Along with their service came petitions and expectations for their freedom. Not only were owners unwilling to grant freedom, the idea of armed or unarmed slaves in their midst was still unacceptable, even if most of that service was in noncombat roles of scouts, guides, cooks, orderlies, waiters, and laborers, for the same reasons they used in the seventeenth century. However, even this small early opportunity for service vanished, with a policy of exclusion adopted by the Continental Army as early as October 8, 1775. Soon after taking command of the Continental Army, General George Washington issued orders to bar all "Negroes" from service, although he eventually and reluctantly conceded that black soldiers already in the army could complete their enlistment. Manpower shortages were critical even then, and some recruiters turned a blind eye in order to meet enlistment quotas.

Most states in the North and especially in the South banned black enlistment from the start of the war or early into the war. Many Americans thought the war would be brief and that white soldiers would be sufficient to defeat the British. As the war continued into its third year, white enlistment fell far short of federal quotas, and states began to reconsider their ban on black soldiers. Recruiters once again turned a blind eye when enlisting. Many Americans liked the idea of sending black recruits to fill the Continental Army in order to reserve dwindling numbers of white men for local militias. Reluctance of white men to enlist by this point in the war made the idea of using black men as substitutes more attractive, and most states in the North eventually allowed black men to serve as substitutes. When states could not meet their federal enlistment quotas, they became more willing to ignore black exclusion to fill their muster roles. General Washington eventually was glad to get full muster roles from states, regardless of the color of the men. The Continental Army did use a few all-black units during the war, such as the First Black Rhode Island Regiment under Colonel Christopher Greene. "Rhode Island's legislature voted in February, 1778, that any slave volunteering for the new battalions would be declared 'absolutely free' and entitled to the wages and bounties of a regular soldier."[4] Connecticut and Massachusetts authorized black enlistment of both free and slave in significant numbers. Even Maryland, Virginia, and Delaware enlisted slaves in spite of the 1775 ban. Only Maryland in the South approved black substitutes. Virginia allowed black men to serve in noncombat roles only. Some southern states, such as Georgia and South Carolina did allow masters to hire slaves out to the military for labor, but they refused to allow any black service at all, even when manpower shortages threatened the very outcome of the war. Manpower shortages did little to change American federal policy regarding the exclusion of blacks, free or slave, from service, but the great manpower need did result in states ignoring the ban. Dunmore's Proclamation in November 1775, however, brought about a change in policy, though temporary and limited. Washington feared blacks would flock to British lines and their promises of freedom. In December 1775, Washington allowed that recruiters could enlist free blacks, if Congress approved the idea. On January 16, 1776, Congress gave partial approval and decided that only those who had served previously could reenlist. No new enlistments were allowed, and on February 21, 1776, General Orders upheld the prohibition on slave enlistments. Extreme circumstances forced the temporary change in policy, but allowing blacks to serve only in critical times became the norm of the American military for decades to come. Black Americans, however, persisted in the idea that military service could lead to freedom.

By 1776, critical need forced the Continental Army to accept any men the states sent, and by 1777, the army was revising the exclusion policy. By early 1779, Congress readied itself to enlist slaves, asking states to raise black battalions. Owners would receive one thousand dollars in compensation for each slave. Any slave successfully completing his enlistment would receive his freedom and fifty dollars. States, except for South Carolina and Georgia, began successful recruitment. The British and the Americans began to court black Americans for service in the war, both promising freedom.

Dunmore's defeat did not stop the flow of black slaves to British ranks. As many as half a million offered to fight for the British during the war, compared to approximately five thousand on the American side. Black

Americans believed their chances of gaining freedom were better with the British. In the end, neither side kept their word. Most black soldiers were returned to their owners or sold into slavery elsewhere. Some made it to British Nova Scotia in eastern Canada or joined a group relocated to Sierra Leone on Africa's west coast. Neither location proved beneficial, with prejudice and harsh conditions the rewards for their efforts. Many perished.

As soon as the war ended, black enlistment and service ended as well, regardless of their status as slaves or freemen. Their hopes for full citizenship in exchange for their sacrifice were dashed. Approximately five thousand of the three hundred thousand troops who had served on the side of the United States were black Americans. This war established the pattern and policy of black exclusion from service in peacetime and in wartime, with the exception of times when the country needed their help to win wars. Repeatedly, they eagerly stepped forward to serve. Repeatedly, they were excluded or enlisted and then discarded at war's end.

After the war, when Indians were the biggest threat to life and property, the Militia Act of 1792 authorized a military of only white men between the ages of eighteen and forty-five. The law remained in effect until 1862, but black Americans found ways to serve in the years between the Revolution and the Civil War. The Marines, which had excluded black service from its creation, continued to do so in the decades after the Revolution, indeed until 1942. The navy, which had allowed blacks in service during the Revolutionary War, initially banned blacks and mulattoes after the Revolution but soon changed their practice because white enlistment did not meet their needs. Conditions in the navy were harsh, and many whites refused that service. However, the navy still restricted blacks to 5 percent of their total manpower and to noncombat roles. When war broke out between the United States and Britain in 1812, black Americans continued to serve in the navy, and they gained increased roles and recognition. Commander Oliver Hazard Perry was initially reluctant to accept them, but soon welcomed them on board his fleet in the Great Lakes. As during the Revolution, slaves saw service as a road to freedom and offered to fight for whichever side made the best promise. As Dunmore had in 1775, Vice Admiral Sir Alexander Cochrane offered escaped slaves a chance to fight for Britain. This not only increased his manpower numbers but also diminished those of the enemy, further weakening enemy strength when the United States had to use manpower to prevent slave escape and to fight the British. The British trained two hundred of the escaped slaves as a unit of marines, who saw combat at Pungoteague, Virginia, in May 1814, and at Bladensburg, Maryland, a few months later. They were present at the burning of the Capitol and the president's house. They served so well that they became a permanent unit in British forces in North America. The fact that as many as five thousands slaves fled to British lines to accept Cochrane's offer did not, as it had during the Revolution, persuade the United States to change policy on black enlistment.[5]

The War of 1812 did not enjoy popular support, with white enlistments falling far short of the twenty thousand Congress authorized. Militia were in short supply as well, and very few officers were available for command. Those who did volunteer in large numbers were free black Americans in the North. The government fell back on its usual practice of excluding them from the army. Since the war took place mostly at sea, the navy was far more desperate for "any thing in the shape of a man" than the land forces.[6] The war on land went abysmally as a result of lack of white participation and exclusion of blacks. The British burned the capitol and captured areas in the Northeast, yet white enlistment did not increase. Though the United States continued its policy of banning black service, three states raised black regiments. In 1814, New York had two thousand black men in two regiments, and Pennsylvania raised a black regiment, but Louisiana, with its large free black population, had enlisted free blacks into the militia from the beginning of the war. Blacks had been an important part of military activity in Louisiana for decades, first during Spanish rule and then under the French. When Louisiana became part of the United States, the long-standing black militia of New Orleans offered their services to Governor William C. C. Claiborne, who accepted. His acceptance created a firestorm of protest in the white community. He did not change his mind, and much of the uproar subsided. In 1812, New Orleans authorized free, property-owning blacks in militia units under the command of white officers, though the units actually had three black officers: Second Lieutenant Isadore Honore, Major Vincent Populus, and Major Joseph Savory. General Andrew Jackson, in command of American forces along the Gulf Coast, did not have the men he needed to repulse the British at New Orleans in late 1814, but he did not call on the black state militia units. On September 21, from his headquarters of the Seventh Military District located in Mobile, he issued a proclamation to free black Americans in Louisiana, calling them to arms in defense of their country, promising to each man who volunteered the same bounty in the form of land and money that each white volunteer received: one hundred twenty-four dollars and one hundred and sixty acres. Volunteers would receive the same pay, rations, and clothing as white soldiers. By the middle of December, between four hundred and six hundred had volunteered. They were organized in two battalions, one battalion under the command of Major Pierre Lacoste, and the other under Majors Jean Baptiste Savory and Jean Daquin. With these troops as part of his force, Jackson repulsed the British attacks in December 1814, and on January 8, 1815, at the Battle of New Orleans. The black battalions served so well that Jackson paid them special praise, but, as in the past, as soon as the war was over, the black units were disbanded, and most did not receive the bounty Jackson had promised.

Broken promises became part of the routine regarding black service. In times of peace, black Americans were barred from carrying arms altogether. In times of war, they were frequently allowed only noncombat service if any service at all. Enemy armies promised freedom in exchange for service against the country that enslaved them. Black Americans stepped forward from colonial days, when they stood shoulder to shoulder with white Americans against Indians, through the Revolution and the War of 1812. Their service did not gain them freedom or full citizenship. Once crises passed, an ungrateful nation returned them to slavery. From 1834 until the Civil War, blacks were barred from enlistment in New Orleans as well as in the rest of the country.

Blacks continued to fight for their freedom, and sometimes that meant fighting against the U.S. government. In 1816, after the defeat of the British at New Orleans the previous year, the U.S. Army had many concerns besides black military service. Americans quickly expanded into the newly won lands to raise cattle and to farm. During this time, the Seminole, Miccosukee, and Creek Indians conducted raids across the border from Florida into Georgia, which alarmed Americans. In addition, American slaves ran away to join other blacks and their Indian allies living in Florida, which brought calls from Americans for the military to clear the lands for settlement, to stop Indian raids, and to stop the flow of slaves southward. Free blacks occupied a fort, soon known as Negro Fort, at Prospect Bluff in Florida. Americans were worried that their slaves would flee to Negro Fort, and indeed that seemed to be the case. The Seminole and Miccosukee Indians of the area welcomed the runaways. Along with an increase in population at the fort, word had it that they were becoming increasingly well armed. General Andrew Jackson, hero of New Orleans and commander of the Southern Military District, ordered General Edmund P. Gaines to dismantle the situation.

In order to establish a post for a base of operations, Gaines needed supplies brought up the Appalachia River from New Orleans and requested that the navy deliver them. Commodore Daniel Patterson and Gaines knew the supply boats would come under fire from the Negro Fort and planned for its destruction. Fighting commenced on April 27. A single hotshot from the gunboat, a shot that had been heated until it glowed, scored a direct hit on the fort's magazine. The entire fort exploded, and nearly all the three hundred people in the fort, including women and children, perished. Destruction of the fort did not end American interests or concerns in the area; in fact, it escalated both and led to a series of conflicts known as the Seminole Wars, in which blacks still fought for their freedom as they had in the Revolution and the War of 1812. In the three encounters of the Seminole Wars in 1817–1818, 1835–1842, and 1855–1858, they joined forces with their Indian allies against the Americans.

The First Seminole War commenced in November 1817, the result of a land and resource dispute between Neamaltha, a Miccosukee leader, and General Gaines. Neamaltha claimed the Americans at Fort Scott encroached on his lands and cut his timber. Gaines claimed that the Miccosukee lands were under American jurisdiction as part of the Treaty of Fort Jackson between the Creek Confederation and the United States. The Miccosukee had not signed that agreement. Gaines sent troops to capture Neamaltha. They did not find the Miccosukee leader, but they destroyed his village at Fowltown. The Indians retaliated with an ambush on an American force sent to escort supplies from the south, along the Appalachia River. Jackson organized a campaign to defeat the Indians and their black allies. The Spanish, with whom the United States was negotiating for possession of Florida, protested the invasion. Jackson took Fort Carlos de Barrancas from Spain in May, 1818, ending with Spain's cession of Florida to the United States under the Adams-Onis Treaty in 1819. On paper, this treaty ended the First Seminole War. In reality, much of the conflict between the Americans and the blacks and Indians in Florida continued. In the meantime, runaways swelled the Seminole ranks.

In 1823, Florida's Indians signed the Treaty of Moultrie Creek to move to reservations. The Indians had large numbers of blacks with them, adopted as slaves and family members. Though some of the runaways were adopted as slaves, the type of slavery was far different from the slavery they had fled. A number of people from the two groups had married and had children, making the American proposals of buying them from the Seminoles or of the Seminoles simply leaving them behind unthinkable. Reservation lands also incorporated many black settlements, providing a safe haven for runaway slaves and a continued source of contention between the Indian tribes and the Americans. Trouble did not end there. Promised annuities of money and food were slow in arriving, if they arrived at all. Americans viewed the long-standing trade relationship between the Indians and Spanish fisherman with suspicion and made concerted efforts to halt that trade, further reducing food supplies. The people on the reservation were on starvation rations, with an alarming number already starved to death, and they raided nearby farms and settlements for food. Whites trespassed onto the reservation to steal, to sell whiskey, and to commit other crimes. Raids increased; the numbers of runaways joining blacks allied with the Indians increased, and so did white calls for military intervention. Americans feared for their lives and their property, especially cattle and slaves. They insisted the military return their slaves to them.

By 1832, the United States government continued with plans to remove the Indians west as part of the Indian Removal Act of 1830. The Treaty of Fort Gibson outlined parts of the agreement for the move. Most of the Seminoles did not agree with the treaty. The nearly five hundred blacks living with the Seminoles posed another major problem. The Americans, however, were determined to force the Seminoles and the blacks with them to make the move. By 1835, the Americans started issuing threats and arresting those who did not comply. By late December 1835, violence escalated to critical levels, and troops were sent to defeat the Indians and blacks and forcibly move them west, thus beginning the Second Seminole War.

In the first skirmish of the Second Seminole War in December, Major Francis Dade lost more than one hundred men to the enemy. Reports of massacre created widespread civilian panic southward toward the Keys. More runaway slaves joined the raiders from plantations throughout the area. Local militia became ineffective as their resolve diminished with each burnt plantation, leaving the regular army and the navy, already undermanned, to face a growing enemy force. American civilians and military personnel were more determined than ever to remove the Seminoles and blacks from Florida. Defeats continued to mount for the Americans, who used ineffective tactics against an enemy expert in guerrilla warfare and who knew the area well. The Americans had to rely on supplies from outside the area, while their enemy enjoyed local supplies and the support of local black communities. The blacks and Indians enjoyed a higher tolerance against the tropical climate because they had lived there for years. American soldiers new to the area suffered severely from the heat and humidity and from dengue fever, bilious fever, and yellow fever. The war dragged on through 1836, 1837, and 1838, with the blacks and Seminoles retaining control of much of Florida. American commanders encountered such high numbers of black enemy that they called it the Negro War instead of the Seminole War. Even resorting to launching attacks on enemy representatives under the protection of the white flag and using bloodhounds to track the enemy in the swamps, commander after commander failed to bring the war to a close through 1839 and 1840. With tensions mounting in Texas, increased Indian conflict in the West, and the war in Florida draining the government of already-scarce resources and funds, the Americans were getting desperate for an end to the war. One of the major disagreements between the Americans and the Seminoles remained the fate of the Seminole Negroes, as they were increasingly called. In an effort to end the war, in 1841, Secretary of War Joel R. Poinsett declared that all Seminole Negroes living with the Indians before the Treaty of Payne's Landing in 1832 would move with the Indians. This idea was unacceptable to the Indians because the agreement would require them to leave behind the Seminole Negroes they considered important to their group. Finally, in May 1841, a commander took the field with a new plan. Colonel William J. Worth implemented tactics to deprive the Seminoles of their planting season and to locate and destroy villages in areas Americans had not yet ventured, depriving them of food stores and sanctuaries. His plan was so effective that the war ended by August 1842. Many of the defeated enemy were rounded up and sent to Indian Territory. Some managed to elude capture and remain in Florida. Americans awaited assurances that all the defeated Indians and blacks would be captured and sent west.

Worth also persuaded Congress to implement a colonization plan to permanently deny Florida to the Seminoles and the Seminole Negroes. The Armed Occupation Act offered free land for those who settled, made land improvements, and stayed for five years. By 1843, isolated incidents of violence occurred, with scattered Seminole and Seminole Negro raids on settlers. By 1849, the incidence of violence expanded. Americans renewed their demands that Seminole Indians, Miccosukee Indians, and Seminole Negroes remaining on reservations in Florida be sent west. These demands led to renewed hostilities in the Third Seminole War.

Pressure from white encroachment and military presence erupted into violence in December 1855, with a Seminole attack on soldiers under Lieutenant George Hartsuff. The Seminoles, Miccosukees, and Seminole Negroes were backed into a corner and tried to simply stay out of the whites' way, but, when forced, they came out fighting in a war they could not win. For three years, both sides conducted inconclusive and costly raids. Once the Indians and blacks realized they had no sanctuary, they surrendered, and by May 1858, they were on their way west.

Beginning in 1849, a number of Seminole blacks fled from Indian Territory across the border into Mexico, in Coahuila. The boundary between Mexico and the United States was the difference between slavery and freedom. After the Civil War, American military commanders believed the Seminole blacks could help in the subjugation of the Indians of the South and Southwest, by serving as guides and scouts to the military. They approached the Seminole blacks to persuade them to return to Texas. The two groups negotiated for land and provisions for the men and their families. Initially, twenty of the men served as scouts at Fort Duncan in Texas. On August 16, 1870, the Seminole Negro Indian Scouts were mustered into service. More of their service is covered in chapter seven.

Though the United States denied black Americans meaningful military opportunity, they still sought freedom through service, even if it meant fighting against the United States. Such an opportunity arose with the Seminole Wars, especially the seven-year Second Seminole War from December 1835 through August 1842. According to historian Kenneth W. Porter, the Second Seminole War was the deadliest of all U.S. conflicts with Indians, "with more than 1,500 regular soldiers and sailors lost. In contrast, from 1866 to 1891, when the many tribes in the West were conquered, total U.S. Army losses were less than two thousand."[7] Unlike the Indian Wars in the West, blacks fought with the Seminoles against the United States. Decades of marriages between the two groups had created second- and third-generation Black Seminoles. As in past wars, they fought for their freedom. If they lost this war, they would undoubtedly be forced into the slavery their ancestors had endured. In the seven years of the war, the United States was unsuccessful at defeating this enemy. The Seminole Wars are important to the history of the Buffalo Soldiers for two reasons. The Seminole Wars involved more than Indians fighting the United States. Black Americans, runaway slaves, and the Seminole Negroes comprised a large part of the fight and fought for freedom from slavery and the opportunity to live in Florida as free men. The Seminole Negroes who fled to Mexico returned to Texas and enlisted as scouts with the Buffalo Soldier regiments in the 1870s.

In all of these wars—the American Revolution, the War of 1812, and the Seminole Wars—blacks participated enthusiastically and with great sacrifice. With each war, they chose the most likely path to freedom. With each war, they were disappointed. When Americans took up arms in 1861, black Americans once again hoped for freedom and once again offered to fight.

CHAPTER 2

The Civil War and Postwar Occupation: "Gentlemen, the Question Is Settled; Negroes Will Fight"[1]

His ring was the only clue to his identity. Andre Cailloux's body had lain on the field of battle for forty-one days. He was born a slave in 1825 but gained his freedom, married, became a cigar maker, and acquired property.[2] In April 1861, the Louisiana Native Guards, comprised of free men, offered to raise a regiment for their state. Governor Thomas D. Moore authorized the regiment in May. Louisiana reorganized its militia in January 1862 and disbanded the Native Guards in February. Moore reinstated them in March. The regiment had one thousand men in thirteen companies by early 1862. Cailloux was elected first lieutenant of Company C. In the face of repeated requests from the regiment's officers, the Confederate government failed to provide the barest of supplies. By January 1862, they still awaited uniforms and arms. As the Union Army and Navy arrived to take New Orleans in May 1862, the Native Guards had no arms with which to meet the enemy. They received word on August 22, 1862, that General Benjamin F. Butler, Union commander of the Department of the Gulf after the capture of New Orleans, issued General Order No. 63, inviting Louisiana's free black militiamen to leave the service of the Confederate government and serve in the Union Army, in the Free Colored Brigade. Butler promised a hundred dollars bounty, 160 acres of land, the same pay as white soldiers at thirteen dollars a month, and food for the men's families. In addition to feeling that the Confederate government had betrayed them, many saw the opportunity to fight for the Union as a way to free family members still enslaved and to win full citizenship. As in the past, black Americans fought for the side they believed would lead to freedom. Southern blacks were fighting more for their homes and families than they were for the Confederacy and its cause. More than two thousand men hurried to enlist with Butler. Most of these were *contrabands*, General Benjamin Butler's term for slaves who escaped to Union lines, but a number, such as Cailloux, were Native Guards. The First Louisiana Native Guards mustered into the Confederacy in 1861, but poor treatment as part of the Confederacy soon led them to accept enlistment into Union forces as the Native Guards.

By September, the Native Guards had officially joined the Union effort. The First Regiment Louisiana Native Guards mustered into the Union Army on September 27, the Second on October 12, and the Third on November 24. Cailloux became Captain of First Regiment's Company E. They were the first black regiments mustered in to fight for the North. All three regiments had black officers. The Second Native Guards saw little combat action, with only one battle victory on their record. They mostly drew guard duty and fatigue duty for various labor tasks, from digging ditches to cleaning their posts. The First and Third also received more than their share of fatigue duty, but they experienced combat as well, joining Union troops in May 1862 in another of General Nathaniel P. Banks's failed efforts, this time against the strong Confederate garrison at Port Hudson, Louisiana, on the Mississippi River. The Union wanted to clear the Mississippi River of all Confederate forces and literally split the Confederacy in half. Union forces had taken Memphis and New Orleans in 1862. They needed to take Vicksburg and Port Hudson to gain control of the Mississippi. Lieutenant General Ulysses S. Grant was assigned to take Vicksburg at about the same time that Banks was to take Port Hudson.

Months passed after initial enlistment of the Louisiana Native Guard into Union forces, and the Union failed to keep its promises to the men. Their families were not receiving food, and the men had yet to be paid. Since they were fighting for the Union, many of their families suffered from anti-Union hostility. Some of them were evicted from their homes for not paying their rent. The men carried a heavy burden of concern for the welfare of their loved ones, but they remained steadfast in their service. Commander of the First Regiment, Colonel Spencer H. Stafford, sent repeated pleas for the government to pay the men and feed their families. His requests fell on deaf, or more likely racist, ears. For the first months, all three regiments drew fatigue duty. They finally received their first pay in March 1863. The officers, such as Cailloux, did receive the same pay as white officers, but the enlisted did not receive the thirteen dollars paid to white troops. Since black troops were originally slated for labor only, their pay had initially been set at ten dollars a month, minus a fee for clothing. When these soldiers transitioned to combat roles, the change in policy to reflect appropriate pay took more than two years. Though disappointed, the men were happy to have any pay to send home to help their beleaguered families.[3]

During these first few trying months, conflict did exist between the Native Guards and local civilians and policemen at their various stations. Locals accused them of theft and rape, though no rape was proven. In December 1862, Captain Emile Detiege shot a new recruit, Charles Joseph DeGruy, for disobedience. Detiege was charged with murder. One persistent disagreement focused on streetcar segregation in New Orleans. Native Guards, including officers, often had to wait for streetcar service until a car designated for black riders was available, even if white cars had plenty of room. Several isolated incidents occurred, some involving Native Guard troops, and most Native Guards continued to complete their assignments, awaiting better treatment, pay, food for their families, and combat duty, even though New Orleans consistently refused to change the rules to better accommodate the soldiers. These days were difficult for the men and officers, who had to worry about family at home and endure racist treatment from local civilians, the enemy, and their own officers.

Banks had replaced Butler as commander of the Department of the Gulf in December 1862. Banks entered military service purely as a stepping-stone to political advancement, perhaps all the way to the White House. Since many Northerners still opposed arming black men, Banks knew that commanding black soldiers and commissioning black officers would hurt him politically, and he set out to purge the Native Guard regiments of their black officers. He decided to reorganize them as his own Corps d'Afrique, under white officers. He tricked the officers of the Third into resigning and intimidated the officers of the Second into following suit. Perhaps only the white officers of the First, Stafford and Lieutenant Colonel Chauncey J. Bassett, stopped Banks from similar action with the First. Banks reorganized the First, Second, and Third Native Guards into the First, Second, and Third Corps d'Afrique. The 1,080 men of the newly organized First and Third were scattered at various posts along the Mississippi when they received orders to head to Port Hudson. Cailloux's regiment left Baton Rouge on May 20, without

Stafford, whose mounting frustration with the racism shown his men had resulted in his arrest on May 16. He had cursed a subordinate for mistreatment of his men. Stafford's absence left his men without capable leadership and vulnerable to abusive officers.

Banks commanded a force of about thirty thousand. Unfortunately, he was not the only incompetent officer in command for the Union attack on heavily fortified Port Hudson. Many of the Native Guard companies, including that of Cailloux, were under the command of Brigadier General William Dwight, an inept and lazy alcoholic. He was drunk well before the battle started at ten o'clock in the morning. Like Banks, Dwight did not think that blacks should be on the battlefield, which may have contributed to his lack of preparation, though drinking was probably the biggest factor. He had failed to scout the terrain, so he did not realize, or perhaps did not care, that access to Port Hudson was very nearly impossible. He informed his officers that their troops would have an easy time of it.

It proved to be some of the most difficult terrain of any battle of the war. The town was located at the top of steep cliffs, below which grew woods thick with underbrush and broken by marshes, creeks, and ravines. Since Banks failed to coordinate his forces and provided no covering fire for their approach, they had to cross the difficult terrain and scale the cliffs under heavy fire. The defenders held every advantage. Their guns covered all approaches. They had constructed abates and rifle pits, and they enjoyed the protection of a moat. The combination of poor officers, well-prepared defenses, and impossible approaches spelled doom for the Union. As they advanced, they immediately fell under withering fire, but Cailloux kept encouraging his men onward. Witnesses claim Cailloux and his men made anywhere from three to six charges, until Cailloux fell dead from multiple wounds. Dwight, still drunk and well back from the battlefield, ordered them to charge again. Their battle lasted from midmorning until nightfall. In a truce the next day, the Union sent details to recover the dead and rescue the wounded, but they rescued only white wounded and recovered only the bodies of white soldiers; they did not recover the black dead and left the black wounded to die where they fell. Banks knew the black dead and wounded were abandoned, and did nothing. After the white dead and wounded of the Union were recovered, he claimed he had no more dead or wounded on the field.

On June 14, Banks sent another assault force, which failed. On June 15, he asked for volunteers for yet another assault. Too few men volunteered, so he changed his mind and settled in for a siege, gaining

Confederate surrender just days after Confederate Lieutenant General John S. Pemberton surrendered to Grant at Vicksburg on July 4. After the surrender, the bodies of Cailloux and other Native Guards, which had been neglected and left in the sun and heat for over a month, were carefully collected. Thousands, including white civilians, soldiers, and the all-white band of the Forty-Second Massachusetts, who played a funeral dirge for Cailloux through the streets of Crescent City, turned out on July 29 for his funeral. But Banks inflicted one final insult upon the black regiments at Port Hudson. His officials did not include the First Regiment on the list of participating regiments, denying them the right to inscribe the battle on their regimental flag.

During the Civil War years, many Southerners still believed slaves, who were the only black Americans they recognized, should never be armed for war, even under desperate circumstances. Banks was not the only Northerner who believed blacks should not carry arms and who tried to ensure their failure. Many incidents occurred demonstrating Northern resentment and mistreatment of black soldiers, from commanders, white soldiers, and Congress. A congressional investigation after the Crater disaster at Petersburg in 1864, for example, found that racism on the part of commanding General George G. Meade resulted in the slaughter of hundreds of black troops and the failure of a plan that could have ended the war earlier.

Numerous white officers and soldiers refused to serve with black soldiers and refused to fight to free slaves. They had enlisted to save the Union, not to end slavery. After Lincoln issued the final Emancipation Proclamation on January 1, 1863, a number of white officers resigned and white soldiers deserted; some actually joined the Confederacy. Perhaps the worst offenses were committed by Congress, who enlisted black soldiers with certain promises and then abandoned their obligations. Congress failed these men regarding pay, protection, and duty assignments. Black soldiers received ten dollars a month, three dollars less than white soldiers, with clothing allotment deducted from that lower pay. They often went many months without receiving pay. When Robert Gould Shaw, commander of the all-black Fifty-Fourth Massachusetts Infantry, Stafford, and others protested and called for equal pay, the administration used the Militia Act of 1862 and the June 1863 General Orders, No. 163, to insist that black soldiers would be paid as laborers rather than combat soldiers.[4] Many perceived that Northern white soldiers would object to equal pay, because it would place black soldiers on the same level as white soldiers. The Fifty-Fourth and Fifty-Fifth Massachusetts Infantry Regiments refused to accept payment until Congress saw fit to pay them the same as whites. In addition to equal pay in the future, they insisted on back pay for the many months they had already served. Lincoln and Congress continued to drag their feet on this matter, until June 1864, when they passed a bill for equal pay, retroactive to January 1864, although the measure would apply only to those who could prove they were free from April 19, 1861. Many black soldiers could not prove they had been free on that date, and many had entered service in 1862. Not until March 3, 1865, was the issue corrected for all, with the Enrollment Act, which provided for equal pay and full back pay from the time of enlistment.

Not only did blacks have to fight for combat pay, they had to fight for combat duty. Northerners planned to use black soldiers for fatigue duty because of the widespread belief that black soldiers would not perform well in combat. Some believed that blacks feared weapons, that they would run in the face of the enemy, and that they would show no aggression on the battlefield. Back regiments often entered battle only as shock troops or in hopeless situations, such as at Port Hudson and Fort Wagner, contexts that threatened to confirm white perceptions. They took what they could get and grimly endeavored to make the best of it. Their conduct provided proof after proof of the absurdity of these beliefs. Black soldiers deserted less, reenlisted more, volunteered for suicide missions, and repeatedly proved themselves in battle.

Along with pay, protection, and duty assignments, ongoing debate focused on officer appointments for these regiments. Most of the time, white officers received preference, but some black men did enjoy the opportunity to serve as officers. The Louisiana Native Guards initially kept their black officers when Butler enlisted them into the Union Army. Three officers in the Fifty-Fourth Massachusetts Regiment and three officers in the Fifty-Fifth Massachusetts Regiment were black. In May 1863, the War Department's General Orders No. 144 created guidelines for officer examining boards for black officers. Overall, most commanders and government officials preferred white officers, and most officers were white. This set the precedent for assigning white officers to all-black units during the Civil War and in future wars until 1948, when President Truman passed Executive Order 9981, finally desegregating the military. The policy of white officers also set the precedent for the process of officer selection from the Civil War onward. Though they wrongly believed black soldiers needed white officers to serve well, many Northerners and Southerners eventually, if grudgingly, recognized the bravery, sacrifice, and fighting abilities of black troops, even when the odds were stacked against them. Others remained unconvinced no matter what.

When the Civil War erupted in 1861, blacks were among the first to volunteer to serve. Most white Americans believed the war would be brief and that white troops would be more than enough to win it. On April 15, 1861, President Lincoln authorized only seventy-five thousand volunteers for ninety days. The Militia Act of 1795 restricted Lincoln to those numbers, but many believed that those troops, combined with the sixteen thousand troops already in the regular army, would provide sufficient manpower and time to defeat the states in rebellion, even minus the men who left the regular army to fight for the Confederacy. Thousands more whites volunteered and had to return home. It soon became evident, however, that seventy-five thousand was far short of the manpower the war would require. In May and again in July, Lincoln made calls for volunteers. By March 1863, he issued the Conscription Act to provide additional manpower to continue the war. Even under those conditions, whites in the Union were still adamantly against arming blacks, for a variety of reasons. White protests against the Conscription Act in 1863 resulted in riots, the most famous being the New York City Draft Riot in July, which targeted blacks and abolitionists. Rioters burned down the Colored Orphan Asylum, killed over one hundred black Americans, and wounded one hundred more. Ohio Congressman Chilton A. White made clear, "This is a government of white men, made by white men for white men, to be administered, protected, defended, and maintained by white men."[5] Allowing blacks to fight for their country might mean an obligation to grant them freedom and full citizenship, might prove that blacks could fight as well as whites, or might result in black violence against whites. Freedom and full citizenship in exchange for military service was exactly what black Americans wanted. Numerous offers from black regiments, some fully formed and equipped, presented themselves to the Union War Department. Men such as former slave and abolitionist Frederick Douglass persistently called for acceptance of the sable arm in the war effort. All the offers and all the demands initially fell on deaf ears. Echoing the American Revolution, history repeated itself as both the North and the South excluded blacks from the beginning of the war. As the war stretched on, however, conditions forced changes in attitudes and practices for the North and the South. These changes began in the North before they did in the South, but by the final year of the war both sides had black men or planned to have black men on the battlefield.

As they had in nearly every past war, black Americans from all parts of the country once again awaited the opportunity that would get them closer to freedom and full citizenship. Their service was initially limited to labor, but both sides finally realized that white Americans could not win this war alone. In desperation, both sides called black Americans to step forward in armed sacrifice as they had in past wars. Most of the combat service was in the Union Army and Navy, with black soldiers fighting in many battles, small and large. Unlike white Americans, they faced additional dangers, such as Northern racism, and Confederate retaliation and violence in the form of no quarter under the Black Flag, the practice of killing a targeted group of people whether in battle or after that battle as prisoners. Even with the additional hurdles, their record is outstanding. Yet at war's end, while they were no longer slaves, they were not full citizens, either, and so the struggle for equal rights continued for decades after the war.

The North initially excluded all blacks, based in part on the 1792 and 1795 Federal Militia Acts. Union Secretary of War Simon Cameron stated in April 1861, in response to offers from blacks to raise regiments for service in the war, "This Department has no intention at present to call into the service of the Government any colored soldiers."[6] Volunteers were rejected, and militia groups received orders to disband. By the summer of 1862, however, arming blacks against the Confederacy was beginning to be more than just a matter of debate. Perhaps the first use of blacks occurred in May 1861, when Union General Benjamin Butler employed runaway slaves, whom he called "contrabands," as laborers in his camp at Fortress Monroe, Virginia. On August 6, Congress passed the First Confiscation Act, which provided a legal basis for actions similar to Butler's. In October, Assistant Adjutant General William D. Whipple authorized extensive use of contrabands for labor, in return for wages of eight or nine dollars a month for men and four dollars a month for women. As in the South, Northerners gave pause at the idea of arming blacks, and the Army was far more reluctant than the Navy, mostly because the Army could afford to be more exclusive. Naval duty was harsh and austere, and many whites simply refused such service, leading to manpower shortages earlier for the Navy. By late 1861, Union Secretary of the Navy Gideon Welles authorized black naval enlistment with a salary of ten dollars a month, but only as servants and laborers. Nearly thirty thousand served in the Navy during the war, approximately 25 percent of the total wartime enlistments.

Union Army commanders disagreed on the use of the sable arm. In the field, some commanders were following Butler's lead in using contrabands for labor, but others refused to allow fugitives within the confines of their camps, and Major General Henry W. Halleck even went so far as to issue General Orders No. 3 in November, stipulating that commanders should not follow the Butler policy and should remove any fugitives already present within their camps.[7] This order created a firestorm of debate and demonstrated how controversial Northerners still viewed black service. Union commanders in Kansas, South Carolina, and Louisiana, however, early on realized the value of using black Americans to fight. Kansas Senator and Brigadier General James H. Lane enlisted blacks to fight in "Bleeding Kansas" as early as October 1861. Congress decided to take advantage of this valuable resource in July 1862, passing the Militia Act of 1862 and the Second Confiscation Act of 1862, legally authorizing black enlistment. Lane accelerated his efforts, appointing Captain Henry C. Seaman and Captain James H. Williams to recruit and enlist as many men as they could. The First Kansas Colored Volunteers soon saw action on October 28, 1862, against Missouri State Militia at Island Mound near Butler, Missouri. Their victory was the first victory for black troops in the war. It also occasioned the start of rumors that Confederates were murdering black prisoners under the "black flag" of no quarter.

After President Lincoln issued the Emancipation Proclamation in January 1863, the First Kansas became the First Kansas Regiment, Colored Volunteers, later the Seventy-Ninth United States Colored Troops (USCT), and the fourth black regiment mustered into the Union army. In May they fought at Sherwood, Missouri, and in Jasper County, Missouri, near Baxter Springs. In June, they headed to Fort Gibson in Indian Territory, where they fought at Cabin Creek on July 1 and 2. They fought in the Battle of Honey Springs, also called the Battle of Elk Creek, on July 17, against the confident and successful Twenty-Ninth and Thirty-Ninth Texas Regiments. Their commander, Colonel James M. Williams, was badly wounded during the battle, but their victory over the Texans convinced many Americans of the fighting abilities of black soldiers. In 1864, they fought with General Frederick Steele in the Camden Campaign and at the Battle of Poison Springs, Arkansas, where they suffered a defeat. Rumors circulated after all these battles that Confederates had murdered black Union captives. The regiment was mustered out of Federal service on October 1, 1865.

Even with Simon Cameron's refusal to authorize private recruitment of blacks and with the Lincoln administration's policy against arming blacks, Cameron was not personally against the idea of black service. On October 14, 1861, the War Department issued orders that authorized Brigadier General Thomas W. Sherman to use "fugitives from labor" in the Union endeavor in enemy territory in South Carolina in "such services as they may be fitted for ... in squads, companies, or otherwise."[8] Sherman was the commander of the Port Royal Expedition in November in South Carolina, with the goal of establishing a beachhead on Hilton Head Island to blockade Confederate shipping. Sherman did use "fugitives from labor" in carrying out his orders, but he used them for plantation labor, not military service. Though they received pay for their labor and a large group of teachers and clergy arrived to teach the fugitives to read, their lives seemed much the same as before Union arrival. Cameron's order to Sherman and subsequent admissions of support for arming blacks in opposition to official administration policy stirred controversy and led in January 1862 to Lincoln appointing Cameron as minister to Russia, replacing him on January 15 with Edwin M. Stanton; however, the possibility of black military service seemed a step closer to reality. Though Sherman did not see sufficient reason to arm blacks, his replacement in the Department of the South, Major General David Hunter, did. Hunter's military objective remained the same as Sherman's, but Hunter was far short of the military manpower necessary to accomplish that objective. Almost immediately after his arrival, he requested permission to recruit, equip, train, and use blacks as soldiers. He did not wait for permission. On April 25, 1862, he declared martial law in South Carolina, Georgia, and Florida, and on May 9, he declared all slaves free and made plans to organize the First South Carolina Colored Regiment. His intentions were good, but his efforts at organizing the regiment involved forced impressment that terrified the potential soldiers, who did not understand what was happening. Months earlier, when Major General John Charles Fremont, on August 30, 1861, proclaimed martial law in Missouri, stating, "The property, real and personal, of all persons in the State of Missouri who shall take up arms against the United States, or who shall be directly proven to have taken an active part with their enemies in the field, is declared to be confiscated to the public use, and their slaves, if any they have, are hereby declared freemen,"[9] Lincoln immediately requested he rescind the order. When he refused, Lincoln dismissed him. At the time of Hunter's declaration, Lincoln awaited answer from the Border States in response to his proposed gradual compensated emancipation. Hunter's action placed the vital Border State decision in jeopardy. Lincoln was not happy. Hunter had acted without consulting or informing his commander in chief. Lincoln would have advised Hunter against the move. As it was, Lincoln declared Hunter's action unauthorized and void.

Brigadier General Rufus Saxton, under orders from the War Department, picked up where Hunter left off in April, creating the First South Carolina Volunteer Regiment. On August 1862, three days after Butler's General Orders No. 63 in Louisiana, Stanton ordered Saxton to "arm, uniform, equip, and receive into the service of the United States such numbers of volunteers of African descent as you may deem expedient, not exceeding 5,000."[10] Though the orders included provision for equal pay and rations, combat pay was not a reality for two more years. Regardless, contrabands arrived in large numbers, even though the memory of Hunter's poor treatment of the black soldiers was fresh. Northern whites still doubted the abilities and loyalties of black soldiers. Then, an event transpired that persuaded all to reconsider. The shift in policy of the Lincoln administration became more evident when Lincoln issued the Preliminary Emancipation Proclamation on September 22, 1862. Both whites who previously doubted the abilities and loyalties of black soldiers and those black soldiers who had received poor treatment as a result of Hunter's actions took note. So did Saxton, who decided to send his men into the field to see how they would perform.

Beginning on November 3, Lieutenant Colonel Oliver T. Beard of the Forty-Eighth New York Infantry took Company A under Captain Trowbridge on an extended and highly successful raid along the coasts of Georgia and Florida. In one week, they killed enemy soldiers, captured prisoners, destroyed large amounts of property, and confiscated more than one hundred slaves. The rescued slaves often immediately volunteered to join the fight. The raid proved the fighting abilities of black soldiers and encouraged others to volunteer.[11] On November 24, Colonel Thomas Wentworth Higginson arrived as the new commander of the First South Carolina. On January 1, 1863, Higginson and his regiment celebrated the implementation of the final Emancipation Proclamation; they also received their regimental colors. Higginson's first expedition with his new command came later that month, when they headed into Georgia and Florida, on the Saint Mary's Expedition to recruit slaves and gather supplies, such as wood and iron. Based on intelligence from Corporal Robert Sutton, who knew the region along the St. Mary River between Georgia and Florida from his days in slavery, much-needed wood was available in plentiful quantity. The mission was for 460 men to take three steamboats up the river and garner the wood and other building supplies. Though they encountered resistance from sharpshooters and cavalry, the mission was highly successful. They did not expect battle, but they met and defeated the enemy at the Battle of the Hundred Pines. On January 31, while they were still in the field, they became the fifth black regiment mustered into Federal service. In March, Higginson's men successfully took and held Jacksonville, Florida, until ordered to abandon the town and return to Camp Saxton. Their wartime service consisted mostly of important raids into the South for recruiting and supplies. They were mustered out of Federal service on January 31, 1866.

Perhaps the best-known demonstration of black fighting determination and ability came from the Fifty-Fourth Massachusetts Infantry on July 18, 1863, with their brave assault on heavy Confederate fortifications (called Fort Wagner by the Union and Battery Wagner by the Confederates) at Charleston, South Carolina. Several Union assaults had failed. After a miserable trip to nearby Morris Island in the rain and with no food for two days, commander of the Fifty-Fourth, Colonel Robert Gould Shaw, accepted the honor to lead his men in yet another assault on July 18. At twilight, they started the attack over nearly a mile of open, sandy ground, sometimes wading through water knee deep, under withering fire from Confederate gun batteries. The forlorn-hope attack ended with Shaw, three officers, and 135 men dead, with eleven officers wounded, and one hundred men missing. The Confederates buried Shaw at the bottom of a pit under his men, an attempt to insult and humiliate him. His family decided to leave him at rest with the men he led.

Because the men of the Fifty-Fourth and their commander attracted war correspondents to the battle at Fort Wagner, the Confederates refrained from their routine postbattle murders. Initially, Confederates forces had taken around one hundred black prisoners, but they did not kill them. They considered the possibility of Northern retaliation, which was never a real threat, the condemnation of Europeans, from whom they still hoped for help, and the effects at unfavorable press would have on their reputations of chivalry and gallantry. On July 31, 1863, Lincoln issued General Orders No. 252, proclaiming Northern retaliation for Confederate mistreatment of black Union soldiers and their commanders, but the South had little to fear. Northerners did not follow through on the order. The Lincoln administration believed retaliation would only incite the enemy to mistreat all Union soldiers, not just black soldiers. Also, retaliation was not politically attractive. After Fort Wagner, however, avoid attention from the press, the black prisoners who survived their battle wounds were sent to a prisoner of war camp in Florida, South Carolina, with conditions so deplorable that most died of starvation, disease, or murder within three months.

By the end of July 1863, more than thirty all-black Union regiments had been formed, including the First Louisiana Engineers, the Second South Carolina, the Fourteenth Rhode Island Heavy Artillery, and the Fifty-Fourth Massachusetts. Some of these thirty regiments, and many more yet to be formed, owed a debt of thanks to orders given earlier that year by Union Secretary of War Edwin Stanton to Adjutant General

Lorenzo Thomas. Stanton was pleased that Rufus Saxton had successfully raised black regiments by the spring of 1863, but he was not pleased that Saxton had raised only five regiments. Stanton wanted more in a hurry.

Because of Thomas's success in the Mississippi Valley, the Lincoln administration created the Bureau of Colored Troops in May 1863, to consolidate and centralize recruiting efforts and muster regiments directly into Federal service instead of state service. The First United States Colored Troops (USCT) regiment mustered into service on June 30, 1863. The First Kansas Colored Volunteers became the Seventy-Ninth USCT; the First South Carolina Volunteers became the Thirty-Third USCT; the First Arkansas became the Forty-Sixth USCT; and the First, Second, and Third Louisiana Native Guards became the Seventy-Third, Seventy-Fourth, and Seventy-Fifth USCT. The creation of the Bureau of Colored Troops was a major milestone in the history of black American military service. Black Americans believed they finally had a real chance to fight for freedom and equality. By the end of the war, approximately 180,000 black soldiers served in 144 regiments, and 38,000 of those soldiers gave the last full measure, some after the war ended. The North made early and rather extensive use of a valuable human resource, but they treated them neither fairly nor well. The North's most grievous failure to these men was not protecting them from the black flag practices of the Confederates.

The South was short of manpower from the start of the war. In 1860, the North had approximately 20 million people. The South had approximately 11.5, with 3.5 million of that population in slavery. Out of necessity, the South used slaves as laborers in the war effort to build fortifications and perform tasks that would free whites for fighting. Owners rented their slaves to the Confederacy or sent them to serve, as laborers only, in their owners' place. All understood, however, that these slaves would be under close guard to prevent escape and that they would be denied access to weapons. The free black men of the Louisiana Native Guards, who volunteered to serve the South as early as May 1861, were allowed to organize but denied the right to carry weapons, even as New Orleans fell to the Union in May 1862. Southern cries to employ black soldiers in combat fell on deaf ears. In January 1864, Confederate General Patrick R. Cleburne requested permission to enlist slaves to fight. Confederate Secretary of War Judah P. Benjamin made a similar request in December 1864. Confederate President Jefferson F. Davis refused both requests. He had lots of support for his refusals. Some Southerners claimed they would prefer to lose the war than to see armed slaves, even if they were fighting for the Confederacy. South Carolina and Georgia had expressed similar sentiments during the American Revolution. Confederate General Clement H. Stevens stated, "I do not want independence if it is to be won by the help of the Negro.... The justification of slavery in the South is the inferiority of the Negro. If we make him a soldier we concede the whole question."[12] When Confederate General Robert E. Lee offered a suggestion similar to Cleburne's and Benjamin's in January 1865, manpower shortages were so critical in the South that, finally, on March 13, Davis reversed his earlier refusals and signed General Orders No. 14, the Negro Soldier Law, permitting commanders to recruit and enlist slaves "to increase the military force of the Confederate States."[13] Some of those enlisted men were training in Richmond when, one month after the order, Lee surrendered to Grant, ending the war before the newly enlisted men could reach the battlefield.

Most Southerners, however, had a vitriolic opposition to black service for either side, but especially for the North. Nearly all Southerners—owners, non-owners, and women—considered the very idea of black soldiers carrying arms an affront to all their ideals. Armed black men were the stuff of their worst nightmares, as they recalled slave uprisings of the past. Some held other misguided beliefs near and dear. They convinced themselves that blacks could never make effective soldiers; they were cowards; they would never raise their hand to their beloved masters. They convinced themselves that those who did carry weapons against them were deluded or tricked and had lost their senses. Once a slave did don the uniform against his former master, the only cure was death, and every Southern state carried the death penalty for slaves in insurrection even before the war started. Southerners were not just annoyed at the idea of fighting against blacks on the battlefield, they were shocked that blacks would fight, and they were humiliated and outraged, and that rage vented itself in repeated fury on the black soldiers and their white officers. As early as November 30, 1862, before Lincoln issued the final Emancipation Proclamation with the enlistment proviso, Confederate Secretary of War James A. Seddon wrote a letter outlining Confederate response, stating, "Slaves in flagrant rebellion are subject to death by the laws of every slave-holding State.... They cannot be recognized in anyway as soldiers subject to the rules of war and to trial by military courts.... Summary execution must therefore be inflicted on those taken."[14] Copies of the letter went out to all district military commanders, including Major General John H. Forney in the District of the Gulf, who told his commanders not to shoot them but to hang them. Confederate commanders believed that all blacks in uniform against the South knew they would be killed if caught. A month later, Davis declared that the law should be expanded to include Union commanders such as Butler and Hunter, who should be shot or hanged immediately upon capture. The Confederate Congress, on April 30, 1863, authorized summary execution of enemy officers commanding black troops, claiming they were inciting servile insurrection.[15] Even though the law stated that black captives would be returned to state authority, in practice, most would be killed either way, whether they made it back to state custody or not. Chances were great that they would never make it to state authorities, especially if Southern commanders had any say. Countless witnesses after many battles related gruesome accounts of Confederates murdering black Union soldiers. These after-battle incidents created problems for Confederate commanders, who agreed that the slaves deserved to die but did not want their name associated with the murder of prisoners, even black prisoners. The best solution to eliminate the problem was to not take black prisoners in the first place.

One of the Confederate commanders, General Edmund Kirby Smith, was exhausted and irritated. Word had it that in March 1863, Union General Ulysses S. Grant had stored supplies at Milliken's Bend, in Madison Parrish, Louisiana, approximately ten miles north of Vicksburg, as part of his Vicksburg Campaign. Jefferson Davis ordered Smith to deny Grant those supplies. Smith sent Major General Richard Taylor in command of General John G. Walker's Texas Division, known as Walker's Greyhounds, to carry out the orders. Taylor objected, citing that they were no longer sure the supplies were still there and that his men would be more valuable in an attack at New Orleans. Smith insisted, and Taylor reached Richmond on the evening of June 5, where he rested for a few hours and moved out in the early hours of June 6. Meanwhile, Union Colonel Hermann Lieb, commander of the black Ninth, Tenth, Eleventh, and Thirteenth Louisiana Infantry Regiments, African Descent, at Milliken's Bend, expected an attack and took his African Brigade and two companies of the white Tenth Illinois Cavalry to scout toward Richmond. They encountered Taylor's pickets, and the two forces engaged in a brief skirmish. Lieb decided to withdraw back to camp to start preparing for an attack. His men had little experience, some of them having enlisted only two weeks earlier. Not all had uniforms, and most did not know how to fire their weapons. Lieb would do the best he could. He did call for help and received word that the ironclad gunboat *Choctaw* was en route to assist.

Brigadier General Henry E. McCulloch's Infantry Brigade of Walker's Division attacked on the morning of June 7, beginning a seven-hour battle and one of the least-known battles of the war. Present with the African Brigade were the First Mississippi, African Descent, and the Twenty-Third Iowa Infantry, who had arrived on the *Choctaw* and were the only white Union infantry regiment in the battle. The inferior training and weaponry of the African Brigade quickly led to fierce hand-to-hand fighting. Exhaustion, heat, and lack of water finally helped bring an end to the battle but not to the carnage. Wounded and surrendering black soldiers suffered death at the hands of the Texans, who, confident at the beginning of the battle, were surprised at the fighting determination of the black men in blue. Casualties were high, with the Ninth alone suffering 23 percent of its ranks killed, the highest of any other unit in the war. A number of Union soldiers thought they heard McCulloch shout "no quarter" to his men as they went into battle, adding fuel to the rumors that Confederates were routinely murdering Union prisoners. McCulloch had captured a number of white officers and black soldiers. Why McCulloch chose to take them captive at this time instead of killing them is unclear. Their fate was precarious. Smith was furious, calling their capture unfortunate. He and many other Confederate commanders and soldiers saw no quarter as the solution. Since these escaped slaves had dared to take up arms against their masters, they deserved death, even if it meant cold-blooded killing after the fighting stopped. It would also send a clear message to other slaves that they should remain in slavery. Since the South claimed that all black men fighting for the Union were simply escaped slaves, they refused to include them in prisoner exchange. The North strongly disagreed. If black soldiers died on the field, however, the North could not question their deaths or demand their exchange. The fate of McCulloch's prisoners remains unknown.

From the time Grant established part of his headquarters at Milliken's Bend, thousands of runaway slaves joined him there. He used the men as laborers to dig canals to bypass Vicksburg's guns. From the time of Butler's decision regarding contrabands, debate on what to do with runaways ranged from sending them back South, to caring for them in Union camps, to arming the men to fight for the Union, to organizing them as free, paid workers on plantations in a government-sponsored, plantation-leasing system. On March 25, 1863, newly appointed Secretary of War Edwin M. Stanton ordered Adjutant General Lorenzo Thomas to the Mississippi Valley to form black regiments. Thomas came through beautifully, with twenty regiments by the end of that year, a total of fifty by the end of 1864, and by the end of the war a total of around seventy-six thousand soldiers comprising more than 40 percent of the war's Union total. A number of these regiments had black noncommissioned officers.

On April 10, 1863, Thomas declared Milliken's Bend the location for implementation of a policy that organized contrabands on plantations along the Mississippi River to cultivate the land so they could provide for themselves and provide surplus for the Union Army. Instead of huddling in filthy, crowded refugee camps with what food and supplies the Union could provide, the fugitives would live together as families and receive pay for their labor, along with food, clothing, housing, and medical care, though treatment from the plantation lessees was not always better than that from the old owners. The men of military age with physical capabilities would be recruited or conscripted if need be and armed to guard the plantations and area posts. The Eighth, Ninth, Tenth, and Eleventh Louisiana Infantry Regiments were formed as part of Thomas's recruiting. Confederate reaction to these developments was harsh, and Lieb's men suffered the full force of Confederate fury. McCulloch might have taken some prisoners, but most black soldiers who survived were bayoneted or shot immediately after the battle. Some were hanged. Grant and the Federals heard the accounts of atrocity, and Grant wrote Taylor a letter inquiring into the matter. When Taylor denied any knowledge of atrocity, Grant accepted his word and let the matter drop.

Even worse in some ways than defeat and the treatment black soldiers received at the hands of their Southern enemies was continued Northern failure to protect them. Rumors of the Confederate black flag had circulated as early as 1862 after the first battle involving black troops at Island Mound, Missouri, and after nearly every subsequent battle. Many witnesses from a number of battles provided testimony of the Confederate practice of no quarter. One exception was the Second Battle of Fort Wagner on July 18, 1863. After the Fifty-Fourth Massachusetts's assault and defeat at Battery Wagner, concern arose over the fate of the Union prisoners. Lincoln finally issued a proclamation protecting all United States soldiers regardless of color and prosecuting any offenders, promising an eye for an eye in retaliation. The South took heed to a certain extent, confining the captured Fifty-Fourth soldiers for the duration of the war, but they refused to exchange black prisoners, leading to the complete breakdown of prisoner exchange—a breakdown that had begun with the discovery that Southern parolees were violating the conditions of their exchange. Meanwhile reports strongly suggested that Confederates continued to murder black soldiers and their officers.

Probably the most widely known murder occurred after the April 12, 1864, capture of Fort Pillow. General Nathan Bedford Forrest took Fort Pillow from a Union white cavalry regiment and a black artillery regiment. After the surrender, the Confederates refused to accept the surrender of black soldiers, killing anywhere from 200 to 262, in cold blood. The Confederates abandoned the fort the next day. Union relief forces discovered the grisly scene and buried all the dead in a common mass grave. One thing was different regarding the Fort Pillow Massacre, as it soon came to be called. A far greater array of witnesses, including war correspondents, soldiers, sailors, civilians, survivors, and even Confederate officers, shared their accounts of the atrocity, and those accounts became widely available. They all described Confederates murdering wounded soldiers, women, and children, even burying wounded soldiers alive. Confederate officers offered their own accounts, admitting details of misconduct on the part of their troops, but they felt justified in the actions because of the laws of their states and the Confederacy.

Murders continued and atrocities escalated, at Poison Spring, Arkansas, and at Mark's Mill, Arkansas, in the Red River Campaign under Banks and Major General Frederick Steele. Once again, Banks performed poorly, and the campaign ended in disaster for the Union. Steele decided to return to his base but found himself outnumbered and critically short of supplies in hostile territory. Then Steele started making his own blunders. He sent Colonel James M. Williams and 665 men, most from the First Kansas Colored Infantry Regiment, to travel sixteen miles and back with a large number of wagons to bring back a supply of corn rumored nearby. Williams estimated that twelve thousand Confederates would be in the way to stop them. His protests to Steele went unheeded. Indeed, they encountered Brigadier General John S. Marmaduke, Brigadier General Samuel B. Maxey, a Texas cavalry division, and Colonel Tandy Walker's Indian Brigade of 680 Choctaw and Chickasaw Indians. The Confederates had over three thousand men when they attacked Williams and approximately eleven hundred Union troops on the morning of April 18, 1864, at a place called Poison Spring. Williams had no choice but to abandon the wagon train and try to retreat, or run, as he told his men. Added to the usual Confederate methods of murder on this day was the Indian practice of scalping. According to witnesses, they especially targeted the black soldiers. Even unarmed runaways who had joined the train did not escape the wrath. They were shot or bayoneted in cold blood. They were scalped, sometimes while still alive. A few made it back to Steele's location, where Steele ordered the extra baggage destroyed before they made a run back to Little Rock. So ended the Camden Expedition of the Red River Campaign.

Atrocity and murder continued until the very end of the war: at Olustee in Florida, in February 1864; Plymouth, North Carolina, in April 1864; Brice's Cross Roads in Mississippi on June 10, 1864; at

Petersburg, Virginia, at the Crater and at Chaffin's Farm in June 1864; at Saltville, Virginia, in October 1864 and many other places. Not only did the North continue to fail to protect their soldiers, the steps they had taken to protest failed. Sheer numbers of prisoners led to the resumption of prisoner exchange in 1864, but the very few black soldiers who escaped murder and suffered captivity remained prisoners until the end of the war, with many assigned to labor in the Confederate cause. Conditions did not improve before the war ended. Amazingly, black Americans still volunteered to serve. They still fought, even harder than before the Confederate black flag appeared on the battlefield, because they knew what would happen to them if captured.

Lee's surrender to Grant to mark the Confederate defeat in April 1865 did not crush Southern fury toward black Americans, especially black soldiers or former soldiers. Still the North failed to protect black Americans. Some black units mustered out soon after the war. The Louisiana Native Guards, the Seventy-Third, Seventy-Fourth, and Seventy-Fifth USCT, demobilized on September 23, 1865. Like all black regiments whose enlistment ended soon after the war, they mustered out and returned home with the hope that their service would result in equality and increased civil rights. They were wrong.

Black veterans held rallies to gain equal rights, such as the vote. In Louisiana, they held memorial services for the fallen Native Guards. They organized veterans' organizations, but white organizations refused to recognize or include them. Not only were whites committed to denying black veterans' rights, some were committed to denying them freedom or even life. On October 29, 1865, several hundred veterans marched in a parade down Canal Street in New Orleans that was to end with a memorial service and a rally for black male suffrage. The rally was disrupted by white violence. At another rally on July 30, 1866, white civilians and policemen targeted blacks. When the fighting subsided, 38 people were dead and 146 wounded, nearly all black. One of the dead and nine of the wounded were Native Guard veterans. Many black Americans and soldiers experienced violence in the postwar years. Until its last members were dead, veterans of the Native Guard fought for equal rights, for their withheld pensions, and for their rightful membership in veterans' organizations.[16]

Even though blacks had fought in nearly every previous American military conflict, the Civil War was the first time not all blacks were immediately released from military service at the war's end. From the Civil War forward, black service was a component of both the peacetime and wartime American military establishment. Their service in the Civil

War was brave and honorable. All 176,895 black Americans in uniform during the Civil War deserve recognition for their sacrifice and service. More than 68,000 of them died, probably two-thirds from disease. In 1861, Congress created the Medal of Honor, the country's highest honor for battlefield acts of bravery and heroism. At least twenty-one black American soldiers received it.

At war's end, the government quickly demobilized troops. Those mustered out first were usually those who had served the longest and those whose enlistments were expired or near expiration. Both of these conditions meant white soldiers were usually mustered out before black soldiers. Because they had enlisted for three-year terms late in the war, probably in 1863 or 1864, black regiments were retained for postwar service. Their first duty was not pleasant. The federal government showed poor judgment in placing black troops in difficult and dangerous situations as occupation forces in the defeated South. The assignment meant continued employment for black men as soldiers, and some did want to stay in the service, particularly as the chances of fair employment outside the Army were poor. The soldiers could help the Freedmen's Bureau reunite families torn apart by slavery, help freedmen find jobs, protect them from angry Southerners, and provide for their immediate needs for food, housing, and education. However, this placed them among angry and racist Southerners who were not ready to accept black Americans outside the bounds of slavery, especially armed soldiers in the uniform of Yankee occupation forces. Southerners in many areas of the South continued to commit violent acts against the freed people, including murder, and their violence did not stop at civilians. Southerners attacked black soldiers and their white officers, in and out of uniform, wounding and killing a number of them. Southerners also targeted soldiers' families. Unfortunately for the occupation troops and their families, the Federal government never did find a solution to protect them or to curb the violence against them. Blacks had to defend themselves and their families in addition to performing their demanding and difficult occupation duties. At times, this led to their own officers disciplining them for defending themselves. To make matters worse, white occupation troops joined in the violence against the soldiers, their families, and the freed people, usually suffering no consequences for their acts of violence. In some cases, violence and lack of government protection and support led to mutiny or acts that the army chose to call mutiny.

Many black regiments received orders to Texas in the summer after the war. Major General Philip H. Sheridan had four responsibilities in Texas. His troops were to control rebels in the Trans-Mississippi region.

They were to patrol the Mexican border. They were to protect black Americans. They were to make the western frontier safe for settlers. Major General Henry W. Halleck, commander of the Department of Virginia, combined all his black troops into the Twenty-Fifth Corps and sent them to Texas to support Sheridan. Mostly, Halleck just wanted to be rid of his black troops. The troops learned as they were boarding transports to Texas that their families would no longer receive food from the government, with the idea that the troops should support their families from their pay. The problem was that they had not received pay for many months and had no money for their families. Some mutinied. Things got worse. The men suffered from illnesses on the trip to Texas, with numbers of them dying. Arrival in Texas did not improve their situation. They were stationed at Indianola, Corpus Christi, and Brazos Santiago, the last, especially, a very unpleasant place. It was dry and sandy, with no fresh water, and infested with bugs and snakes. In addition, they had no suitable housing. To make things worse, at any one time at least half of the men suffered from scurvy. They endured months of extreme food and water shortages, no living quarters, and repeated outbreaks of disease. Other problems arose as occupation continued. Soldiers and officers often resorted to drinking too much and participating in forbidden extracurricular activities, such as relations with prostitutes, leading to discipline and health problems. Worse than these conditions, however, was the resentment of local whites to the presence of the black soldiers. Whites frequently accused the soldiers of imagined crimes and offenses, and they also subjected the soldiers to unprovoked violent attacks then blamed the soldiers for instigating the violence. Discipline for soldier offenses, real or not, was mixed, from lax to extremely harsh. Harsh discipline, such as hanging men by their thumbs, bucking and gagging, and the sweatbox, led to the breakdown of morale and additional mutinies, some of which resulted in the execution of soldiers.

The Federal government used black militia units in addition to black regulars as occupation troops. These men experienced the same conditions and challenges as those in the army. In Mississippi, whites recorded the names of black militia members in so-called "dead books" and fired weapons into units as they drilled. Whites also seized weapons from rail transports on their way to supply the black units in Florida, South Carolina, and Arkansas. Black militia leaders, in occupation service for the Federal government, were murdered: Jim Williams of York County, South Carolina, and Charles Caldwell of Mississippi, to name two. Five black militia members were murdered in the armory in Hamburg, South Carolina. Even in the face of such difficulty, some occupation troops took advantage of the free time and opportunity to access education. Literacy rates rose. Black soldiers added their voices to the call for equal rights and the vote.

Congress wanted to reduce the army to the prewar number of sixteen thousand, so, as the months passed, the black regiments mustered out. In December 1867, the 124th USCT was the last black Civil War regiment to muster out. They had served well and sacrificed, and as they returned to civilian life, many wondered what was in store for them. Unfortunately, most of what lay ahead included racism, violence, and a constant struggle for equal rights. Many black Americans feared for their property, their safety, and their lives. In one incident near Fort Pickering outside Memphis, in May 1866, white police and civilians killed forty-six black Americans in a frenzy of racist violence. Black Americans did not get to vote until ratification of the Fourteenth Amendment in 1868, three years after the end of the war. They were also denied education equal to whites.[17]

Not all black troops wished to return to civilian life, but when blacks volunteered for service in the postwar regular army, controversy arose. Many, including General Grant, opposed the idea, even some who admitted the USCT regiments had done well in the war. Others took steps to make that service a reality. Massachusetts Republican Senator Henry Wilson introduced a plan to Congress for inclusion of blacks in the regular army. In the summer of 1866, Congress followed suit and added six black regiments. Out of a total of ten cavalry regiments, two would be black, the Ninth and Tenth Cavalry Regiments. Out of a total of forty-five infantry regiments, four would be black, the Thirty-Eighth, Thirty-Ninth, Fortieth, and Forty-First Infantry Regiments. All five artillery regiments would be white. Another army reorganization in the spring of 1869 reduced the total number of cavalry and infantry regiments. The four black infantry regiments consolidated to two. The Thirty-Eighth and Forty-First became the Twenty-Fourth. The Thirty-Ninth and Fortieth became the Twenty-Fifth. The two cavalry regiments, the Ninth and Tenth, remained. The following chapters will examine the organization and formation of those regiments.

One final sad note regarding black service during the Civil War is that many white historians excluded their service from accounts of the war. In 1928, Mr. W. E. Woodward went so far as to state, "the American negroes are the only people in the history of the world, so far as I know, that ever became free without any effort of their own.... [The Civil War] was not their business. They had not started the war nor ended it. They twanged banjos around the railroad stations, sang melodious spirituals, and believed that some Yankee would soon come along and give each of them forty acres and a mule."[18] James M. McPherson commented, "In spite of the large number of articles and books dealing with the Negro's active part in the Civil War that have been published since 1928, the belief still persists among many laymen and some historians that the slave was a passive, docile, uncomprehending recipient of freedom in 1865, and that the four and one-half million Negroes in the United States played no important or effective role in the tragic drama of civil war."[19] Fortunately, in recent years, the black Americans who served in the Civil War have received much more attention from historians. These brave soldiers also paved the way for the next black opportunity to serve.

CHAPTER 3

New Beginnings and New Trials: Creation, Organization, and Overview

Indians in the West had seen American soldiers before, but not like these. They had encountered the Americans through decades of struggle and negotiations, usually with devastating costs to their families. These Americans still wore blue, but their skin was black and their hair curly like the buffalo. The return of the U.S. Army after the Civil War ushered in decades of renewed conflict and struggle. Four regiments of black infantry and two regiments of black cavalry arrived in the West after 1866 and became part of the conflict and struggle. They found themselves subjugating Indians, protecting whites from Indians, protecting Indians from whites, negotiating between American citizens and their government, battling natural disasters, and taming the West for settlement. They explored, mapped, built roads and telegraph lines, and helped the West develop economically as well. They sacrificed and experienced much hardship. Through all of this, their most difficult problems were isolation, boredom, and racism. This chapter examines the formation and organization of the first all-black infantry and cavalry regiments in 1866 and their reorganization in 1869.

Indians started referring to the black American soldiers they encountered after the Civil War as Buffalo Soldiers. The term Buffalo Soldiers usually brings to mind black American soldiers in the American West and Southwest in the Indian War years, from 1866 to 1891, fighting Indians and protecting settlers. The stories of these years for each regiment, the Ninth and Tenth Cavalry and the Twenty-Fourth and Twenty-Fifth Infantry, follow in the next four chapters and focus on the subjugation of the Indians and the conquest of the western frontier. This chapter examines the formation, organization, and recruitment of these regiments after the Civil War.

Many black Americans tried to enlist in the years after the Civil War. Impairment and disease disqualified many from being physically fit. Insufficient numbers of qualified physicians aided some of the men in concealing conditions such as hernia or lameness. The rosters contained few physically qualified, and even fewer who could read. Appointment of officers was difficult and critical to the success of the men. Provision of regimental chaplains to provide much-needed education contributed to individual and regimental accomplishments. The men had to adapt to the hot and dry climate of the West, and they had to repair or even rebuild their posts when they arrived. Additionally, the Indians, who came to respect the black regiments' tenacity and fighting abilities, were not the only ones to recognize the sacrifice and bravery of black Americans. Even in the midst of racist attitudes, the United States honored a number of these men with the Medal of Honor. Another group of black soldiers deserves a place with the Buffalo Soldiers. The Black Seminole Scouts served with the Buffalo regiments for eleven years, and four of them received the Medal of Honor. Part of their story is included in this chapter. Finally, examples of their service and activities outside the Indian Wars conclude the chapter.

The U.S. Army occupied the West before the Civil War, with troops stationed along strategic lines of forts. With the outbreak of the war, troops abandoned the forts and went east to fight in the armies of the North and South. After they left, Indians once again claimed the land, hoping the white men were gone for good. After the war, Americans looked west, for a new start. They began arriving soon after the war, in increasing and alarming numbers. They came to establish farms and ranches, to get rich in the gold fields, to forget the war, and to escape from eastern civilization. They demanded their government protect them from the Indians and open the West for settlement, all of the West, even lands designated as reservations for the Indians. Much of the responsibility to meet these demands fell to the new black regiments.

After the Civil War, many black regiments whose enlistments had not expired received orders to head to Texas to help Major General Philip H. Sheridan control rebels in the Trans-Mississippi region, patrol the Mexican border, protect black Americans throughout the South, and make the western frontier safe for settlers. Major General Henry W. Halleck, commander of the Department of Virginia, combined all his black troops into the Twenty-Fifth Army Corps and sent them on transport ships to Texas to support Sheridan. Mostly, Halleck just wanted to be rid of his black troops, but many of the remaining enlisted men at the end of the war were blacks whose enlistments expired later than the enlistments of most whites. Some white officers, such as Halleck, and members of Congress wanted to be rid of the black regiments or to station them away from populated areas. They sent them to the West and Southwest, such as the 125th USCT, who marched from Kansas to Santa Fe for duty at various forts in New Mexico. Still others remained in occupation throughout the South.

As in the past, the end of the war meant tough decisions regarding military strength and responsibilities. The United States traditionally did not have a large peacetime military force, for a variety of reasons. Americans were reluctant to financially support a military force it did not need. The United States had traditionally used militia and volunteers in times of war rather than a professional force. Americans did not trust the idea of a standing, professional military, especially in times of peace. They also thought geography provided enough protection to allow them to demobilize after war and still have time to prepare forces when needed. The prewar army had roughly sixteen thousand soldiers. Union ranks had swelled to approximately two million. In the summer of 1865, Congress had to assess the country's military needs and determine how large a force they required to meet those needs. The postwar military was responsible for Union occupation of the former Confederate states. Other duties included patrolling the border with Mexico against threats from bandits, marauders, and the possibility of French forces entering from the South. Some of the most difficult and most pressing assignments called for large numbers of troops in the American West to protect railroad workers, to explore and map the West for settlement, to protect settlers, and to subjugate Indians. Congress, in its traditional approach to a small standing military, estimated a small force to cover all these responsibilities. Their initial very low estimate soon proved inadequate. Along with numbers far too low to meet the country's needs, many in Congress were advocating a return to the traditional all-white military.

After the war, not all black soldiers wished to return to civilian life, and not all congressmen and commanders wanted to exclude blacks from the peacetime army. Massachusetts Republican Senator Henry M. Wilson, in January 1866, proposed an army bill that increased the size of the postwar army and, for the first time in the country's history, included black Americans in the peacetime army. Even after observing the wartime service of black troops, many officers and leaders, including Lieutenant General Ulysses S. Grant, still doubted black soldiers' abilities and effectiveness and saw their service as either completely undesirable or to be limited to labor duties. Proponents of black enlistment argued that black troops were at least equal to white troops if not superior to them, noting black's wartime service in battle and that their desertion rates were far lower than those of white soldiers. Debate raged through the winter and spring. Finally, on July 28, 1866, Congress passed the Army Reorganization Bill. The bill increased army numbers to roughly fifty-four thousand, the largest peacetime army in the country's history, even though the actual strength was only about twenty-five thousand during the Indian War years of 1866–1891. Congress included six black regiments in the regular army. Out of a total of ten cavalry regiments, two would be black, the Ninth and Tenth Cavalry. Out of a total of forty-five infantry regiments, four would be black, the Thirty-Eighth, Thirty-Ninth, Fortieth, and Forty-First Infantry. All five artillery regiments would be white.[1] Black American soldiers who wanted to remain in military service had the chance to do so.

Congress intended the newly created black regiments to perform the same regular duties as white regiments, with the same pay of thirteen dollars a month, food, clothing, and housing. When they completed their enlistment, they would receive a reenlistment bonus and a pay raise to fourteen dollars a month. They had to be healthy, single, and between the ages of eighteen and thirty-five. They did not have to pass a literacy requirement. The average black volunteer was twenty-three years old, illiterate, and identified himself as a laborer or farmer. On paper the only differences between white and black regiments were that each black regiment would have a chaplain who would instruct the soldiers in basic academics and literacy skills and black regiments would have two veterinary surgeons instead of one. Actual differences extended beyond these provisions. The black regiments persistently received assignments at isolated outposts and forts, in harsh climates. They invariably lived in inferior housing far below the conditions of that of the white regiments. They did not routinely rotate to more populated areas to recharge, even though white regiments rotated regularly. Above all, they battled racism at every turn.

From the beginning, white officers commanded black units. This practice started during the Civil War. Politicians and commanders mistakenly thought that only white Southern officers understood and knew how to lead black Americans, since many already had experience with them in civilian life. Military leaders and Congress in 1866 thought it only made sense to continue that practice. As it was, no black officers were available for command anyway. Many officers were graduates of the United States Military Academy (USMA) at West Point, and since its establishment in 1802, no black American had even applied for admission. Of the available white officers, many shunned the idea of serving with a black regiment. Numbers of them, such as George Armstrong Custer, actually accepted lower rank just to receive assignment with a white regiment. The ones who were willing to serve with the black regiments were often only doing it for easy promotion and did not possess the attitude or leadership skills the new regiments needed. The Buffalo Soldiers suffered greatly from the poor leadership of some, but thankfully not all, of their officers. Fortunately, the officer corps slowly began to admit blacks. Between 1870 and 1889, twelve of twenty-five black applicants gained admittance to the USMA, but it was a difficult journey for the first black cadets. Only three of those cadets graduated, and they endured treatment from their fellow cadets ranging from ostracism to hazing because of the color of their skin. White cadets, and some officers, adamantly refused to accept them, and West Point Commander Major General John M. Schofield let racism and hazing run rampant. One cadet in particular, Johnson Chestnut Whittaker, was admitted to the academy in 1876. In 1880, he was found beaten, bloodied, and tied to his bunk. An inquiry declared he had done these things to himself, and he was court-martialed and expelled in 1881. The court-martial ruling was overturned in 1883, but Whittaker was not readmitted and remained expelled for academic reasons.[2] Three black cadets finally endured to graduation. Henry O. Flipper gained appointment in 1873 and graduated in 1877. He started his career with the Tenth Cavalry and was doing well until he was falsely charged with embezzlement in 1901 and court-martialed for that charge as well as for conduct unbecoming when he tried to defend himself. He spent the rest of his life trying to clear his name. Finally, in the 1970s, he was exonerated of the charges and honorably discharged—too little, too late. John Hanks Alexander entered the academy in 1883 and graduated in 1887. He served with the Ninth Cavalry before becoming a professor at Wilberforce University in Ohio, in 1894. Tragically, he died from a seizure shortly after arriving at Wilberforce. Charles Young graduated from West Point in 1889. He built an impressive career over thirty years and became a full colonel. When he was in line for battlefield command in World War I, many white Americans remained unwilling to accept the idea of a black American in command of white soldiers. Racism brought down Young's star and brought his career to a very sad end. His story appears in Chapter 9. During most of the years of their service, the Buffalo regiments served under white officers, some good and some bad.

Fortunately, the regimental commanders were men of integrity who wanted to command black soldiers and wanted their regiments to be successful. Some of them had previous experience commanding black soldiers; others did not. Two of them, Colonel Edward Hatch and Colonel Benjamin H. Grierson, were appointed on General Ulysses S. Grant's personal recommendation. Both had served with Grant during the Civil War. Hatch started the war as a captain in the Second Iowa Cavalry. In just a few short months, he was leading the regiment as its colonel. When Grierson was eight years old, a horse kicked him in the head, nearly killing him and leaving a large scar on his face. He was not fond of horses. He was a music teacher before the war, but he enlisted at his earliest opportunity. Ironically, he was assigned as a major in the Sixth Illinois Cavalry. Grierson became one of Grant's best cavalry commanders during the war. Hatch served with Grierson when he commanded the famous cavalry raid through Mississippi in 1863 in support of Grant's Vicksburg campaign. Grierson's raid became quite famous in the history books and in Hollywood, with John Wayne playing the role of Grierson in *The Horse Soldiers*. Hatch received command of the Ninth Cavalry, and Grierson received command of the Tenth Cavalry. Grant's endorsements proved correct. Both men served their regiments well for many years. Colonel William B. Hazen commanded the Thirty-Eighth Infantry until the reorganization of 1869. Colonel Ranald S. MacKenzie, another excellent cavalry leader, commanded the Forty-First Infantry. When the Thirty-Eighth and the Forty-First combined to form the Twenty-Fourth Infantry in 1869, MacKenzie became the new regiment's commander. In 1870, he took command of the Fourth Cavalry, leaving the Twenty-Fourth to Colonel Abner Doubleday, then to Colonel Joseph H. Potter in 1873, and Colonel Zenas R. Bliss a decade later. All these officers served the regiment well. Colonel Joseph A. Mower commanded the Twenty-Fifth Infantry until 1870, when he died. A series of commanders passed through the regiment until Colonel George L. Andrews took command in 1871 and stayed for twenty years. These officers were white, and they were dedicated to their men. Officers of white regiments practiced racism against the men, as did occasional officers of the Buffalo regiments who were poor officers who ended up in command in black regiments because it was easier to receive an appointment in the black regiments than in white regiments.

Along with the misguided belief that only white officers could effectively command black soldiers, another damaging Southern tradition made the transition to military service difficult. Antebellum state laws in the South had made it illegal to teach slaves to read and write, so literacy levels were horribly low. Some commanders, such as Grierson and Mac-kenzie, tried to maintain literacy as an enlistment requirement, but not enough black literate men were available, and all the regiments had to enlist numbers of illiterate men. This meant recruits could not fulfill the duties of clerks and noncommissioned officers until they became literate. In most of these regiments, white officers performed the clerical duties until enlisted men could step into these roles.

One solution to the low literacy rates was to assign each regiment its own chaplain to give the men access to basic education. During the Civil War, black regiments usually had white chaplains. After the Emancipation Proclamation in 1863, black chaplains began serving in a more professionalized manner. They reorganized education materials and schedules, requiring attendance, and they expanded education opportunities to include the soldiers' family members. In 1866, however, the Buffalo regiments received white chaplains, partly because the demand for pastors was great and too few of the newly freed slaves were qualified to fill the position. The white chaplains made tremendous progress for the Buffalo Soldiers. They established schools at the forts and posts. They collected books and other materials. They scheduled classes around duty rosters to make sure the men were free to attend. Eventually, five black chaplains served with the regiments, from 1884 to 1907. Four were former slaves from the South, and one was born free in the North. Former slave and Civil War navy veteran, Henry V. Plummer started service in 1884 as a chaplain with the Ninth. His service to his men was exemplary, but he was unpopular with whites because he spoke out against racism and other controversial issues. He became more and more unpopular with local civilians and the white officers of the Ninth, and in 1894, after ten years of service, he was dismissed. College graduate and former slave, George W. Prioleau, replaced Plummer with the Ninth. Prioleau avoided controversy and focused on fulfilling the religious and educational needs of his men. He retired in 1920. Another former slave, William T. Anderson, served as chaplain for the Tenth Cavalry, beginning in 1897. Like Prioleau, he was educated and dedicated to the religious and educational development of his men. Even more, though, he was a physician who saw to the physical health of his men. He served tirelessly in the West, in Cuba, and in the Philippines before he retired in 1910. Allen Allensworth, a former slave born in Louisville, Kentucky, on April 7, 1852, started his service with the Twenty-Fourth Infantry in July 1886. Several accomplishments set him apart from other chaplains. He attained the rank of Lieutenant Colonel, the highest of any black chaplain. He also established educational systems and standards that both civilians and the military adopted. He developed teaching strategies, included both the soldiers and their families in the lessons, and included vocational training in his curriculum. He retired in 1907. Chaplain to the Twenty-Fifth Infantry was Theophilus G. Steward, born free of racially mixed parents in the North in 1843. He joined the Twenty-Fifth in 1891. He went with the regiment to the Philippines and helped the military set up a number of schools for the Filipino children. He retired in 1907.[3] The men they served realized the importance of education, and many took every opportunity they could to go to class or to study on their own when they could not attend. They soon took over clerical and noncommissioned-officer duties that white junior officers had performed since the beginning of the regiments. The transition brought the officers and men into closer working relationships and strengthened the bonds between the two groups. Through education, the Buffalo Soldiers evened the playing field with their white counterparts. In the coming years, they would outperform them in some aspects.

The soldiers themselves could make a difference when it came to education, but other factors lay beyond their control. William H. Leckie, in his groundbreaking and important study *The Buffalo Soldiers*, claimed that these regiments nearly always received the worst equipment, the worst weapons, clothing, food, and horses. They also received insufficient quantities, and delivery was chronically late. Anecdotal evidence supports Leckie's claims. Grierson and others complained of not enough good horses. However, so did commanders of white regiments, and William A. Dobak and Thomas D. Phillips, examining new evidence in *The Black Regulars, 1866–1989*, found no proof that black cavalry were intentionally or systemically denied horses.[4] Instead, an overall shortage of good horses meant that cavalry regiments constantly competed for horses, while infantry regiments had to rely on mules to mount their troops.

Evidence of systemic discrimination against the men of these regiments is elusive, but their repeated assignment to isolated outposts and forts in the American West and Southwest was a reality and suggests that Americans tolerated or even supported the idea of blacks in uniform, as long as they were stationed far away from whites. These assignments meant extreme isolation and hard labor. Most of the posts and forts needed repairs, which the men did themselves, often short of supplies and materials. At other times, black troops arrived at their designated locations and had to build their post from the bottom up. Frequently, during their first weeks and months at these posts they lived in tents or other temporary structures that provided no protection from the elements. The military was already spread far too thinly in the West, and having to spend time and energy on building and repairs meant black troops had less time for other duties. Black troops comprised approximately 10 percent of the infantry and 20 percent of the cavalry that Sheridan, commander of the Division of the Missouri, had out West. Out of the twenty-five thousand men in the postwar regular army in 1874, Sheridan had 17,819 men to fight ninety-nine Indian tribes numbering 192,000 people covering a million square miles. Within those million square miles, Sheridan's troops were to make sure that Indians remained on reservations and whites stayed off them. They were also detailed to help during natural disasters, quell domestic disturbances, and protect government property during labor strikes in the 1870s, 1880s, and 1890s.

On June 27, 1865, the War Department's General Orders No. 118 reorganized the United States into five military divisions and eighteen geographic departments. The 1866 army experienced further changes to that organization. The Division of the Mississippi, under Major General William Tecumseh Sherman, in 1866 became the Military Division of the Missouri, and Sherman was promoted to Lieutenant General. His division was headquartered in St. Louis, Missouri, and contained four geographic departments: the Department of Arkansas; the Department of the Missouri, which included Colorado, Kansas, New Mexico, and Indian Territory; the Department of the Platte, which included Iowa, Nebraska, Wyoming Territory, Idaho Territory, and Utah Territory; and the Department of Dakota, which contained Minnesota, Dakota Territory, and Montana Territory. In March 1869, Sherman was promoted to general and made commander of the army, a position he held until 1883. Major General Philip H. Sheridan was promoted to lieutenant general and assigned command of the Division of the Missouri, with its headquarters moved from St. Louis to Chicago, Illinois. In 1870, a fifth department, the Department of Texas, was added.

When the black infantry and cavalry regiments were created, these department commanders received the first charges for recruitment. Sherman and Sheridan each received orders to raise one black infantry regiment and one black cavalry regiment. Under Sherman, Colonel William B. Hazen raised the Thirty-Eighth Infantry at Jefferson Barracks, Missouri, and Colonel Benjamin H. Grierson raised the Tenth Cavalry at Fort Leavenworth, Kansas. Under Sheridan, in the Department of the Gulf, Colonel Joseph A. Mower raised the Thirty-Ninth Infantry, and Colonel Edward Hatch raised the Ninth Cavalry. Colonel Nelson A Miles raised the Fortieth Infantry, and Major General George H. Thomas raised the Forty-First Infantry. Enlistments were five years for cavalry and three for infantry. The enlistment for cavalry was longer because it took longer to train cavalry. Each company would contain sixty-four privates. Initially, enlistment would be closed to civilians; instead all recruits would be United States Colored Troop veterans. These men were already somewhat trained, and getting first chance to enlist in the new regiments would reward them for their Civil War service.

Commanders for each regiment personally conducted the recruiting. By September Mower had recruited three hundred in New Orleans for the Thirty-Ninth, and Hatch had seven hundred men for the Ninth in Louisiana by November. By the end of October, however, Grierson of the Tenth had fewer than forty recruits, and Hazen of the Thirty-Eighth had only twenty-seven. Finding enough officers was an additional problem for all the new regiments, and this lack of officers in turn hindered recruiting. Illiteracy stopped enlistees from performing recruitment duty. A shortage of doctors for physical examinations created further delays in reaching regimental quotas, and inadequate screening meant that unfit men were enlisted.

Grierson reassured his recruiters that high standards of fitness and literacy were worth the delay in filling the regiment. Colonel Ranald S. Mackenzie, replacing Thomas in the Forty-First, agreed and preferred more selective recruitment to quickly reaching regimental numbers. The shortage of officers also hindered training. The regiments, fortunately, did gain some key officers. Lieutenant Colonel Wesley Merritt served with the Ninth. Lieutenant Samuel L. Woodward served with the Tenth. Slowly, all the regiments reached their authorized numbers by the end of 1867. However, normal attrition and the end of three-year enlistments took a toll on the numbers and prompted the need for more recruiting.

In March 1869, Congress passed another army reorganization bill which reduced the overall army strength and consolidated the four black infantry regiments to two. In April 1869, in New Orleans, the Thirty-Ninth and Fortieth consolidated to the Twenty-Fifth under Colonel Mower. In Texas, the Thirty-Eighth and Forty-First consolidated into the Twenty-Fourth under Colonel Mackenzie. The 1869 act extended infantry enlistments from three to five years, adding to recruitment difficulties because some men were willing to enlist for three and then re-enlist if they desired, but they were not quite as willing to enlist for five years from the start.

From the beginning, these men faced difficult challenges. They had to adapt to new environments. The heat and drought of the West and Southwest were hard on man and beast. They had to complete a variety of duties in their new surroundings. They built and repaired telegraph lines, guarded railroad workers, built and maintained wagon roads, scouted previously unknown areas, guarded stage coaches and stations, built or repaired their own housing and posts, provided escorts to wagon trains, railroad survey crews, telegraph construction crews, and military and civilian dignitaries, hauled water, cut wood, fought Indians, and sometimes fought trespassing settlers. Many of these duties required skills that most of the men had to learn. Perhaps their biggest enemies were isolation, boredom, and racism. These bitterest of foes were present everywhere they went and made everything else more difficult.

Though mostly involved in frontier duty, regimental troops were also sent to quell civil disorder and domestic disturbance, a detail the men themselves found distasteful. A brief examination of three of these incidents, the Colfax County War in New Mexico in 1877, the Lincoln County War in New Mexico in 1877–1878, and the Pullman Railway Strike in 1894, demonstrates the nature of the assignments and how the men experienced them.

In March 1876, the Ninth Cavalry arrived in Colfax County, New Mexico, after disagreement over a two-million-acre land grant left several civilians dead. Captain Francis Moore took thirty men of Company L from Fort Union to Cimarron to stop the violence and arrest those responsible. The source of the violence, however, had begun years earlier, around 1843, when two Americans, Charles Beaubien and Guadalupe Miranda, received a two-million-acre land tract from the Mexican government. When the land became part of the United States in 1848, the U.S. first recognized Beaubien and Miranda as the owners, followed by recognition of Beaubien's daughter and her husband, Lucien Maxwell. In 1870, a British firm hired a group of Colorado businessmen under the name of Maxwell Land Grant and Railway Company to buy the tract for them, since, as foreigners, the British investors could not legally purchase it themselves. Secretary of the Interior Jacob Cox disputed the deed to the Maxwell Company and allowed the General Land Office to issue the land to homesteaders and ranchers who had already been using it for decades. Conflict continued between the homesteaders and ranchers and the Maxwell Company over ownership, but homesteader discovery of gold complicated everything, raising the stakes for all involved. Both sides sought legal remedy, but in the meantime, the Maxwell Company started issuing eviction notices, implementing them with violence when necessary. The situation only worsened when those being evicted learned that some high-level politicians were holding hands with the Maxwell Company. When Reverend F. J. Tolby, an outspoken opponent of the Maxwell group, was found murdered, people suspected the Maxwell cohort and their political friends. Murder escalated, with each side taking revenge for their fallen by murdering those they believed responsible, amid additional accusations of political fraud and corruption. Finally, in March 1876, Moore and his men of the Ninth arrived, only to find more trouble from alcohol and racism than from the ongoing conflict they were sent there to stop. The only result of their presence in Cimarron was trouble for themselves. Against orders, some of Moore's men involved themselves in altercations with cowhands from Texas and Cimarron civilians who apparently did not approve of black Americans in Federal uniforms. Several soldiers ended up dead in the streets; another was tried and hanged for murder. The troopers left Cimarron in April and left New Mexico in 1881. The British investors sold their rights to the land to Dutch investors. The U.S. Supreme Court, in 1887, confirmed ownership of the entire original tract to the Maxwell Land Grant Company, and the Colfax County War ended.

Too often, bad officers put black troops in impossible situations, sometimes to advance their personal agendas, sometimes out of pure ineptitude. In Lincoln County, New Mexico, the Ninth Cavalry's Lieutenant Colonel N. A. M. Dudley became personally involved in the Lincoln County War even after he had received orders to stay out of the situation. Once again, the causes of the war had started years earlier, in the 1870s. Business partners Lawrence G. Murphy and James J. Dolan and a group of political associates that included bank president and U.S. District Attorney Thomas B. Catron established a lucrative scheme to cheat the government, the Indians at the Mescalero Agency near Fort Stanton, the troops at Fort Stanton, and the civilians of Lincoln County. Murphy and Dolan—"the House," as they called their business—garnered the contracts to provide the fort and the reservation with beef, grain, food, and other supplies then systematically cut corners on quality and quantity and lined their pockets with the increased profits. Independently, cattleman John S. Chisum and businessman John J. Tunstall arrived to set up shop in Lincoln. Chisum was interested in supplying beef to the fort and the agency. Tunstall had local business interests. They soon teamed up and, with the help of local lawyer Alexander A. McSween, offered serious challenges to the House. Needless to say, with so much at stake—and with local law-enforcement backing the Murphy/Dolan camp—violence erupted. Tunstall, who had hired gunmen such as William Bonney, also known as Billy the Kid, to protect him from the House's hired men, was ambushed and murdered. Bonney and others with Tunstall witnessed the murder but could not prevent it. Each side formed an armed camp. In February 1878, calls for help from local citizens tired of the violence reached Fort Stanton, where three companies of the Ninth Cavalry and one company of the Fifteenth Infantry, about 150 men, were stationed.

Captain George A. Purington of the Ninth sent men from his companies to help Deputy U.S. Marshall Robert Widenmann serve arrest warrants to members of the Murphy/Dolan camp for the murder of Tunstall. Violence escalated. Things took a turn for the worse when Lieutenant Colonel Dudley became commander at Fort Stanton. A heavy drinker with a bad temper, Dudley earlier had been court-martialed on two separate occasions. When professional gunslingers arrived for both sides, and men from each camp were found dead in the streets, Dudley sent troops into town to curb the violence and, when this measure failed, called for reinforcements. Around this time, however, Colonel Hatch received word from Secretary of War Henry Knox that the use of federal troops to perform local law enforcement violated the Congressional Posse Comitatus Act passed in June 1878. The law was new and not fully clear, but Knox advised Hatch to avoid further use of troops in the Lincoln County War. Hatch relayed those orders to Dudley, who promptly and persistently disobeyed them. He ordered his troops into Lincoln during the last two weeks of July. Tunstall's murder had opened the floodgates, with Bonney and others vowing revenge against Tunstall's murderers. Shootouts between the rival factions occurred on the streets of Lincoln, placing uninvolved citizens in harm's way. These shootouts were the reason for Dudley's continued unauthorized involvement, and it nearly cost the life of at least one of his men, Private Robinson, who was nearly caught in the crossfire delivering a message from Dudley to the latest in a series of sheriffs, a man named Peppin. As a result of frequent shootouts, Dudley entered the town in force with a howitzer and cannon in tow and added to the violence, or at the very least did not stop the Murphy/Dolan men. During this final shootout, McSween, Bonney, and Tunstall's remaining hired gunmen, now calling themselves the Regulators, were firing on Dolan's men from the cover of McSween's house. Dolan's men set fire to the house, eventually forcing out the occupants. McSween was shot in his front yard, as his house and other properties burned to the ground. After the smoke cleared, the Lincoln County War was essentially over. Many of Dolan's men were dead. Dolan had exhausted his funds hiring gunmen and was financially ruined. Tunstall and McSween were dead. Chisum was in no mood to continue the fight, and the people of Lincoln County wanted peace. Dudley had sided with the House, but he had not brought his weapons to bear and had essentially not affected the outcome. The men of the Ninth had followed the orders of a terrible commander, who was acquitted of all charges in the matter in his third court-martial!

Worse than officers such as Dudley were officers who endangered and abused their own men. Some officers, such as General Nathaniel P. Banks and General William Dwight at the Civil War Battle of Port Hudson on May 27, 1863, appeared to intentionally place their black soldiers in danger on the battlefield. Others, such as Edward M. Heyl, who in July 1866 joined the Ninth Cavalry as first lieutenant and received promotion to captain later that month, made no attempt to conceal their racism. Heyl quickly established a reputation for brutality toward his men. In April 1867 at San Pedro Springs, Texas, he thought some of his men had not followed quickly enough his orders to take care of their horses, so he ordered them to be punished by hanging from their wrists. When one private broke free, Heyl beat him with his sabre. When Sergeant Harrison Bradford protested Heyl's behavior, the tension escalated into gunfire that killed Bradford and a lieutenant named Seth Griffin. Locals called it a mutiny and blamed the black soldiers.[5]

On many occasions, black troops also had to protect themselves from local civilians. One of numerous examples is that of the Tenth Cavalry at Fort Concho, Texas, in 1877. Soldiers went to Nasworthy's Saloon in nearby San Angelo. Texas Rangers objected to their presence and pistol-whipped the soldiers, who later armed themselves and shot up the town, killing a bystander.

In August 1885, the Twenty-Fifth was stationed at Fort Meade in Dakota Territory when Corporal Hallon was taken from the nearby Sturgis City jail and lynched for the murder of Dr. Lynch. The evidence against Hallon was circumstantial at best. Fellow soldiers marched into town, formed up, and fired into Abe Hill's saloon and a citizen's house, killing a man in the saloon. The soldiers then marched back to the fort. Whether the shooting was related to the lynching is unclear. Officers arrested four soldiers. The townspeople demanded removal of the black soldiers and their replacement with white soldiers. General Alfred H. Terry refused their demands, noting that if the citizens of Sturgis City wanted less violence, they should eliminate the saloons and brothels.

In May 1888, the Twenty-Fifth Infantry was stationed in Montana Territory, in Forts Shaw, Missoula, and Custer. In June, local civilians lynched Private Robert Robinson. He and a white soldier from the Third Infantry quarreled over Robinson's mistress, Queeny Montgomery, who apparently had been unfaithful to Robinson. During the fight between the two men, Robinson injured the other man and ran. When townspeople tried to capture him, he killed one of them. Sun River Sheriff Downing placed Robinson in the local jail, but he was found lynched in an alley the next morning. Robinson did not help himself with his own actions, but he knew of his probable fate at the hands of the locals and chose to fight. His killers were never apprehended. All too often, black soldiers bore the brunt of blame and received the punishment. Incidents such as these happened so frequently that they felt their only option was to take matters into their own hands.[6]

The soldiers had other contacts with civilians as part of their service. The regiments were used to protect federal installations and mail deliveries during labor strikes. The summer of 1877 witnessed the first national labor strike. It involved railway workers and spanned nearly a dozen states. President Rutherford B. Hayes called in federal troops to control the mobs and protect property. Another railway strike, the Pullman Strike, in 1894, led President Grover Cleveland to once again call in federal troops. The strike centered in Chicago but spread to affect other parts of the country as well. Railway employees resorted to a strike against the Pullman Palace Car Company over continued pay reductions with no financial reduction in rents. Many families were literally starving.[7] The troops were supposedly present to protect federal installations and the mail, but they actually broke the strike. Illinois Governor John P. Altgeld protested the president's use of federal troops in his state, but his protest fell on deaf ears. Violence from the strike in Chicago reached other areas when the American Railway Union called for a sympathy strike against all railroads that used Pullman cars. Brigadier General William R. Shafter received orders in July to take officers and men of the Twenty-Fourth Infantry to one of the affected areas, Los Angeles, California, to ensure safe delivery of the mail. Shafter and five companies arrived in Los Angeles on July 5, restored order and kept the trains running, even the trains with Pullman cars. The Twenty-Fourth left Los Angeles on July 24. After the strike, the Supreme Court ruled that the president had the legal right to send federal troops into a state without its consent.[8]

Sometimes, the regiments were detailed to protect Indians from whites. Other times, they provided disaster relief. The Ninth Cavalry had the distasteful duty to escort Victorio's Mimbres Apaches to the San Carlos Reservation, a place they hated, because whites had already encroached on their former home. To make the most of available resources, the Apaches lived in subtribes scattered across the Southwest. Victorio's group was mostly known as the Warm Springs Apaches or the Mimbres Apaches because they lived near the Ojo Caliente, or Warm Springs, and also frequented the region near the Mimbres Mountains, both in New Mexico. The government decided to move the Indians instead of the white trespassers, even though the San Carlos location was dangerous and deadly to the Apaches, especially the Mimbres. The U.S. government placed the Mimbres next to traditional Apache enemies, which put families at risk from attacks from neighbors. Their part of the reservation also had insufficient water that contained harmful minerals, making it harmful for drinking. Game was nonexistent, and danger in the form of snakes and scorpions was part of their daily existence. The government claimed that the move would protect Mimbres from attack from white settlers who had encroached on the land they had called home for many years. This relocation was not pleasant for the Apaches or for the men of the Ninth. Later, the Ninth repeatedly escorted white civilian "Boomers" trespassing onto Indian Territory in Oklahoma with plans to stake out claims and settle with their families. They were not always pitted against settlers. Most of the time, they were a help to settlers. They fought fires and saved both settlers and their homes. They rescued settlers from natural disasters, such as in 1881, when the Twenty-Fifth saved as many as eight hundred settlers and their cattle from spring floods in Dakota Territory. They even pooled their own money and other resources to help those who had lost their homes.

Not all the assignments involved fatigue duty, violence, or boredom. General Nelson A. Miles wanted to explore the possibility of using bicycles for military purposes. In 1896, Lieutenant James A. Moss of Company F of the Twenty-Fifth Infantry led twenty-one men as a bicycle unit for a distance of one thousand miles, from Fort Missoula, Montana, to Yellowstone National Park and back. The next year, Moss took his men nineteen hundred miles from Fort Missoula to St. Louis, Missouri. Through rain, heat, and snow, they arrived at St. Louis on July 24, 1897, after a trip of forty-one days. Though the project was deemed a success, the idea of a bicycle unit was not immediately implemented, but the Twenty-Fifth did use bicycles again after the Spanish-American War, to control riots in Havana. Lieutenant Moss went on to serve as an officer in the all-black 367th Infantry Regiment, 92nd Division, in the American Expeditionary Force in World War I. In contrast to this assignment, other duties were more sobering. In October 1889, Company A of the Twenty-Fifth placed 106 headstones at Custer Cemetery in South Dakota to mark graves or remains moved from the site of old Fort Phil Kearney, Wyoming. In the spring of 1890, another company of the Twenty-Fifth marked the cemetery boundaries and erected new headstones.

Most of their service, however, did involve fatigue duty, violence, and boredom. The four regiments served in the West and Southwest for twenty-five years and fought more than two hundred battles and skirmishes to help subjugate the Indians and open the continent to white settlers. Though white regiments rotated east to better climates and to enjoy time closer to civilization, the black regiments remained isolated on the frontier. Perhaps the only exception occurred in May 1891, when Troop K of the Ninth transferred from Fort Robinson, Nebraska, to Fort Myer, just outside Washington, DC, the first time since Reconstruction that black soldiers had served east of the Mississippi River. They served there for three years, despite protests from local white civilians. They rejoined their regiment at Fort Robinson in October 1894. Until the outbreak of the Spanish-American War, they remained in the isolated outposts.

Along with persistent isolation, the name the Indians gave them—Buffalo Soldiers—also set black regiments apart from their white counterparts. According to Arlen Fowler, author of *The Black Infantry in the West, 1869–1891*, the name Buffalo Soldiers was first given to the Tenth Cavalry during the Cheyenne War of 1867–69. It was later applied to the Ninth and then to the Twenty-Fourth and Twenty-Fifth. The soldiers did not know if the Indians referred to their hair being much like that of the buffalo or to their fighting prowess and determination, also much like that of the buffalo.[9] According to Dobak and Phillips, the men did not refer to themselves as Buffalo Soldiers in diaries or letters. However, these regiments and many later black regiments used the buffalo as part of their regimental insignia and their identity.

Other black Americans served with the Buffalo Soldiers during the Indian War years. The Black Seminole Scouts had a long history of fighting experience, reaching back to their ancestors in slavery. Spanish King Charles II's Edict of 1693 encouraged runaways from the British colonies, offering freedom in exchange for conversion to Catholicism and enlistment in the militia. Slaves took advantage of this opportunity and established black communities in Florida. Fort Mose, located just north of St. Augustine, was established in 1738 and became a target for the British in 1740 when war broke out between Britain and Spain. The British took the fort, but the Fort Mose Militia, with black soldiers, Spanish soldiers and Indian warriors under Captain Francisco Menendez, recaptured the fort, which remained in Spanish possession for the next eighty years.[10] These early colonists forged alliances with the Seminole Indians, either as slaves or as members adopted into families. The Seminoles practiced a type of slavery far different from the slavery the runaways experienced under the British and later under the Americans, with practices similar to kinship and tribute systems, in which "slaves" paid tribute to their "owners" with part of their harvest. Slaves under such a system enjoyed many rights and freedoms. Children from this relationship formed a new group; many names identify this group, Black Seminoles, Seminole Negroes, Maroons, Seminole Maroons, and Seminole

Blacks, to mention a few, with no one name perfectly applicable. One of the earliest recorded Black Seminoles was John Horse, also known as John Cavallo, John Cowaya, Juan Caballo, and Gopher John, the son of a black mother and a Seminole father, born in 1812. As an adult, he provided valuable service to his people as an interpreter and negotiator. He also served as a guide for the U.S. military.[11]

British colonists sent slave catchers into Florida after runaways. When Spain ceded Florida to Britain, many black settlers fled to Cuba. Some remained with the Seminoles. When Britain became distracted in the war against her rebellious American colonies, slaves again took the opportunity to seek refuge in Florida. Later, Americans from the United States sent their slave catchers. The Americans coveted Florida for several reasons. They wanted to deny Florida as a refuge for runaways. They wanted military control of the area to subjugate the Seminoles and the Miccosukees. They wanted to expand slavery and agriculture into the region. Their desire to gain Florida became a source of constant tension between the two countries. The Americans brazenly tried to seize Florida, starting with Amelia Island and planning to take more until they had the entire area under the United States flag. This posed a double threat to the blacks and Black Seminoles, since slave catchers decided to capture people based solely on their skin color. American militia and federal forces in Florida vowed to kill all armed black soldiers they could find. Those black soldiers fighting against American forces played a huge role in defeating the Americans in their first attempt to take Florida.

After the signing of the Treaty of Ghent in December, 1814, ending the war between England and the United States, Black Seminoles, runaways, and free blacks, along with their Indian allies, fortified the fort the British had built on Prospect Bluff and renamed it Fort Negro. It became a major destination for runaways. General Andrew Jackson ordered General Edmund P. Gaines to destroy the fort. Its destruction contributed to the outbreak of the Seminole Wars. Part of that story is in Chapter 1. During the Seminole Wars, John Horse became a prominent Black Seminole leader. In 1838 and 1849, the United States relocated many but not all of the Seminoles, Miccosukees, and Black Seminoles, including John Horse, to Indian Territory. The Black Seminoles were promised freedom if they surrendered and relocated. The Seminoles found conditions in Indian Territory to be not what they expected and blamed the Black Seminoles, who were innocent of the charges but who had acted as interpreters during the treaty negotiations. The Black Seminoles did not deceive their allies, but once in Indian Territory, they found themselves in danger from the Seminoles and from the Creek Indians, already established in that location. The Creeks claimed all the Black Seminoles were their slaves to use or sell. They kidnapped and sold all they could capture. By 1848, despite all the pleas for help from the government, their children were being kidnapped and sold at an alarming rate. To make matters worse, U.S. Attorney General John Y. Mason decided in June of 1848 that the Black Seminoles should not be granted freedom but should be returned to slavery under the Seminoles, who were now hostile and not willing to practice the same kind of slavery they had practiced in Florida. The Seminoles were also in no position to protect the Black Seminoles from the Creeks. By late 1849, John Horse and a leader named Wild Cat determined to lead their people to Mexico. They reached Mexico in July 1850. They eventually settled at Nacimiento and lived there for the next two decades. During these years, they gained a fierce reputation on both sides of the border as trackers, fighters, and scouts.

In 1870, Captain Jacob C. DeGress, commander at Fort Duncan, met with the Black Seminoles to discuss their return to American soil and their enlistment as scouts for the U.S. Army. The American military at this time was spread far too thinly to secure the South and Southwest, and they certainly did not have the scouting expertise of the Black Seminoles. The Black Seminoles met again with Captain Frank W. Perry and later claimed Perry had made an agreement with them that they would be enlisted as scouts for full scout pay. They and their families would receive housing, rations, and tools for farming. After their service, they would receive land on which to settle permanently. Perry died and left no documentation of the agreement. In July 1870, the Black Seminoles travelled to Fort Duncan to establish terms and enlist. The first scouts were mustered into the Black Seminole Scouts on August 16, 1870.[12] They were stationed at Fort Duncan and at Fort Clark. At about the same time, Major Zenas R. Bliss took command at Fort Duncan and was much impressed with his new scouts. They mostly performed labor until 1872, when they received a new unit commander, Lieutenant John L. Bullis of the Twenty-Fourth Infantry, who would remain their commander until 1881. During that time, they served with the Fourth Cavalry, the Twenty-Fifth Infantry, the Ninth Cavalry, the Twenty-Fourth Infantry, and the Tenth Cavalry. They participated in Mackenzie's Remolino Raid into Mexico against Lipans who raided into the U.S. and used the Mexican border as refuge. Of the fifty men under Bullis's command, four of them received the Medal of Honor. During the Red River War, Private Adam Payne of the Black Seminole Scouts won the Medal of Honor when he held off Kiowa attackers to allow the four other scouts with him time to regroup and make a run for it. Three other Black Seminole Scouts, Sergeant John Ward, Private Pompey Factor, and Trumpeter Isaac Payne, received the medal for saving Bullis's life in 1875, when the four men were pursued by dozens of well-armed Comanche Indians. Bullis's horse shied in the fracas, and the other three, already well away, went back and rescued him. After the Red River War, the Black Seminole Scouts served with the Twenty-Fourth under Lieutenant Colonel William R. Shafter as they cleared the Llano Estacado of any remaining Indians. That story is in Chapter 6.

The Black Seminole Scouts assisted the army in several early successes, but by 1874, their people were starving because the government would provide rations only for the family members of the scouts, and the Black Seminoles had people with them who were not direct family members. They also had not received land for a permanent home, and appeals to the government fell on deaf ears. Shafter, Bullis, Hatch, and others made pleas on their behalf, but by mid-1875, no relief was in sight. In addition to the destitute plight of their people, the Black Seminoles and the Black Seminole Scouts came under hostile attack from local civilians who resented their presence, especially at Fort Clark. One night, an ambush set for John Horse wounded him severely and killed Private Titus Payne. Medal of Honor winner Adam Payne was murdered—by another Medal of Honor winner hired to arrest Payne as a bandit. Pompey Factor received his Medal of Honor but no pension because his service record was lost. By 1877, few of the Black Seminole Scouts were Black Seminoles. When the army no longer needed their services in 1881, the men and their people were evicted from Fort Clark. Without government permission, many joined other Seminoles and Black Seminoles in Indian Territory. The government claimed that since no copy of Perry's initial agreement with the Black Seminoles existed, the government was not obligated to provide land for a permanent home. As a result of their service, marauding Indians mostly remained south of the border. The work of the Black Seminole Scouts assisted in the success of the Buffalo Soldiers against the Indians in the South and Southwest. Their service opened the American West for settlement, but the Black Seminoles had no jobs, no homes, and no way to support their families. Their absence in the field made finding and apprehending the enemy much more difficult for the Buffalo Regiments.

The Buffalo Soldiers faced many tough challenges in the field and at their posts. One result of their isolation was limited opportunities for fun and entertainment. A great source of entertainment was baseball. The regiments formed teams and played each other, played white regiments, and occasionally played white civilian teams. They gained a reputation for their skill and athleticism. The game and their success grew. They played college teams and some professional teams. The games took them away from the isolated posts to stadiums where they played in front of large crowds. The games were an outlet to relieve boredom but also gave the troops a sense of accomplishment and built bridges between the soldiers and civilians and between whites and blacks. The men also had basketball and football teams and participated in shooting, boxing, horsemanship, and track and field.

Regimental bands were another great source of pride and entertainment for the men. The most famous band of the black regiments was that of the Fifteenth New York National Guard, renamed the 369th Infantry as part of the Ninety-Third Division in Europe in World War I. The story of James Reece and his band is in Chapter 9. All four Buffalo Regiments during the Indian War years had a band. They provided entertainment for the men and their officers, but local communities frequently invited the bands to play weekly concerts and play during parades and at celebrations. The band members worked hard, traveling the country to play a full schedule of state fairs and other events. Their service as musicians fostered positive relationships between white and black Americans—occasionally the only positive relationship the two groups shared. Colonel Benjamin H. Grierson of the Tenth Cavalry was a musician and took a personal interest in his regiment's band. From the early days of recruitment and organization, Grierson sought musicians. Instruments were in short supply, and he asked for small contributions from the men to purchase instruments. Like the other regimental bands, that of the Tenth found itself busy playing for regular duty and for entertaining on post and around the country.

After the Indian War years, the regiments continued in the West and Southwest, but they occasionally did travel for service in other places. They played key roles in the Spanish-American War, in the Philippine Insurrection, and in the Punitive Expedition into Mexico. Though the Ninth, Tenth, Twenty-Fourth, and Twenty-Fifth were denied service in World War I, they continued to patrol the Mexican border and served in the Philippines and Hawaii during that time. Some of the noncommissioned officers of the regiments did serve in Europe as officers in black regiments of the American Expeditionary Force, and they served in World War II and the Korean War, though not always in the roles or locations they sought. Desegregation of the military in 1948 meant that the Korean War marked the last days of the black regiments, and the last days of the Buffalo Soldiers. Their sacrifice and loyalty continued to be among their hallmarks throughout that time. Racist treatment continued during all these campaigns and wars, making their service even more astounding when they had to fight the enemy on the battlefield and racism both on and off the battlefield. During this same time, black Americans also served in the navy. From 1865 to about 1895, the navy averaged five thousand to six thousand sailors in service a year. About five hundred to eight hundred at any given time were black because naval rosters were still difficult to fill. Black sailors were used mostly as cooks and stewards. Before the 1948 desegregation legislation, racism and discrimination existed for black sailors, but it was different from the experiences of black soldiers. The navy could not provide separate facilities, and the men had to work together in cramped spaces. All branches struggled after 1948 to comply with the new law, but they eventually made strides in the right direction.

Throughout the years, many of these soldiers gave the last full measure and earned the country's highest military honor for heroism, the Medal of Honor, though some had to wait far too long for the recognition. Societies have always sought ways to honor their soldiers who sacrifice to save others. General George Washington established the Badge of Military Merit, a purple heart made of cloth, in 1782. Only three men received it, and it fell into disuse until 1932, when it became the now-familiar Purple Heart, acknowledging those wounded in battle. During the Civil War, Congress established the Medal of Honor in July 1862 to honor gallantry in action. Other medals and awards exist to honor lesser deeds, but the Medal of Honor has been and remains the highest honor the United States can award. Black soldiers received that award in the Civil War and in every subsequent war. A number of them received the award long after the act that merited the honor. Some recipients' stories are included in these chapters, and a list of black Medal of Honor recipients appears in Appendix A. "Since the Medal of Honor's inception 88 African Americans have earned the distinction: Civil War—Army 18, Navy 8; Indian Wars—Army 18; Peacetime, 1872–1890—Navy 8; Spanish-American War—Army 5, Navy 1; World War I—Army 1; World War II—Army 7; Korea—Army 2; Vietnam War—Army 15, Marine Corps 5; Totals—Army 66, Navy 17, Marine Corps, 5."[13]

While the following accounts of Medal of Honor recipients reflect leadership and sacrifice, many more stories equal to these exist. These few offer a glimpse of the bravery and valor of all the recipients. During the Civil War, Sergeant William H. Carney of the Fifty-Fourth Massachusetts Infantry, a former slave, became the first black recipient of the Medal of Honor. He carried the flag into battle at Fort Wagner on July

18, 1863. He was wounded five times. He held the flag high as he was carried from the field. Attendants treating his wounds offered to carry the flag for him. He refused. Once his wounds were bandaged, he walked back to his unit, still carrying the flag. During the Indian Wars, on May 13, 1880, twenty-five men of Ninth Cavalry's Company K, under the command of Sergeant George Jordan, were staying the night at Sanders Stage Station in New Mexico after a day-long march. Men and horses were exhausted. They planned to rest for the night and head back to Fort Tularosa the next morning. A rider arrived with news that Victorio and his warriors were getting ready to attack a small town near Tularosa. Jordan and his men mounted and conducted a forced march to the town. They arrived in time to fortify the town and gather the people to a place of safety. Victorio arrived and made several charges, which the soldiers repulsed. Victorio gave up and rode away. Jordan received the Medal of Honor for saving the townspeople. During the Spanish-American War, on July 1, 1898, Sergeant Edward L. Baker Jr. was charging up San Juan Hill with the rest of the Tenth Cavalry when he saw a fellow soldier fall into the river with a serious wound. The man was unable to get himself out of the water. Baker ran into the river under heavy enemy fire and hauled the wounded man to safety. Baker received the Medal of Honor for disregarding his own safety and saving another soldier.

During World War I, few of the black American soldiers in Europe saw combat, because Americans were adamantly against black American soldiers on the battlefield. Most were assigned to labor detail. The Ninety-Second Infantry Division (the Buffalo Division) and the Ninety-Third Infantry Division both saw combat. The Ninety-Third fought with the French Army and performed well. The American military strongly suggested that the French not award any black American soldiers for valor, a suggestion the French ignored. Four black soldiers received recommendations for the Medal of Honor. Three were downgraded to the Distinguished Service Cross, and the three soldiers received that award. The fourth recommendation, for Corporal Freddie Stowers of the Ninety-Third's 371st Regiment, disappeared and resurfaced in 1988. Stowers was killed in action in September, 1918, during the act for which he was eventually awarded the Medal of Honor, and was laid to rest in France. In 1991, President George Bush awarded Corporal Stowers's Medal to his surviving family members. His citation reads:

Corporal Stowers, distinguished himself by exceptional heroism on 28 September 1918 while serving as a squad leader in Company C, 371st Infantry Regiment, 93rd Division. His company was the lead company during the attack on Hill 188, Champagne Marne Sector, France, during World War I. A few minutes after the attack began, the enemy ceased firing and began climbing up onto the parapets of the trenches, holding up their arms as if wishing to surrender. The enemy's actions caused the American forces to cease fire and to come out into the open. As the company started forward and when within about 100 meters of the trench line, the enemy jumped back into their trenches and greeted Corporal Stowers' company with interlocking bands of machine gun fire and mortar fire causing well over fifty percent casualties. Faced with incredible enemy resistance, Corporal Stowers took charge, setting such a courageous example of personal bravery and leadership that he inspired his men to follow him in the attack. With extraordinary heroism and complete disregard of personal danger under devastating fire, he crawled forward leading his squad toward an enemy machine gun nest, which was causing heavy casualties to his company. After fierce fighting, the machine gun position was destroyed and the enemy soldiers were killed. Displaying great courage and intrepidity Corporal Stowers continued to press the attack against a determined enemy. While crawling forward and urging his men to continue the attack on a second trench line, he was gravely wounded by machine gun fire. Although Corporal Stowers was mortally wounded, he pressed forward, urging on the members of his squad, until he died. Inspired by the heroism and display of bravery of Corporal Stowers, his company continued the attack against incredible odds, contributing to the capture of Hill 188 and causing heavy enemy casualties. Corporal Stowers' conspicuous gallantry, extraordinary heroism, and supreme devotion to his men were well above and beyond the call of duty, follow the finest traditions of military service, and reflect the utmost credit on him and the United States Army.[14]

Another example of recognition long overdue is Sergeant Henry Johnson, who singlehandedly defeated numbers of enemy Germans in World War I. Many have championed his cause for a number of years, and he is just now getting closer to receiving the Medal of Honor.[15] His story is in Chapter 9.

Though the Buffalo Soldiers are mainly known for the military legacy they left during the Indian Wars, their service is much more varied and expansive than that. This chapter mentions but a very few incidents of that service. After the Indian Wars, they continued to serve in varied capacities, until complete integration during the Korean War closed the last chapter of their story. Black Americans went on to serve with distinction in an integrated military. The following chapters focus on the Indian Wars, while the last chapters examine black troops' lesser-known service in later engagements. Our story will end with their last days together as regiments.

CHAPTER 4

A Different Kind of War: The Ninth Cavalry

Captain Frank T. Bennett looked at the grim faces of his men of the Ninth Cavalry. They had provided escorts dozens of times, but this one was different. Their commander, Colonel Edward Hatch, had petitioned for six months on behalf of their charges, Victorio and his Mimbres Apaches a subtribe of the Apaches who traditionally lived around the Ojo Caliente and Mimbres Mountain regions of New Mexico. Hatch, Indian agent Dr. Walter Whitney, even General William Tecumseh Sherman, commander of the army, and General John Pope, commander of the Department of the Missouri, agreed with Hatch, and had tried for years to persuade the Interior Department to allow Victorio to remain at Canada Alamosa. Victorio had agreed to treaty terms several times, in exchange for food, supplies, and permission for his people to remain at Canada Alamosa. The Bureau of Indian Affairs never sent adequate food, so the Apaches were in a state of chronic starvation. The men of the Ninth initially received orders to punish the starving Apaches if they left the reservation to find food. Government annuities often did not arrive on schedule or were not nearly enough to adequately feed the people. Indians left the reservation to hunt food for their hungry families, but the Ninth had orders to apprehend them and return them to the reservation, even though no food was available to them. They spent years in that endeavor, rounding them up each time they left, with several skirmishes throughout that time. In one incident, Lieutenant Henry

Ninth Cavalry, Company D, sharpshooter collar insignia, Crawford, Nebraska, 1880–1890, C. C. McBride, photographer. (Library of Congress)

H. Wright, in command of six enlisted cavalrymen of the Ninth and several Navajo scouts, became surrounded and unable to escape the enemy. Corporal Clinton Greaves charged the Indians and broke through their line, allowing Wright and the others to escape possible capture and death. Corporal Greaves received the Medal of Honor.

The endless scouting patrols and frequent skirmishes did not change the fact that many times the Indians left the reservation and committed depredations to acquire food. They often stole horses and rustled cattle, and if settlers tried to prevent them, the Indians usually killed them or took them hostage to sell or trade for cattle or horses. Locating them and forcing people in such desperate condition back to the reservation was difficult, but it was the Ninth's duty. When these efforts failed to reduce the frequency of raids on local farms and ranches, the Ninth received orders in the spring of 1877 to move the Apaches to the more remote area of San Carlos—to forcibly escort the starving people from their homeland to a place that they hated and a place that would be even more dangerous and detrimental to them. The government placed them on the most inhospitable part of the reservation, with inadequate food and water sources. Government rations were often late and insufficient to feed all the Indians. Their neighbors on the reservation were a group of Apaches with whom they shared long-standing animosity and with whom they now competed for scarce resources. Some of the people were so weakened from hunger that they could not walk and had to ride in wagons. Pleas on their behalf for better treatment came from former conscientious Indian agents and from officers such as Hatch, but those pleas fell on deaf ears.

John P. Clum, Indian agent at San Carlos, exercised an undue influence over the government's decision to relocate the Apache. Twenty-three-year-old Clum had been in the Signal Corps, but it was his affiliation with the Dutch Reform Church that led President Ulysses S. Grant to appoint him, as part of the Peace Policy, as the civilian agent at San Carlos. Clum went to the Ojo Caliente reservation to arrest a group of renegade Chiricahua Apaches, another subtribe. While he was there, however, he recommended that Victorio's people, the Warm Springs Apaches, be relocated to San Carlos along with the renegade Chiricahuas. The government gave full support to this bad decision and assigned the Ninth Cavalry to execute the move.

Victorio was in an impossible situation and was desperate. His name belongs on an impressive list of Chiricahua Apache leaders, such as Cochise, Mangas Coloradas, Loco, and Nana. Victorio's people lived mostly in New Mexico, Mexico, and Arizona. His band of Chiricahua was the Mimbres, also known as Warm Springs, Coppermine, or Ojo Caliente Apaches. The Ojo Caliente Reservation in New Mexico was in Canada Alamosa, the valley the Mimbres repeatedly requested the government to designate as their permanent home. Victorio preferred peace but did not shrink from war to protect his people and their way of life. He had the reputation of a cold-blooded killer. He had many enemies, from settlers to military officers to leaders of other subtribes, and by the mid-1870s, they wanted him dead. He was probably born around 1825, during a time of turmoil, and for most of his life, it seems Victorio knew little but strife.

The Mimbres' desire to remain on their homeland was at the heart of their problems. Several issues made their staying unlikely. The Santa Rita copper mines existed on their land. They had little interest in mining the copper, but both whites and Mexicans regularly trespassed across Indian territory to work the mines, some of whom claimed ownership. Though ownership was unclear, Chihuahuan banker Francisco Manuel Legume obtained a grant from the Spanish crown and extracted the ore using local Mexican slave labor. He promised food and supplies to the Apaches if they allowed him to work the mine, food and supplies that never arrived. Through the years, white and Mexican desire for the copper and non-delivery of promised food and supplies inevitably led to conflict and violence with the Apaches, who were repeatedly forced to choose between raiding and starving. When white and Mexican pressure on Apache resources meant dwindling game, the Apaches resorted to raiding local settlements and ranches. In 1835, in response to what the Mexicans called depredations, such as cattle rustling, murder, and kidnapping, Sonora reinstituted an earlier policy of extermination against the Apaches. Indian hunters only had to produce scalps as proof to receive a bounty. In 1849, bounties increased to two hundred pesos for an adult male, but any scalp would do, including those from women and children and Mexicans. There was no shortage of scalp hunters, and Sonoran officials paid out thousands of pesos for scalps each year.

Trouble for Victorio escalated in 1837 with the massacre of Mimbres Apache chief Juan Jose Compa and some of his people at the hands of an American scalp hunter from Kentucky named James Johnson. Compa was a beloved and capable leader, and his people wanted revenge. Apache custom called for retaliation, which came in the form of swift and bloody raids, leaving a trail of dead settlers and Mexicans. The Mexicans abandoned the Santa Rita mine in the wake of so much violence. Many of the raids took the Apaches into Texas. These two groups had experienced so much hostility over the years that both groups felt only hatred for each other. Many Texans, who viewed Indians as a threat to their families, homes, and livestock, believed the only solution was extermination. The raids to revenge Campo's death renewed the violence. Mirabeau B. Lamar, president of Texas from 1838 to 1840, declared war on the Indians, "an exterminating war upon their warriors; which will admit of no compromise and have no termination except in their total extinction or total expulsion."[1] After the war with Mexico from 1845 to 1848, the American government, realizing large numbers of whites would flock to the newly won western territories, tried to connect with the Apaches, to establish and arrange for resettlement onto reservations. The Apaches were reluctant to establish any kind of relationship, still smarting from the Johnson massacre. American Jack Hayes, named Indian subagent for areas of New Mexico in 1849, failed to establish communications with the Apaches and declared, "the Apaches are treacherous, warlike and cruel, and need severe chastisement before they can be made to know the policy of observing good faith with white people." "Special Agent George Bailey of the Interior Department reported to Commissioner of

Indian Affairs Charles E. Mix in November 1858, that, 'the testimony of all who have any knowledge of the Apache concurs in pronouncing him the most rascally Indian on the continent. Treacherous, bloodthirsty, brutal with an irresistible propensity to steal, he has been for years the scourge of Mexico ... and grave doubts are expressed whether any process short of extermination will suffice to quiet him.'"

During the Civil War, Confederate Lieutenant Colonel John R. Baylor called for the extermination of all Indians, with orders to his Arizona Guards and Arizona Rangers to "use all means to persuade the Apaches or any other tribe to come in for the purpose of making peace, and when you get them together kill all the grown Indians and take the children prisoners and sell them to defray the expense of killing the Indians." Union Colonel James Henry Carleton ordered "all Indian men ... killed whenever and wherever they could be found."[2] The Apaches were not innocent victims, but they did not completely deserve their bad reputation, and much of what they did was in reaction to the treatment they received from their enemies. Through the years, Mexican and white bandits and rustlers blamed their crimes on the Apaches. Ranchers were more than willing to lay blame on the Indians, since they received reimbursement from the government if their losses were the result of Indian raids. Some ranchers even arranged for whites to steal their livestock, so that they could make a claim for government reimbursement and make a profit. The Apaches had nowhere to hide. Apache hatred and distrust of both Americans, especially Texans, and Mexicans only grew over the years. A permanent place to live on their homeland might have prevented most or all of these problems.

Eventually, their situation compelled them to agree to treaties and reservation life but not at Ojo Caliente. They first agreed to a treaty in 1852, which Congress ratified in 1853. The Apaches were faithful to the treaty agreements, but Congress was not. Settlers and miners rushed into the newly won western territories when war with Mexico ended and when gold was discovered in California. This put pressure on available resources and pushed the remaining wildlife out of the area, which further reduced food supplies. In addition, the United States nearly always failed to provide food and other promised supplies. The Apaches stole to avoid starvation, continuing raids into Mexico in order to feed their families. A new treaty in 1855 limited the Apaches to smaller reservations, but Congress failed to ratify it until 1870. One part of this treaty, however, greatly disturbed Victorio and his Mimbres Apaches. The treaty introduced the idea of removal from their homelands. The idea persisted for years, with Victorio, who had been their leader for years, making it known that they would not agree to a move.

With the outbreak of the Civil War, many Americans, including the soldiers, headed east. These war years did not eliminate conflict between Apaches and whites, and certainly not between Apaches and Mexicans. When the war ended and Americans redoubled their interest in the West, trouble escalated again. The United States sent most of their postwar military, including the new all-black regiments, to the West to subjugate Indians and open the West for settlement. In July 1867, Congress created the Indian Peace Commission charged to place Indians on reservations away from roads, settlers, and railroads. They were to find more humane and more economical ways to treat the Indians while removing them from contact with white Americans. President Grant implemented several actions, which came collectively to be known as the Peace Policy or Grant's Peace Policy, at the beginning of his administration. Unhappy with the trouble, expense, and lack of progress of Indian subjugation, Congress made significant changes, such as replacing military agents with civilians, revising treaties and improving reservations, and concentrating Indians onto pieces of land to make controlling and supplying them more efficient. Some of these actions were honest efforts to help the Indians. By the late 1860s, Indian agents and subagents were doing a poor job at best caring for the Indians. They were to maintain peace, keep the Indians on reservations, and distribute food and other supplies. Some of these men were simply not up to the job; others were corrupt and exploited the Indians.

The poor reservation system with its ineffective agents and subagents led to increased violence, both from and against the Indians. Because of the pressure on game and the failure of the government to provide promised annuities, they raided local ranches and homes for cattle, horses, food, and captives. Rustlers continued to blame Indians for their crimes. Settlers wanted clear access to land that was free of Indian inhabitants. Americans disagreed on what to do about the Indians. The military wanted to subjugate and control them, though some military personnel agreed with the settlers, who wanted to exterminate them. Others, especially Easterners, wanted to assimilate them. All of these ideas involved reservations in some capacity. Grant's Peace Policy was designed to reform the treaty and reservation system and to replace inept or corrupt agents with Christians who were honest and would have the Indians' best interests at heart. The civilian agents would locate and design reservations, distribute rations, and prepare the Indians for assimilation into white culture. The Apaches experienced a procession of these new civilian agents, but they were inept, and none of them improved the Apaches' circumstances. Only two agents, Dr. Michael Steck and

Lieutenant Charles Drew, even came close to improving conditions for Victorio and his people, such as improving access to water, making sure annuities arrived and were distributed, and even allowing the men to leave the reservation to hunt extra food for their families. Unfortunately, Steck left for another job, and Drew died in the field.

By August of 1869, the American government again contemplated moving the Mimbres Apaches instead of letting them remain at Canada Alamosa, near Ojo Caliente, which had unofficially served as their reservation for many years and was located in their homeland, but they decided against it. Poor treatment of the Apaches continued in November of 1870, when Indian Commissioner Ely S. Parker instructed Colonel Nathaniel Pope to "select a tract near Fort Stanton for a Southern Apache reservation, one far enough from their homeland to guarantee they would be dissatisfied with it."[3] The Board of Indian Commissioners independently sent Vincent Colyer, a representative tasked to find a suitable reservation site for all the Apaches. Colyer did not serve as an agent to the Apaches, but his decisions hurt them perhaps more than all the agents combined except for Clum. Colyer visited several possible sites and interviewed Indians. When he arrived at Canada Alamosa in August 1871, the person he should have met above all others, Victorio, was in Mexico. Victorio would have made it clear to Colyer that Canada Alamosa was where his people belonged and that no other place would do, especially San Carlos, the place they dreaded the most. The land at San Carlos was dry with water that was in short supply much of the year. Temperatures rose to well above one hundred degrees in the summer. Canada Alamosa had good water, good land, in a location the government could easily and inexpensively provide supplies. Instead, Colyer selected a site in the Tularosa Valley, about ninety miles from the Apaches' home and so isolated that the government would have great difficulty and expense sending supplies. This single decision promised a decade of suffering and bloodshed. All the Apaches would relocate to the new Tularosa Reservation by the end of 1870. The United States did not know or did not care that many factions of the Apaches were long-time enemies, resulting in outright refusal on the part of many of them to relocate to Tularosa. Victorio protested so vehemently that the Mimbres were allowed to remain at Canada Alamosa for a while longer.

A while longer ended in May and June of 1871, when they were forced to move to Tularosa. Victorio's people were assigned to a location on Tularosa that the military had abandoned because of the high danger of malaria to soldiers. By October, unhealthy conditions had reduced the Mimbres by about 25 percent. They did not have enough food; they had inadequate medical care; they did not like Indian Agent Orlando F. Piper; and they did not get along with the other Apaches at Tularosa. Violence between the groups meant the women and children, especially, were in constant danger of attack. They pleaded to return to Ojo Caliente. Their reasons did not persuade the government, but something else did. The location of Tularosa made it easy for young warriors to slip into Mexico for raids and then slip back onto the reservation. What could have been a return to their home and an improvement for the Mimbres turned into a disaster. They finally received permission to leave Tularosa in 1874 and go back to Ojo Caliente, but within a year, the government again considered moving them to a more concentrated reservation to make it easier to control and supply them. Their new home was far worse than Tularosa. The very thought of the San Carlos Agency in Arizona filled them with dread. The climate was very dry and harsh, and they knew life there would be difficult. By the summer of 1876, it was a reality.

Frederic Remington described the San Carlos reservation:

> [It is a] vast tract of desert and mountains, and near the center of it, on the Gila River, is a great flat plain where the long low adobe buildings of the agency are built. Lines of white tents belonging to the cantonment form a square to the north. I arrived at this place one evening after a hot and tiresome march, in company with a cavalry command. ... The San Carlos is a hotter place than I ever intend to visit again. A man who is used to breathing the fresh air of New York Bay is in no condition to enjoy at one and the same time the dinner and the Turkish bath which accompanies it.[4]

Soldiers dreaded duty at San Carlos as well, commonly referring to it as "Hell's forty acres." It had many areas with no water at all, no trees for shade in temperatures that averaged between 100 and 120 degrees, and scarce game. The water that did exist was not fit to drink. Large numbers of rattlesnakes, scorpions, and tarantulas made it their home. Owen Wister, author of *The Virginian*, wrote: "Take stones and ashes and thorns, with some scorpions and rattlesnakes thrown in, dump the outfit on stones, heat the stones red hot, set the United States Army after the Apaches, and you have San Carlos."[5]

The dreadful assignment of escorting the Mimbres to San Carlos was not the first escort for the Ninth, nor was it their first encounter with Indians. The Ninth had a long history of both since their creation in July 1866, as one of two all-black cavalry regiments. In August 1866, when President Ulysses S. Grant issued orders for General William T. Sherman, commander of the Military Division of the Missouri, and commander of the Division of the Gulf, General Philip H. Sheridan, to organize two regiments of cavalry, he handpicked the officers he preferred for command of those regiments. He recommended Colonel Edward Hatch, who had commanded cavalry in the Civil War and had served under Colonel Benjamin H. Grierson on Grierson's famous 1863 cavalry raid into Mississippi as part of Grant's Vicksburg Campaign. Hatch immediately established his headquarters in Louisiana and began recruiting. By November 1866, he had several hundred recruits but no officers. Many white officers refused to serve with black regiments, preferring a lesser rank with white regiments. George Armstrong Custer had accepted a lesser rank to serve with a white regiment, the Seventh Cavalry. Finally, Lieutenant Colonel Wesley Merritt and Major Albert P. Morrow, both able officers, joined the Ninth. Merritt came on board and stayed until July 1876, when he took command as colonel of the Fifth Cavalry. Morrow joined on March 1867 and stayed with the regiment for fifteen years. The recruits, still pouring in, were largely unqualified in a number of ways. Most were illiterate, and many were physically deficient. Some had served in the Civil War. Postwar conditions did not favor black men in civilian roles, with rampant, widespread, and violent racism and no opportunities. Military service offered an attractive alternative, and many tried to enlist knowing they were physically unfit. The term of enlistment for cavalry was five years. The army offered steady and respectable work, with much higher pay than the rare civilian jobs, and soldier benefits included food, shelter, clothing, medical care, and education. The enlisted for the Ninth came from Louisiana, Kentucky, South Carolina, and Texas. They included George Gray, a Kentucky farmer who died of tetanus at Fort Clark, Texas; William Sharpe, a laborer who died from an Indian arrow on the Pecos River; Emanuel Stance, a five-foot-tall nineteen-year-old from Charleston, South Carolina, who won the Medal of Honor; and Washington Wyatt from Virginia, who was murdered in Austin Texas at age twenty and whose murderer was never apprehended.

In addition to the physical infirmities, such as lame limbs, hernias, and dysentery, that they bought with them, they had to endure crowded conditions in unhealthy camps. In October and November alone, twenty-three died of cholera. As a result, desertions rose and morale plummeted, making recruiting more difficult. In spite of the difficulties, especially the shortage of officers, Hatch miraculously had all twelve companies organized by February 1867. Still woefully short of officers, he received orders in March 1867, to move the entire regiment to Texas, ten companies to San Antonio and two to Brownsville. They had a shaky start, with soldiers near the point of mutiny before they reached their first posts. The travel was difficult, with shortages of food and supplies. The men suffered from illnesses on the trip. They also experienced racism from civilians, officers, and Congress. By summer, however, they arrived at their new assignments at Fort Davis and Fort Stockton, just as the need for soldiers in West Texas sharply increased. The Ninth started years of service against marauding Indians, Mexican and white bandits and rustlers; they would perform endless border patrols over harsh terrain in a punishing climate. By late 1875 and early 1876, the entire regiment was stationed in New Mexico, where they remained until December 1881.

Fort Stockton had been vacant since the start of the Civil War, and it was rundown. Upon reoccupation, the Ninth had to repair and rebuild the fort. Since many forts were in similar shape, building materials were few. Hatch sent his men into the Guadalupe Mountains to establish a sawmill and provide lumber for building and repairs. Forts were far apart, with poor roads and little communication connecting them, and the troops had to guard vast distances. In addition to making the fort livable, they found themselves fighting Indians right away. The area surrounding Fort Stockton was busy with Indian activity. The fort sat astride the Comanche War Trail, which passed through the Staked Plains and southern Texas into Mexico. The harsh conditions on the Staked Plains, also known as the Llano Estacado and the Great American Desert, made it difficult for humans and animals alike. Captain Randolph B. Marcy of the Fifth United States Infantry encountered the Staked Plains while exploring the Red River in 1852 and made this comment:

> Its elevation above the sea is two thousand four hundred and fifty feet at the head of Red River. It is very level, smooth, and firm, and spreads out in every direction as far as the eye can reach, without a tree, shrub, or any other herbage to intercept the vision. The traveler ... sees nothing but one vast dreary, and monotonous waste of barren solitude. It is an ocean of desert prairie ... and absence of water causes all animals to shun it; even the Indians do not venture to cross it except at two or three points, where they find a few small ponds of water.[6]

Descriptions such as this and early maps from the Topographical Corps of Engineers provided the only information soldiers and commanders of regiments had until Ranald S. Mackenzie and William R. Shafter conducted extensive exploration of the area. The soldiers stationed at Fort

Stockton carried the major responsibility for patrolling the war trail near the fort and scouting for the Comanche raiders who routinely used the trail and the Staked Plains to conduct raids into Mexico to steal cattle and horses and to capture Mexican women and children and then evade pursuit. Raiding season was usually in late summer or early fall, under the Comanche Moon, or Blood Moon, a signal to both fearful Mexicans and anxious Comanche that the time was right for the Indians to head south. They usually spent a few months gathering herds and captives, staying just across the border so they could make a quick flight to safety if soldiers arrived. The raiders were experts at stealing animals and taking captives, and their skill at retreat up the Comanche War Trail made it nearly impossible for anyone to follow or apprehend them. They were among the few who knew every inch of the Staked Plains, including where to find water even in dry years. They also developed skills that virtually no pursuer could challenge. They could ride hard and fast for many hours, do without food for days, and do without water for extended periods. This made it more difficult and more terrifying for their captives and enhanced their prestige and reputation as fearsome raiders and warriors.

Water was always one of the most difficult challenges for the troops out West. The forts needed close and reliable water sources. Fort Stockton was fortunate to be near Comanche Spring. Indians and travelers relied on its abundant supply of good water. Hatch recognized its value to his troops and his enemies. Hatch was not the only one to secure water and deny it to enemies; Grierson and the Tenth Cavalry effectively denied water to Victorio in 1879 and 1880, assisting the Ninth in evicting Victorio from American soil for good. Hatch and his men located the other water sources in the area and strategically placed troops to control all of them, providing water to travelers and denying it to Indians. Troops rotated guard duty at these locations, enduring long, isolated, and tedious days and weeks. They also established and manned outposts, such as the one at Fort Lancaster, a key site for protecting the U.S. mail route, a favorite target for raiders. Two of the Ninth's enlisted, Corporal Samuel Wright and Private Eldridge Jones, died guarding a mail coach in October 1867. Most of the time at Fort Stockton and its outposts was dedicated to endless patrols and scouts, escorts, guard duty, post repair and improvements, and the construction of miles of road and telegraph lines, with relatively few Indian sightings but plenty of other enemies: boredom, the heat, inadequate rations, fatigue, disease, racism, and persistent lack of water. The times they did encounter Indian enemies were usually gruesome, such as in April 1872, when Ninth cavalry troopers discovered nine dead men next to a burning freight wagon. The freighters had died in the most horrific ways, some burned alive. The troopers pursued the Indians but did not capture them. Most of the time, the Indians escaped without a trace, taking valuable supplies and animals—and captives—with them.

In May 1871, companies of the Ninth Cavalry and the Twenty-Fifth Infantry were sent to reoccupy Fort Hudson in Texas. This outpost was located in an area especially dangerous to settlers and travelers, keeping the Buffalo Soldiers busy on patrols and scouts for marauders and raiders. They all heard about what came to be known as the Warren Wagon Train Raid that same month. As many as one hundred Kiowa raiders under Satanta, Satank, and Big Tree watched as General Sherman and a small escort passed by their ambush site. Sherman was on an inspection tour to assess military needs in the area and determine the best approach to the "Indian problem." He needed to decide whether to go along with the methods of Peace Policy advocates or to recommend a return to the

Ninth Cavalry on review, 1898. (Library of Congress)

policies and methods the military used and preferred. In 1868, Sherman had expressed his preference against the Peace Policy in a letter to Grant. The Peace Policy would move Indian affairs from military control to civilian control, and Sherman was strongly in favor of military control of all Indian matters. He found a perfect example to support his argument when he visited the Navajo that year. As a result of the Peace Policy, the Navajo were moved to Bosque Redondo near Fort Sumner, New Mexico. The 1600-acre reservation had been established in 1863 for more than nine thousand Navajo and five hundred Mescalero Apache based on the recommendation of the Indian Affairs Commission, with the idea that the government could more easily and efficiently contain and supply them. Sherman had visited the Bosque and called it "a mere spot of green grass in the midst of a wild desert. "The Navajos," Sherman said, "had sunk into a condition of absolute poverty and despair."[7] His letter announced his intention of moving the Navajo back to their original country immediately. As he continued his investigation in 1871, he was almost the victim of an Indian ambush. The Kiowa were waiting to ambush a wagon train when they spotted Sherman and his escort. The Kiowa let him pass unmolested only because they knew the Warren wagon train would pass that same route later that day and would provide better supplies than Sherman's small party. Sherman arrived at his destination completely unaware of his near miss. When Sherman heard the story of the massacre of Henry Warren and six of his men—how one of them had been tied to a wagon wheel and burned alive—he was even more convinced that the Peace Policy was not the solution. The three Kiowa leaders were later arrested. Chapter 5 covers more of this story.

Some companies of the Ninth were stationed with Colonel Mackenzie's Fourth Cavalry at Fort McKavett near the San Saba River in central Texas. They performed frequent patrols to guard water sources and protect settlers. On May 20, 1870, Sergeant Emanuel Stance commanded a routine patrol. Spotting a group of Indians with a stolen horse herd, Stance's men gave chase. They did not capture the Indians, but they did recover some of the stolen horses. That night the soldiers camped at Kickapoo Springs, a Fort McKavett outpost, and headed back to the fort the next day. Along the way, they prevented the Indians from attacking a wagon train. During the skirmish, the Indians tried to flank the soldiers. Stance's quick thinking thwarted the attack and drove off the Indians. Along with saving his men and the wagon train, they recovered additional stolen horses. Sergeant Stance won the Medal of Honor for his decisions and actions.

The other early assignment for the Ninth was at Fort Davis, in the heart of Apache country, with danger in every direction from the many

Apache subtribes who lived in the region around the fort. As with many installations at this time, Fort Davis had been abandoned at the start of the Civil War, but Lieutenant Colonel Wesley Merritt and four companies of the Ninth took possession in July 1867, and immediately began repairs to the buildings. With no vegetables to eat, the troops developed scurvy. They spent much of their first year rebuilding the fort, planting a vegetable garden, patrolling the area within their command, and escorting the mail route between Fort Stockton, San Antonio, and El Paso. The Fort was near the Comanche War Trail, but Apaches, Mexicans, and white rustlers were responsible for most of the trouble in the area. By 1877, both reservation and nonreservation Apaches were conducting frequent raids, and by 1879, Victorio was a major problem.

While stationed at Fort Davis, the Ninth Cavalry received the assignment to travel to Ojo Caliente in the summer of 1875, to stop Apache raids. They found the Apaches starving, in poor health, and angry. Once again, promised food had not arrived, so the Indians continued raiding literally to survive. The Ninth and other regiments, including the Buffalo Soldier Tenth Cavalry and Twenty-Fifth Infantry, needed to find the Indians and get them back onto the reservations. Time and experience had shown the difficulty of both. Hatch and the Ninth spent months searching for the elusive Indians, who moved between hiding places on both sides of the U.S.–Mexico border. They played a cat and mouse game with American and Mexican forces, whose governments refused to join forces against the Apaches. When the Apache were finally subdued, the men of the Ninth did not look forward to the unpleasant duty of escorting the downtrodden Apaches to their inhospitable new home.

Trouble, however, started before the move to San Carlos. When the Indians learned of the arrival of troops to escort them from Warm Springs to the reservation, many Indians fled to the nearby Black Range of the San Mateo Mountains. Captain Bennett and his men had to search the hills and round up as many as they could capture before they could begin the trip. Finally, on October 25, they departed for Fort Apache and the San Carlos Agency, over seven hundred miles away, with 169 Indians, only about half the number they expected to move. Victorio and others had escaped into the surrounding mountains to avoid capture, but they could not take all their people with them. Things only got worse. The trip was miserable. Those who had escaped trailed the escort, calling to their loved ones to try to escape. The ones the cavalry had captured were the young, the old, and the weak. They were in poor condition, undernourished to the point of collapse, with ragged clothing and few possessions. The cavalrymen witnessed the suffering but followed orders and kept them moving. In the first week of November, it rained and snowed for days. The six wagons, each with a six-mule team, struggled in the slippery ice and mud, until they could go no further. The Indians were freezing, with insufficient clothing and supplies against the weather. The enlisted men shared what they could, but they did not have much to spare themselves. Telegraph lines were down again, making it impossible for Bennett to call for help. Finally, on December 1, Bennett delivered his charges to San Carlos, ending a thankless job. The Ninth and the Apaches would, however, meet again, and soon.

In September 1877, Victorio and his people were suffering more than they could stand. He needed to find a way for his people to survive, and that would not happen at San Carlos, so the Mimbres Apaches fled the reservation. They left with no weapons or food, and most wore rags insufficient for the harsh weather. Of course, they committed raids and depredations along their escape route, and the Ninth was called out to capture them and return them to San Carlos. The Indians fled to Fort Wingate and surrendered to Colonel P. T. Swain, pleading for permission to return to Ojo Caliente. The men of the Ninth, under command of Captain Bennett and Captain Moore, returned them to San Carlos, without Victorio and the handful of warriors with him, who did not surrender until February 1878. After months of negotiations, through which Victorio hoped to persuade the government to offer his people the chance to return to Ojo Caliente or even to Canada Alamosa, Victorio learned that San Carlos would be his people's permanent home.

The Ninth stayed busy apprehending Indians, Mexicans, and whites committing raids along the frontier. They also received assignments to settle conflicts between civilians, such as a dispute over salt between Mexicans and Americans near El Paso, and a land dispute in 1875 and 1876, in Colfax County, New Mexico, between opponents of land baron Lucien B. Maxwell and Maxwell's hired gunslinger Clay Alison. The Ninth also became involved in one of the most famous conflicts of the West, the Lincoln County War in New Mexico.

The Buffalo Soldiers' role in the incident that came to be known as the Lincoln County War might have resulted in a better outcome except for a change in leadership, namely Lieutenant Colonel Wesley Merritt's transfer and promotion in 1876 to command the Fifth Cavalry and his replacement in the Ninth with Lieutenant Colonel N. A. M. Dudley, an officer with a trail of trouble behind him and a history of dispute with Hatch, his new commander.

The causes of this war reached back years earlier. The presence of military forts and troops meant big business for local communities,

sometimes providing their very lifeblood. The military made large pur-
chases from local producers of meat and other food, building supplies,
fuel, stock, and services—services the military approved and those the
military did not. The military created a market for goods and services
that contributed significantly to the economic development of the West.
It also improved transportation routes and communications, which fostered settlement and commerce. The presence of forts and troops resulted
in fewer Indian depredations and provided opportunity for both large
and small businesses to thrive, from cattle ranchers and shopkeepers to
saloon owners and prostitutes. People and businesses took great pains
to make sure government funds kept coming, and some found ways to
make huge profits.

From the very beginning of the nation, Americans did not trust or think
they needed a large standing army. The Founding Fathers had struggled
with the idea of protecting citizens without infringing upon their liber-
ties. They resolved the problem by sanctioning local law enforcement or
citizens to come together to quell insurrection or pursue outlaws. States
carried the statute under various wording, but the posse comitatus statute
was not uniformly applied or understood. In remote areas, law enforcement officials and citizens were often in short supply. Sometimes citizens favored the lawbreakers and refused to help apprehend them. Other
times sheriffs, citizens, or governors called on federal troops to intervene.
Troops not only quelled domestic disturbances and apprehended outlaws
but also came to the rescue during natural disasters, such as floods and
fires. They provided much of the labor that drove Westward expansion,
building wagon roads and exploring and mapping the frontier.

After the Civil War, Southerners in particular demonstrated a love/
hate relationship with the military. They resented the presence of federal occupation troops. They wanted the troops there to control Indians,
freedmen, and outlaws, but they resented any effort on the part of the
troops to control white behavior. They especially resented that role for
black troops.

Americans in the Southwest accused the military of protecting Indians
and mistreating whites who wanted access to Indian lands. The military struggled with these issues for years, especially since there were not
enough troops to meet the military needs of the country. In a letter to
General Grant in 1868, General Sherman expressed frustration with citizens demanding non-military use of troops in Arizona and New Mexico:
"It was never contemplated that our soldiers should be employed in
hunting down simple murderers and thieves, but this seems to have been
their habitual use here for twenty years. When a citizen loses a horse,

or some cattle or sheep, instead of calling on his neighbors to go and help find them, he rides fifty or a hundred miles to some military post to report the fact, and forthwith publishes some paragraph to the effect that the Regular troops are of no account."[8]

Congress passed the Posse Comitatus Act in 1878 in an effort to placate citizens unhappy with the military authorization and use of federal troops. The intent of the Act was to reduce the use of federal troops unless under congressional or presidential authority. Settlers wanted troops to protect them from attacks from Indians and Mexicans, but they did not want federal troops interfering in any other part of their lives, such as disputes between ranchers or settlers. The law was new and not fully clear, so the Secretary of War responded to Hatch's request for clarification and advised him to avoid further use of federal troops in the Lincoln County War.

Meanwhile, Victorio and his people were trying to make the best of an impossible situation at San Carlos. Victorio resigned himself to the idea that his people would live at San Carlos and decided to stop his efforts to change that. A quirky incident led to a new chapter in hostilities between the governments of both the United States and Mexico and the Mimbres Apaches, and the Ninth's involvement continued, this time trying to control the Apaches while being careful not to offend the Mexican government with American military presence in Mexico. At San Carlos, Victorio knew that officials from Grant County had warrants for his arrest for murder and theft. When a hunting party, including a judge and prosecuting attorney from Grant County, traveled near San Carlos, Victorio mistakenly thought they were there to serve the warrants, arrest him, and take him to trial. He once again decided to run, leaving the reservation in August 1879. He left a trail of murder, theft, and destruction in his wake, even stealing horses from Company E of the Ninth. Several companies of the Ninth pursued Victorio's Apaches, who repeatedly eluded capture by crossing into Mexico when the soldiers got too close. Following into Mexico was not an option for the cavalry troops. The United States did not want to exacerbate strained relations with the Mexican government. Depredations continued, with Americans demanding the capture or death of Victorio. With the help of Colonel Grierson's Tenth Cavalry and companies of the Twenty-Fifth Infantry and the Twenty-Fourth Infantry, the Buffalo Soldiers denied Victorio access to water and made it impossible for him to remain in the United States. He crossed into Mexico for the last time in August 1880. At this point, the Mexican government granted the United States military limited access to pursue Victorio into Mexico, but Mexican troops under

Colonel Joaquin Terrazas disagreed with their president's decision and took up the pursuit themselves rather than cooperate with the Americans when it became clear that Victorio was once again in Mexico.

Victorio's struggle ended on October 14, in the Tres Castillos Mountains, when troops under Terrazas surrounded and killed Victorio and most of those with him. They scalped the dead and displayed the trophies to adoring crowds as they marched into Chihuahua City. A *Chicago Times* correspondent reported:

> The whole city turned out.... We could discover some black objects against the sky like waving plumes of the knights of old.... These waving plumes are the ghastly scalps of the fallen enemy, held aloft to the gazing crowd.... They are on poles about ten feet long, carried four abreast. We count them, seventy-eight in number, sixteen of which [appear to be] women and children. The whole head of hair had been in most cases taken.[9]

In Victorio's final years, the Buffalo Soldiers, especially the men of the Ninth Cavalry, played a significant role in the continued troubled relationship between the Mimbres Apaches and the Americans. The soldiers were committed to following orders, but they also saw firsthand the condition and treatment of the Indians, and Victorio's situation was not unique. The Ninth would no longer pursue Victorio, but they would see extensive service in the coming years, including service against other Apaches, such as Nana, who was not present at Tres Castillos and who continued to fight for his people. They also found themselves fighting on behalf of the Indians.

In August 1877, the Indian agent at the Mescalero Agency requested help from Buffalo Soldiers at Fort Stanton to recover cattle that Texas rustlers stole from the Indians at the agency. The troops also evicted white squatters who had taken up residence on the Ojo Caliente Reservation almost before Bennett and his men were out of sight.

In Indian Territory in Oklahoma, they were assigned to stop whites from trespassing on Indian lands. The assignment was isolated, and in Indian Territory the men had even less human contact than they had at other posts where civilians lived nearby. The distance also made access to services more difficult. The army provided some but not all of the things soldiers needed and wanted. When a prostitute arrived on Indian Territory, the soldiers happily made frequent visits, but their officer made it clear no civilians were allowed in Indian Territory and ordered the soldiers to escort her off the reserve, which they reluctantly did. The soldiers were delighted when she returned disguised as a man, but this time, their commanding officer arrested her.

While the prostitute incident was an isolated and minor event, large numbers of white Americans from all regions were appalled that the government would deny them access to lands in the West, including lands set aside for reservations. This conflict between the government and white citizens had existed for decades. The war with Mexico resulted in a huge expansion of territory for the United States. After the Civil War, thousands looked West for new opportunity, in the gold fields and the towns that sprang up around the gold fields, and in lands ideal for farming and grazing, regardless of legal claim to the land. The government debated how to distribute the land, whether to sell it or grant it, but reservation lands were not part of the consideration. They were strictly off limits to whites. Both citizens and politicians were attracted to the idea of free white settlement on some of these lands, including parts of Indian Territory. Citizens and politicians in favor of allotment advocated a certain number of acres to each Indian family with the excess reservation land made available for white settlement.

One of the most persistent advocates of this plan was David L. Payne, born on a farm in Indiana in 1836. In 1857, he and his brother Jack left home to seek their fortune. Like so many others, they headed west. David, especially, managed to make a living and acquire a homestead through various endeavors. He fought as part of various regiments in Kansas during the Civil War and the Indian wars afterward. He was elected to the Kansas House of Representatives and appointed postmaster at Leavenworth, Kansas. The federal Homestead Law of 1862 had opened the door for millions of American settlers in Kansas, Nebraska, and Texas in the years after the Civil War. By the 1870s, Payne had his eye on Oklahoma in Indian Territory, reservation homeland to the Five Civilized Tribes and numerous other groups of Indians. Americans, especially former soldiers, clamored for permission to homestead on Indian land in Oklahoma. Federal law prohibited all civilians from accessing any of the land in the Territory, with absolutely no exceptions. Payne was one of many Americans who believed the government was wrong. He and his partners claimed that cattlemen were using the lands in the disputed territory already, with either the government turning a blind eye or giving its blessing.

In 1887, the Ninth went to Cheyenne, Wyoming, to guard Interior Department agents as they tore down fences cattlemen had illegally placed on government land. During the Boomer years in Indian Territory, the government did not send troops to evict cattlemen or their herds, but during the 1870s and 1880s, they evicted homesteader groups again and again. By the late 1870s and 1880s, homesteader movement groups appeared and disappeared with frequency, even after President Rutherford B. Hayes confirmed that Indian Territory would remain closed to white settlement. In 1879, Payne teamed up with Elias C. Boudinot, a homesteader of similar mind, who may have represented railroad interests. Opening the Territory to white settlement would provide tremendous business opportunities for the railroads, so they may have been willing to provide funds for the endeavor. By now, potential homesteaders were called Boomers, and Payne was an avid and capable leader of Payne's Oklahoma Colony, a group intent on settling in Indian Territory. He organized their supplies and planned the schedule for settlement, all for a fee from the prospective settlers. He was also involved in the Oklahoma Town Company. Both of these organizations were in defiance of the laws that prohibited white settlement on or use of reservation land. Both organizations collected fees from potential settlers in exchange for promises of 160-acre lots or town lots. The agreements required each member to sustain himself in the Territory for at least one year, with a required list of supplies. The number of potential settlers quickly grew from 1,500 to nearly 4,000 by early 1881. The government was trying to find legal language to stop the Boomers, but the real burden fell to the military. The government sent black soldiers from Fort Sill, Fort Reno, and Camp Supply to enforce the law and guard the borders of the reservation. This assignment, more than others, placed the Buffalo Soldiers in extreme isolation. Settlers, cattlemen, and others frequently trespassed. Most of these were not violent criminals, but patrolling for trespass and escorting those who did kept the soldiers busy.

The government sent the black soldiers of the Ninth to Indian Territory to keep the Boomers and others out of Oklahoma. As in the Colfax County War and the Lincoln County War, the black troops found themselves representing the government against its citizens. Their assignment against Payne's group of trespassers placed them in a delicate situation, especially in light of the Posse Comitatus law and experiences of other military regiments whose orders pitted them against white civilians. Some angry civilians actually filed charges against the officers and soldiers for various forms of abuse and misconduct in performing their duty in following their orders to remove the whites from the Territory, using force if necessary. Officers incurred exorbitant court and lawyer costs and suffered damage to their careers. In light of these charges, Hatch and the Ninth were advised to perform their orders with care regarding their treatment of the Boomers during removal, eviction, or arrest.

Between May 1880 and October 1885, the cavalry removed Boomers from Oklahoma ten times. The Ninth did the bulk of this work, and they performed admirably in the face of unfair criticism and unwarranted abuse from civilians, newspapers, and politicians. In May 1874, when Lieutenant M. H. Day and men of the Ninth arrived to escort Boomers from Indian Territory for the sixth time, anger flared on both sides. The Boomers, who referred to the black cavalrymen as Yellow Legs because of the yellow stripe on their uniform trousers, refused to leave and resisted when the soldiers tried to arrest them. They drew weapons on the troops and threatened to shoot them. Day heatedly ordered his men to fire their weapons at the nine hundred settlers. The startled troopers refused the order. Day threatened to arrest his men. They still refused. The Boomers cooperated with no further threats. Day later realized his rash behavior and filed no charges against his men. In August 1882, Lieutenant C. W. Taylor and men of the Ninth received the unpleasant task of yet another Boomer escort out of the Territory. When the Boomers once again resisted, Taylor had Payne and others tied to wagons. The troops loaded and hitched the wagons, untied Payne and his men from the wagons but loaded them, still bound, into their own wagons. The troops drove the wagons off the reservation and freed the men from their restraints. The Boomers protested and later filed charges. Both military and civil investigations cleared the men of the Ninth and their officers of any wrongdoing. Payne died in November 1884, and by June 1885, the Boomer invasion was over. The Ninth transferred to Wyoming, Nebraska, and Utah. Their service related to settlers in Oklahoma was not over, however. The government transitioned to an allotment system and opened Oklahoma to settlement in April 1889, squeezing the Indians onto a smaller reservation. They believed the Indians no longer needed as much land as in the past. In the past, they needed more land to hunt. The government hoped they could make the Indians into farmers on small, individual plots of land. The Buffalo Soldiers were present to make sure the "Sooners" followed the rules for settling the land recently opened for whites.

In 1887, the Ninth transferred their headquarters to Fort Robinson, Nebraska. Sad news hit the Ninth in March 1889. Colonel Hatch, the Ninth's commander since its creation in 1866, had a carriage accident and died from complications on April 11, leaving Colonel Joseph G. Tilford in command. Also in 1887, the Ninth received a West Point graduate in its officer ranks. This particular officer, Second Lieutenant John H. Alexander, caused quite a stir, since he was the second of only three black West Point graduates. Henry O. Flipper graduated in 1877, Alexander in 1887, and Charles Young in 1889. West Point did not boast any additional black graduates for nearly fifty years. For three years, Alexander shared a room at the academy with Young. Alexander was sent to Fort Robinson, then to Fort Duchesne, Utah. Young was first assigned to the Tenth Cavalry but was reassigned to the Twenty-Fifth Infantry while en route to join the Tenth. In October 1889, he was again reassigned, this time with the Ninth. Alexander was not at Fort Robinson when Young arrived. He was still stationed at Fort Duchesne. Acting commander of the Ninth while Tilford was ill was Major Guy V. Henry; he protested Young's transfer to the Ninth, claiming too many black officers would hurt the regiment's reputation. But in May 1886 a new congressional law created havoc for Young. Cadets could join regiments as "supernumerary," which meant that regiments could have two additional lieutenants (called "subalterns") until positions opened within the regiment. Young's assignment as a subaltern in the Tenth, however, placed him in line to command white troops, which was a worrisome enough prospect for Young's superiors that he was soon reassigned to the Ninth, where no such possibility existed. Young carved out an impressive career. Details of his service are in Chapter 9. Alexander served seven years with the Ninth. Unfortunately, he died suddenly of an apparent seizure in Springfield, Ohio, on March 26, 1894. Flipper joined the Twenty-Fourth Infantry, and his story is contained in Chapter 6.

At about the time of Hatch's death and Tilford's promotion to commander, the Ninth was once again involved with Indian subjugation, this time to subdue the Sioux, Cheyenne, and others at the Pine Ridge agency. Blunders and misunderstandings led to the Wounded Knee disaster at the Pine Ridge agency in December 1890. An inexperienced and nervous new Indian agent called for the military to disarm Indians he considered threatening and dangerous. When the men of the 7th Cavalry attempted to disarm the Indians, a shot rang out, and the soldiers fired on the Indians with Hotchkiss guns, killing more than two hundred. Events leading to the massacre could have been avoided. Even though other land was available, civilians wanted to settle on the Pine Ridge reservation lands and insisted the government make these lands available to them. The government complied, shrinking the reservation and compressing the Indian population onto an alarmingly small space, with insufficient resources for food and water. Settlers flooded onto the land. Almost immediately, rumors circulated of Indian reprisals and attempts to oust the whites. Most of the early rumors were just fear taking the shape of rumors, but by 1890, more than rumor was circulating. Four troops of the Ninth, under the command of Major Henry, relocated to the Pine Ridge Agency in November. The government was not providing enough food, and the Indians were literally starving to death. Some of the Indians conducted small raids in the area in reprisal or for food, and the troopers of the Ninth were sent to force them back to the reservation, a familiar and distasteful task. At that time, a Nevada Paiute named Wovoka brought a native theology known by the name Ghost Dance to Pine Ridge. Wovoka promised the Indians would once again rule the lands as they had in the past. He distributed shirts he designed, calling them Ghost Shirts and promising they would make the wearer impervious to white man's bullets, making the Indians invincible, and taught them the rituals of the new theology. Unfortunately, the Pine Ridge agent, Daniel Royer, was new, nervous, and inexperienced. He thought the Ghost Dancers were planning an uprising. Like the civilians in the area, he became alarmed and panicked with the Ghost Dance activity. Not only was Royer in a state of fear, the Indians did not respect their new agent and did what they could to intimidate and defy him. By November, panic had spread, and civilians and Royer sent urgent calls to Tilford at Fort Robinson for military intervention. By the middle of December, nearly fifteen hundred infantry and cavalry, including the Ninth, surrounded the agency. Things went from bad to worse when the Indians on the reservation heard of the death of Sitting Bull, killed at the Standing Rock agency. Many left Pine Ridge to join a growing number of warriors. The Ninth left Pine Ridge to track down those who had escaped the reservation. They were still in pursuit when news reached them that the Seventh Cavalry under Colonel James Forsyth had massacred between two and three hundred Sioux at Wounded Knee Creek on December 29. Most of the Sioux were unarmed, and many were women and children. The day after the massacre, the black soldiers made a miserable return to Pine Ridge. Meanwhile, another Forsyth blunder resulted in his men of the 7th Cavalry being trapped in a canyon and under fire from attacking Sioux. Henry and his exhausted men and horses of the Ninth hurried to their rescue. When things calmed down and the threat of violence passed, most of the troops were sent back to their stations. Four troops of the Ninth remained at Pine Ridge until the end of March to assist the Indians through the winter and make sure things remained peaceful. They and the Sioux endured a miserable winter of terrible cold and snow, but things remained quiet.

With the Wounded Knee massacre, the Indian War years of 1866 to 1890 became part of the past. Between 1868 and 1890, the Ninth fought sixty Indian battles. After their service at Pine Ridge, they settled into a routine of drills, patrols, competitions, and post maintenance. They also suffered racial violence from those they were charged to protect. In 1892, they established Camp Bettens in northern Wyoming to reduce conflict between large cattlemen of the Wyoming Stock Growers Association and a group of smaller ranchers. The large herd owners accused the white soldiers in the area of siding with the smaller ranchers in settling grazing and water disputes against the large ranchers and requested the black troops to neutralize the situation. In the small town of Suggs, Wyoming, whites objected to the presence of black soldiers in their local bar and taunted the Ninth until they fought back. Private Willis Johnson was killed. The Ninth transferred to Fort Robinson immediately after the incident. Their next assignment also involved domestic violence, when they were sent to Wyoming and Montana to make sure that strikers against the Pullman Company did not prevent delivery of the U.S. mail. They rode the mail trains and encountered no trouble, returning to Robinson in the late summer. Even with these events and other minor incidents, the Ninth experienced quiet years until the outbreak of conflict with Spain in Cuba. The Ninth served with the Tenth, the Twenty-Fourth and the Twenty-Fifth in Cuba and the Philippines. That story is in Chapter 8. Details of their service during the Great War are in Chapter 9. Their service experiences in World War II and the Korean War are in the epilogue.

CHAPTER 5

Ready and Forward:
The Tenth Cavalry

The Tenth Cavalry had spent endless, mind-numbing hours in the last few years guarding this and other water holes, but today was different. Sweat ran down their backs and into their eyes as they kept watch for any movement on the horizon. These men belonged to the Tenth Cavalry and Twenty-Fourth Infantry, the Buffalo regiments, and they, along with the Ninth Cavalry and the Twenty-Fifth Infantry, had played cat and mouse with the fearsome Victorio and his Mimbres Apaches, a part of the Mescalero Apaches, for the past year. The Apaches had a reputation for being some of the fiercest and most dangerous of the Indians of the Southwest. According to historian Robert Wooster, "by mid-nineteenth century, Comanche attacks, Spanish slavers, and disease had reduced the Mescalero population to fewer than three thousand."[1] However, even with reduced numbers, Victorio's Apaches were still conducting deadly raids, possibly more fierce in nature because they were more desperate. Victorio had been unhappy with the Americans for years. He and his people wished to stay near their homeland at Ojo Caliente in northern New Mexico. Over the years, one issue after another made that wish less probable. Finally, in 1878, they were relocated to the San Carlos Agency in Arizona. On an inhospitable piece of land, they suffered from starvation, disease, and violence from other reservation Apaches. Victorio repeatedly fled the reservation, returning against his will, but with nowhere else to go. He used hiding places in the Guadalupe Mountains of Mexico but often had to head north into New Mexico to raid for necessary supplies. For Americans, he was one of the most feared and hated Apaches, leading warriors in lightning raids to murder, scalp, and steal. In August 1879, Victorio left the reservation and terrified the settlers of the territory in another series of raids. The army, mostly the Ninth Cavalry, with Colonel Edward L. Hatch in command, chased him for more than a year. Their efforts were frustrated because Victorio always stayed close enough to the Rio Grande to cross the river and escape into the mountains, knowing the Americans did not have Mexico's permission to follow him across the border.

In the spring of 1880, General Philip H. Sheridan wanted General Edward O. C. Ord to send the commander of the Tenth Cavalry, Colonel Benjamin H. Grierson, with men from the Tenth to New Mexico to assist the Ninth in pursuit of Victorio. The Tenth had encountered the Apaches a number of times in the past, but, like the Ninth, failed to capture them. On July 30, Victorio's warriors attacked Grierson and six men between Quitman and Eagle Springs, at a small watering hole called Tinaja de las Palmas. Lieutenant Leighton Finley came on the run with fifteen men of the Tenth's Troop G. Captain Charles D. Viele and Captain Nicholas M. Nolan arrived and joined in a four-hour skirmish that chased the Apaches to the Mexican border. On August 3, Corporal Asa Weaver led troops against the Apaches at Alamo Spring. Grierson objected to the idea that the Tenth simply join the Ninth in further pursuit. He thought pursuit ineffective and unduly hard on men and animals. He also thought Victorio's next move would be into Texas. He was right. Grierson proposed a different idea. Both Grierson and Hatch understood the critical importance of water sources in the American West. Their regiments spent years locating, mapping, developing, and guarding every water hole they could find. Rather than chase the Indians, Grierson decided to cut off their access to water. He stationed men of the Tenth Cavalry and the Twenty-Fourth Infantry to guard all the water holes within Victorio's reach. They took the field in July 1880 ... and waited.

They waited at the water hole known as Eagle Springs, in West Texas in the middle of the Chihuahuan Desert. Captain John C. Gilmore with Company H of the Twenty-Fourth came under attack as they approached nearby Rattlesnake Springs with supplies. The Indians very nearly captured the supplies, but the men returned fire and chased them off. The men spent the next few extremely hot days conducting scouts to deny the Indians access to several mountain passes. They scouted ... and waited. Captain Thomas C. Lebo and Company H raided one of Victorio's mountain refuges in the Sierra Diablo and captured a small herd

Reproduction of drawing by Frederic Remington, 1889–1906, Tenth Cavalry, sitting around campfire. (Library of Congress)

of cattle and other supplies. Grierson's plan was working. Victorio was experiencing shortages of both food and water. On August 5, word arrived that Victorio was on the move, probably headed to Rattlesnake Springs. Grierson left Gilmore in charge of the supplies at Eagle Springs and took his men on a sixty-five mile forced march for Rattlesnake Springs, using the mountains as a screen from Victorio. They arrived before Victorio. On August 6, Victorio and his warriors were so desperate for water that they decided to try to fight their way to the spring. Several companies of Buffalo Soldiers joined the men already guarding the spring. They repulsed the attacks and prevented Victorio from escaping further into Texas. On August 14, Victorio was forced to head back into Mexico, never to return to the United States. On October 19, 1880, Victorio and most of his band died at the hands of the Mexican Army in the Tres Castillos Mountains of Mexico.[2]

The men of the Tenth were used to boredom and isolation. They were used to the harsh climate of the American West. They were certainly used to the constant struggle over water. They were also used to discrimination and racism. They had experienced all of these things from the time they enlisted with the Tenth. Section III of the Army Reorganization Act of 1866 authorized two black cavalry regiments, the Ninth and Tenth. Grierson commanded and organized the Tenth at Fort Leavenworth, Kansas, beginning in July 1866. Grierson was an unlikely cavalry commander. At the beginning of the Civil War, he was a musician struggling to make a living for his wife and two sons. He incurred massive debt and had to live with his parents. When the war broke out, he enlisted as an unpaid aide to the commander of an Illinois infantry regiment. In May of 1861, he was an unpaid aide-de-camp at the rank of Lieutenant for Brigadier General Benjamin M. Prentiss and the Tenth Illinois Infantry.

Reproduction of drawing by Frederic Remington, 1889–1906, Tenth Cavalry, on a mountain ledge. (Library of Congress)

Through hard work, he was promoted to major and, later, colonel of the Sixth Illinois Cavalry in October 1861. He accepted the transfer to cavalry with a bit of reluctance. Grierson's face still bore a large scar from when a horse kicked him in the head and nearly killed him when he was eight. He was not especially fond of horses. Colonel T. M. Cavanaugh was the regiment's commander, an inept political appointee who only cared about the title. Grierson took control upon his arrival in November and improved conditions and training at the camp. He did not receive pay, however, until January 1862, when the regiment was mustered into service. He saw no action in the early months of 1862. When the enlisted men went into open revolt against Cavanaugh in April, Grierson became colonel of the regiment. He immediately demonstrated strong leadership skills. His actions in 1862 gained him favor with Grant and Sherman, with Sherman calling him the "best cavalry leader." One of Grierson's commanders, Lieutenant Samuel Woodward of Company G, performed well remaining calm under fire and proving himself a capable leader of his men, and Grierson added him to his staff. They would remain together for decades.[3] In the spring of 1863, Grant used Grierson to lead a raid through Mississippi as a diversion for Grant's plans regarding Vicksburg. The raid was extremely successful and gained Grierson promotion to Brigadier General. In late 1864, he led another successful raid into Mississippi, gaining promotion to major general and command of a cavalry division in Alabama.

When Congress enacted the Army Act of 1866, Grant personally recommended Grierson as commander of the Tenth Cavalry, which he accepted. Sheridan held a strong dislike for Grierson and preferred Merritt and Custer, but Sherman liked Grierson and supported the appointment. Sheridan's dislike of him meant Grierson was occasionally passed over for commands and promotions during the remainder of his career, but he was the right man for the job. He took a personal interest in the regiment and in the men. He knew Sam Woodward was a good officer and asked him to serve as adjutant. Grierson held high standards for all recruits, enlisted and officers. At the end of 1866, he had only sixty-four enlisted men. By the end of January 1867, he had seven officers and eighty enlisted. He knew that the regiment would need only the most qualified men to succeed. Even with such high standards, not enough enlistees had the skills to serve as noncommissioned officers, but some illiterate enlistees served as sergeants while they learned to read. This strengthened bonds between officers and enlistees in ways not possible in other regiments, because officers had to do much of the clerical work until enlistees could do it.

Finding qualified men and officers was not his only problem. Conditions at Leavenworth made recruiting difficult and training impossible. When he arrived at Leavenworth in 1866, the post's commander, Brevet Major General William Hoffman, made no secret of his extreme racism and determined to make things as difficult as possible for Grierson and the Tenth. He assigned them quarters in a swampy area without adequate housing. He refused them permission to parade. He denied them proper and sufficient equipment. He leveled unending false and petty charges against them. He ordered Grierson to keep his men at least ten to fifteen yards away from white troops. These conditions were hard on Grierson and his men, but things got worse when insufficient food and inadequate quarters exposed the men to sickness and disease.

Under such difficult conditions, Grierson endeavored to get his regiment formed and transferred as soon as possible. He told his recruiter in Arkansas, Captain J. W. Walsh, to organize Company D at Fort Gibson in Indian Territory before it reached full strength and to draw supplies for a full regiment. He planned to fill the company later. Getting enough good horses was another huge problem, one that nearly every cavalry regiment in the West faced at the time. Even with all the problems, Grierson made progress. By February, March, and April, Grierson had several companies ready for assignment. Hoffman continued his efforts to impede the Tenth's progress, but there was little he could do once the companies were ready to leave Leavenworth. In June, Grierson notified Hoffman that the word *colored* would not be used regarding his regiment, that they would be known as the Tenth Regiment of Cavalry U.S. Army. Problems continued, one of the worst being a cholera outbreak in June and July, but Grierson and his men remained stalwart. On July 30, the regiment received orders to transfer to Fort Riley, Kansas. By the end of August, Grierson transferred his headquarters to Fort Riley, had companies in the field in Indian Territory, and had the rest on duty at various posts and camps along the Kansas Pacific Railroad in central Kansas. When Woodward arrived at Riley in September to serve as adjutant, acting adjutant Captain Henry Alvord began a twenty-year command of Company M. Between August 1867 and April 1868, the last four regimental companies formed at Fort Riley. During those same months, Grierson took care to form a regimental band, finding ways to fund instruments. By the spring of 1868, the band had gained a wide following and enjoyed a busy schedule. It was a source of pride for Grierson and for the Tenth. The Tenth served at Fort Riley from August 1867 until April 1868. In March 1869, the regiment moved to Camp Wichita in Indian Territory and built Fort Sill from the ground up. They served at Fort Sill for five years.

The regiment had barely completed the move to Fort Riley when Grierson's work was soon tested. To replace federal garrisons withdrawn during the Civil War, the men of the Tenth were needed on the Central and Southern Plains to fight Kiowa and Comanche warriors who had been raiding throughout the Texas frontier and Indian Territory. In 1864 and 1865, trouble had erupted between whites and Cheyenne in Colorado in the Central Plains. The Treaty of Little Arkansas in October 1865, which ended the fighting, placed these Indians on reservations in Texas and Kansas; both states refused to honor the treaty and accept reservations. Violence erupted anew between the Kiowa, Comanche, and Cheyenne against the Texans. In April 1867, General Hancock conducted an expedition to intimidate the Indians, but the expedition actually fostered anger among the Indians instead, and the violence continued. Grierson sent Companies D, E, and L to Indian Territory. Five companies of the Tenth were protecting workers and property along the

Kansas-Pacific Railroad, a frequent target of Indian raids. The men were glad to be away from Hoffman and busy with new assignments. Leaving Leavenworth did not, however, mean the end of racism and deprivation. Their new posts were in disrepair, they were continually awaiting supplies, and local civilians did not welcome them with open arms.

The regiment's first conflict came in August 1867. A large group of Cheyenne had attacked a railroad camp and killed seven men. Captain George A. Armes took Company F in pursuit. The trail led up the Saline River. On August 2, about seventy-five Cheyenne warriors attacked the thirty-four soldiers. Armes dismounted his men and fought the enemy for at least six hours, with more Cheyenne joining the fight. The soldiers were completely surrounded. Armes noted that the Cheyenne were using the new Spencer carbine and had plenty of ammunition. Armes was wounded in the hip, but Sergeant William Christy was killed, shot in the head, marking the first of many combat deaths for the Tenth. Armes estimated the enemy force to number as many as four hundred. Finally, they retreated, and he and his men limped back to camp. They would soon meet that same enemy again. Cheyenne raids continued. On August 20, Captain Armes and Company F, along with volunteers from the Eighteenth Kansas Cavalry, headed out to find the raiders. They became separated and fell under attack near Beaver Creek. Armes was certain he saw some of the most notorious Cheyenne leaders, Roman Nose and Satanta, as well as Charlie Bent, who sometimes served the military as a scout, among the enemy. The fighting had raged for more than a day when the Indians finally withdrew, and Armes headed back to Fort Hays with a number of wounded and dead. The Eighteenth Kansas lost sixteen wounded and two dead. Armes and Company F lost thirteen wounded and one dead, Private Thomas Smith. According to Armes, who was never lavish with praise, in both of these encounters, his rookie soldiers fought with "courage and perseverance under dangers the most trying."[4]

On August 1, 1868, Company I and Captain G. W. Graham were conducting another of the seemingly endless scouts for raiders when they came under fire from approximately one hundred Cheyenne on Big Sandy Creek. The next month, Captain Louis H. Carpenter and Company H went in search of the same group of Cheyenne. On September 22, two soldiers from Fort Wallace were riding to Captain Carpenter with a message when they encountered two frantic and bloody men. Jack Stilwell and Pierre Trudeau were not rookie scouts, but they told the two black soldiers a fantastic story of their harrowing experience and asked the men to return with them for assistance. The event was triggered by a shortage of cavalry in the area, a shortage so acute that General Sheridan had ordered his aide, Major George A. Forsyth, to raise a regiment of cavalry and scout for raiders. They took the field in early September. They struck the trail and were confident of finding the Cheyenne. On the morning of September 17, the Cheyenne found them and attacked with a fury. Hundreds of warriors surrounded Forsyth and fought all day. Stilwell and Trudeau needed the soldiers to hurry to the rescue. By the 23rd, Carpenter had covered many miles without discovering the location of Forsyth. Finally, they found recently buried Indians with evidence suggesting they died in battle. One of the dead turned out to be Roman Nose. They knew they were getting closer, but Carpenter did not find Forsyth until the 25th. Reuben Waller, a soldier in Carpenter's Company H, described the scene as they arrived at the sandbar island in the Arikaree Fork of the Republican River where they battle had raged. The stench of death greeted them long before they saw the aftermath with their own eyes. The scene they found on arrival was gruesome and nearly beyond description. Fifty dead and bloated horses formed a ring on the outer part of the island. Their bodies were covered with black flies. They had been dead for ten days. Inside the circle of horses were dead and wounded men in terrible shape. Among the dead were scouts, surgeon J. H. Mooers, and Lieutenant Fredrick H. Beecher, for whom the island and battle were subsequently named. Among the wounded was Forsyth, wounded so badly that he was not expected to survive the day. The men of Forsyth's command had run out of food and water on the second day of their ordeal. They had started eating their dead horses at that time. As the horses rotted, they continued to eat the decayed flesh for another week. They were literally starving when the Tenth rescued them. The Tenth treated the wounded enough to travel and made it back to the fort. Though not involved in the battle, the black soldiers conducted a gallant search and rescue. Without them, all of Forsyth's command would have perished.[5]

Raids continued, and Sheridan decided to conduct a decisive campaign to subjugate the hostile Indians. Not all Indians were participating in raids, so Sheridan ordered all Indians not fighting to register at Fort Arbuckle to be considered friendly and receive exemption from any attack from Sheridan's men. Captain Alvord and Company M arrived at Fort Cobb to assist with the enrollment. When he arrived, several hundred Indians were waiting to register for exemption. Alvord found that he did not have enough supplies on hand to take care of all of them. Many more Indians were in the area but had not yet registered. Alvord requested additional supplies and more troops from Fort Arbuckle to scout the area around Fort Cobb and persuade people to come to the fort and register. Meanwhile, Sheridan planned a four-column winter campaign against the hostiles. Companies B, F, G, and K of the Tenth were part of the column under command of General W. H. Penrose, whose column would act as a "beater" column and drive the hostile Indians toward Lieutenant Colonel George A. Custer's column, which would engage the Indians in combat. The other columns would prevent escape of the hostiles. With enough rations for forty-three days, they left Fort Lyon on November 10. With them was James Butler "Wild Bill" Hickok, acting as a scout. Less than a week out, the column was hit with a major winter storm, which left men and horses freezing and hungry. Horses died, and men suffered frostbite. Despite all the hardship, the column successfully completed its mission. Custer's column defeated the Cheyenne on the Washita and another column under Lieutenant Colonel A. W. Evans subjugated a large group of Comanches on the Red River. The Tenth with Penrose had driven the Indians into the attack columns and prevented their escape.

The winter campaign had been difficult for several reasons. Large groups of Indians were dispersed over large areas. Sheridan lacked the manpower to cover such large areas. Forts Gibson, Arbuckle, and Cobb were located too far east to be effective. By the time news of raids arrived and men of the Tenth left their forts in pursuit, the distances they had to cover meant they would never capture the raiders. Sheridan sent Grierson and parts of the Tenth to a site near Medicine Bluff Creek, further west in Indian Territory, in November 1868. Grierson had scouted the area earlier and recommended it as a potential location for a new fort closer to the raiders. He and his men, loaded with supplies, arrived in cold and muddy conditions. The area had good timber, water, and fuel, but the soldiers would have to build the entire fort. They had to cut and prepare the lumber; cut local stone; build stables, corrals, storehouses, and barns; and construct barracks for the men and quarters for the officers. They dubbed their new home Camp Wichita.

Grierson moved his headquarters from Gibson to Camp Wichita in March 1869. The men built what would later come to be known as Fort Sill while they watched over restless Comanche, Kiowa, Arapahoe, and Southern Cheyenne in Indian Territory. They were charged with controlling the Indians, but they were also responsible for controlling whites. They had to prevent whites from trespassing onto the reservation to sell whiskey to the Indians. They had to stop white homesteaders and ranchers from settling on reservation land or using it to graze herds. They had to protect their own cattle and horse herds and those of the Indians from white rustlers. In addition to all those duties, they provided protection for stagecoach stations and escort for coaches and supply trains. They were to protect mail carriers, but the area around Forts Gibson and Arbuckle were so dangerous that soon no white men would deliver the mail. The troopers were assigned that task. One soldier, Private Filmore Roberts, left Arbuckle but never reached Gibson. He was labeled a deserter until his skeleton, with the mail still strapped to it, was found four months later. The men proved themselves capable foes, so much that they received the name Buffalo Soldiers, probably from the Cheyenne, during these years.

Conditions were fairly quiet for the first few months. The biggest problems for the men were not Indians or whites but disease, a shortage of men, and a shortage of good horses. That changed beginning in January 1870, when Indians started raiding wagon trains and nearby farms and ranches. The raids increased in number and continued through the rest of the year and into the next. Most of the time, by the time word arrived at Fort Sill and the men saddled up and left the fort, the raiders were long gone. Another problem turned out to be the changing U.S. policy toward the Indians, especially the reduction of military capabilities and authority that was part of the Peace Policy. Continued depredations brought overwhelming outcry from settlers for military intervention to control the Indians, but the army's hands were tied.

An event in April 1871, the Warren Wagon Train Massacre, was another strike against the Peace Policy. General Sherman, in response to settler demands for the government to stop the Indians, toured the West and visited several forts and outposts. He found little trouble until April. Soon after he arrived at Fort Richardson, a mangled and bloody man arrived with a gruesome story of massacre. Thomas Brazeale was a teamster on a wagon train travelling the same road Sherman had travelled just hours earlier. Dozens of Indians attacked the wagon train, killing at least six men in grisly ways. One was tied between two wagons and roasted to death. Brazeale and four others had escaped to tell the story. The same Indians had watched Sherman and his party pass the day before, but they knew the wagon train was headed that way and decided to wait for the richer target. Sherman headed to Fort Sill. Grierson discovered from Quaker Indian agent Lawrie Tatum that three prominent leaders and warriors of the Kiowa, Satank, Satanta, and Big Tree, had bragged about the wagon train massacre. The three were on the reservation collecting annuities. When the chiefs wanted to meet Sherman, he, Grierson, and Tatum gathered on the front porch of Grierson's residence for the meeting. Grierson positioned his men in case of trouble. When

Sherman demanded the arrest of the men responsible for the teamster massacre, fighting erupted. The Buffalo Soldiers remained calm and quickly gained control of the situation and arrested Satank, Satanta, and Big Tree. After the months of raiding and the teamster massacre, the government returned authority to the military to enter reservations to arrest marauders. Satank tried to escape on the journey to his trial and was killed. Satanta and Big Tree were tried and sentenced to death. Grant asked the Texas governor to commute the death sentences to life in prison at the Texas State Penitentiary. Satanta and Big Tree arrived in Huntsville in November 1871. Depredations continued through 1871 and into 1872. Part of the unrest was the continued imprisonment of Satanta and Big Tree, but the military held firm in refusing their release. Meanwhile, the men of the Tenth stayed busy with other enemies as well. White rustlers and Comancheros, Mexicans who did much of their trading with the Comanches but committed raids as part of their business, struck in a series of raids in 1871 and 1872. The Buffalo Soldiers went on endless scouts and pursuits to apprehend them and recover stolen stock and captives.

The Commissioner of Indian Affairs committed a huge blunder in early 1873 when he promised to release Satanta and Big Tree to the reservation. This promise did not bode well for the Tenth. Grierson had moved his headquarters back to Fort Gibson in March. He had also received a temporary appointment to serve as Superintendent of the Mounted Recruiting Service, located in St. Louis, Missouri. Since the appointment was temporary, Lieutenant Colonel Davidson took command of the regiment in Grierson's absence. Davidson was not a good choice, especially in times of trouble. The release of Satanta and Big Tree added to the responsibilities of the regiment, and they were already overloaded. The military had used the prisoners as leverage to bargain for good behavior from the reservation Indians. Their release would take away that advantage. Tatum resigned, knowing the level of trouble ahead. Headquarters moved back to Fort Sill, closer to the reservation. The release of the chiefs was delayed until August 1873, which kept things in check for the moment. As Tatum expected, trouble erupted when they were finally released. Satanta's presence during the Red River War was a parole violation that sent him back to Huntsville. He committed suicide in 1878. Big Tree stayed out of trouble, did not go back to prison, and died in 1929.

The Tenth had served on the Central Plains for their first eight years in uniform, but conditions were worsening in Texas, and in 1873 several companies of the Tenth transferred to Texas, to Fort Griffin, Fort

Concho, and Fort Richardson. They replaced the Ninth Cavalry, who transferred to New Mexico Territory and Arizona Territory. The other Buffalo regiments, the Twenty-Fourth and Twenty-Fifth Infantry, were also in Texas at this time. Texans did not welcome the Buffalo Soldiers and resented black men in uniform in their state. The soldiers were more concerned, however, with apprehending raiders, which occupied their time from the moment they arrived in Texas. As had been the case earlier, depredations were too many and too frequent for the soldiers to cover adequately. Several companies were still at Fort Sill, which spread the troops even more thinly. At both Sill and Gibson, raids increased. Sherman sent a message to commanders to remind them that soldiers could enter reservations in pursuit of raiders, but the military had to be careful not to harm friendly Indians. Once again, friendly Indians were required to enroll at Fort Sill in July and August 1874. Trouble erupted at the nearby Anadarko Agency during the enrollment period, when several Indians arrived but refused to enroll. The leader was a Nokoni named Big Red Food, who acted strangely enough that soldiers were alert for trouble. Violence erupted in gunfire, but the troopers gained the upper hand and regained control of the fort and agency. Once the friendly Indians were enrolled and out of harm's way, Sheridan planned a winter campaign in which the Buffalo Soldiers played a major role. Five columns would sweep the entire area for renegade and hostile Indians, relocating them back on the reservation in what became known as the Red River War of 1874 and 1875.

The war was a success for the U.S. military, with most hostile Indians returned to the reservation by early 1875. Colonel William R. Shafter, commander of the Twenty-Fourth Infantry, received orders to take men from his regiment, from the Twenty-Fifth Infantry, and six companies from the Tenth Cavalry and sweep through the Staked Plains for remaining Indians. They left Fort Concho in the sweltering heat of July. The Staked Plains was a formidable and hostile place in the best of times, but in the hottest and driest part of the year, it could well be impossible. Shafter sent Captain Nicholas Nolan and two companies from the Tenth to scout an area, capture any Indians they found, and return. Nolan spotted Indians but failed to apprehend them. Shafter sent him back to Fort Concho and planned to press charges against him for not capturing the Indians. Ironically, Shafter also failed to apprehend the Indians. The rest of that story is in Chapter 4. The Tenth experienced two other significant events that year. Grierson returned to take command, which saved Nolan from a court-martial because Grierson negotiated a lesser charge with Shafter. The companies still at Fort Sill transferred to Texas.

Indians on the Staked Plains were not the only worry for the Tenth. During the next couple of years, they made frequent patrols into Mexico to apprehend raiding Indians, Mexican bandits, and white rustlers. For the last half of 1876, companies rarely received rest. As a result of escalated raids from bandits and Indians from Mexico, the government and military had granted permission for troops to cross the Rio Grande in pursuit. In July, two companies of the Tenth joined Shafter in a skirmish with Lipan Indians near Saragosa, Texas. Captain Thomas C. Lebo and several companies of the Tenth continued to pressure the Indians. They crossed into Mexico in August and destroyed Kickapoo villages. The Tenth sent companies into Mexico for the rest of the year, sending a clear signal that raiders and bandits could no longer escape across the border and elude the veteran Buffalo Soldiers.

After a brief winter rest, patrols into Mexico continued, stretching the undermanned regiment to the breaking point. The soldiers preferred field activity to garrison duty, but there simply were not enough of them to guard the hundreds of miles of border against so many enemies: Mexican bandits and revolutionaries, Comancheros, Mescalero Apaches, Comanches, white rustlers, Lipan, and Kickapoo. Men and horses were in a persistent state of exhaustion. The climate meant they were usually suffering from heat and dehydration or blizzard conditions. In addition to chasing raiders and bandits, they still had other duties, and they performed them well.

Of all the armed threats during 1876 and 1877, probably the largest single incident involved a group of Quahadi Comanches under the leadership of Black Horse. The Buffalo Soldiers had met Black Horse before, when he surrendered at Fort Sill at the end of the Red River War in 1875. He had been on the reservation since that time. Trouble started in December 1876, when Black Horse gained permission from the Indian agent at Fort Sill to hunt buffalo in Texas. This was a common arrangement, especially since government rations and annuities were often late and usually insufficient to keep the Indians from starving. Whether Black Horse changed his mind about the reason for leaving the reservation or whether he lied to the Indian agent is unclear. Many Indians were justifiably outraged about the senseless white slaughter of the buffalo, and Black Horse was no different. The anger over the loss of such a valuable resource certainly drove his actions.

In the 1860s, the market valued only the hides of the adult male buffalo, so aside from killing to provide meat for railroad crews, white hunters limited their hunting to killing adult males during the winter months when their coats were the most luxurious. The market expanded in the late 1860s to include a high demand for all hides, including calves, taken at any season. By 1871, Bat Masterson and his brothers decided to join one of the hundreds of hunting outfits making lots of money during the years of the Great Slaughter. He became a skinner at age seventeen and described the process. The hunter usually ran an outfit. Since one hunter could kill many buffalo in a short period of time, he typically owned four or five wagons and hired three or four skinners. In the early years, there were millions of animals, and hundreds or even thousands of hunting parties worked near the herds at the same time. Hunters knew which animals to shoot first to prevent the herd from running. Grazing animals did not run even as others fell right next to them. The hunter shot dozens of animals in a day. His Sharps .50-calibre often overheated, and he had to swab the barrel with water to cool it down and continue firing. The work of the skinners was long, dirty, and bloody. Skilled skinners could skin an adult male in as little as five to ten minutes. They sliced the animal's belly from head to tail, made strategic cuts through the skin inside each leg, and cut through the skin around the neck. They tied a rope to the skin at the back of the neck, tied the other end of the rope to their saddle horn, and ripped the skin off quickly. Sometimes, they harvested the tongue to eat, but most of the time, they left the remainder of the animal to rot. Hides were loaded into the wagons, taken to camp, and staked to dry in the sun. As soon as they finished one group, the hunter had another group waiting for them. These activities continued for seven days a week for weeks on end. The buffalo hide industry ruined the lives of Indians whose physical and cultural survival depended on the buffalo. In a single month, one hunter could kill thousands of buffalo.[6]

Black Horse and nearly two hundred of his people travelled to Yellow House Canyon on the Staked Plains and waited to ambush any and all buffalo hunters. They did not have long to wait. They discovered and attacked buffalo hunters throughout the area. In February, veteran buffalo hunter Marshall Sewell and three skinners out of Rath City were camped near the Indian camp. One morning, Sewell approached a buffalo herd and killed dozens. The Comanches watched in horror, growing angrier with each shot. Herman Lehmann was with the Comanches as they watched. He was a captive who had been with the band since his abduction and adoption at age eleven in 1870. He had achieved warrior status since that time. He described the buffalo slaughter that morning. "The plains were being thoroughly combed by the buffalo hunters, who were killing buffalo for their hides. We would often see great wagon loads of hides being hauled away, and would find the carcasses of thousands of slaughtered buffalo. It made us desperate to see this wanton slaughter of our food supply."[7] They captured Sewell and inflicted horrific torture while they slowly killed and scalped him. In fact, they double scalped him, taking two scalp locks from his head instead of one, which horrified whites but expressed the rage of the Indians as they saw the waste of resources left in the wake of the hunters. The three skinners watched from a distance and headed back to Rath City for help. Fighting between buffalo hunters and Comanches was nothing new, the most famous being the attack at the small town of Adobe Walls, a former trading post for buffalo hunters, in June of 1874. Indians knew the town supported buffalo hunters and knew buffalo hunters were present at Adobe Walls on that day. Angry over the continued senseless slaughter of the buffalo, approximately seven hundred Indians decided to attack the buffalo hunters at Adobe Walls. The 29 buffalo hunters held an excellent defensive position and had the large-calibre Sharps rifles they used to kill buffalo. They held out for three days with only four killed. The Indians gave up the fight and retreated. Charlie C. Rath moved his mercantile operation designed to serve buffalo hunters from Adobe Walls to Rath City after the Adobe Walls fight. Both sides were ready to continue the fight started at Adobe Walls. The buffalo hunters gathered men and ammunition and started after Black Horse. The Comanches and the buffalo hunters engaged in the Battle of Yellow House Canyon on March 18. The buffalo hunters were badly outnumbered and soon retreated. When news of the Battle of Yellow house Canyon reached Forts Griffin and Richardson, Buffalo Soldiers took the field to apprehend the Indians. At Lake Quemado, Texas, in May, they skirmished briefly. The Indians surrendered and returned to the reservation.

On every patrol and scout during these years, Grierson made sure his men always located and mapped every available water source. He and his men came to know the country nearly as well as their enemies did, but a patrol in 1877 demonstrated the dangers even for experienced men. All the Buffalo Regiments were well versed in deprivation, especially water, but the incident that came to be known as Nolan's Patrol or the Staked Plains Horror was arguably the worst experience of this kind that any of the Buffalo regiments endured, even worse than Shafter's column experienced in 1875 (detailed in Chapter 6). In the spring and early summer, Mescalero Apaches raided American farms and ranches throughout the border states of Texas, Arizona, and New Mexico at will and escaped into Mexico. The United States had too few soldiers to make a concentrated, extended pursuit. Companies of the Tenth stationed at Fort Concho, near the Texas panhandle, continued routine patrols of the Staked Plains for these marauders but rarely made contact with them.

Captain Nicholas M. Nolan and Company A went after Mescalero Apaches who had attacked stagecoach stations between San Antonio and El Paso. They left the fort on July 14. Just a few days out, they came across twenty-eight buffalo hunters who were tracking the same Indians as Nolan. They two groups decided to join forces. Nolan welcomed a seasoned tracker, Jose Tafoya, who was with the hunters. They established a base camp and prepared for an extended patrol. On the 19th, Nolan, forty soldiers, and twenty-two hunters left the base camp in the direction Tafoya suggested. By the 24th, they had not located the Indians. They had also not located the water Tafoya predicted. The men had made do with little water many times before and believed Tafoya's next prediction of water would bring them relief. By the 27th, they had not located the Indians, their water was running low, and all Tafoya's predictions about water had led to dry holes. The men were becoming anxious. Their horses were struggling to stay on their feet, and some of the men had fallen from their saddles with heat stroke. Nolan had been part of Shafter's 1875 command ordered to sweep the Staked Plains of Indians after the Red River War. He was familiar with the landscape, but he also knew that the land features of this particular region, especially water sources, changed drastically from year to year. 1877 was a drought year, much drier than 1875. The water sources they had used during Shafter's campaign were no longer there. Even the usually reliable Tafoya was struggling. Each time he predicted water at a particular place, they arrived to find no water at all. Finally, he went ahead to check another water source and simply did not return. The men were in bad shape by this time, with several unable to continue. Nolan left those too sick to travel and continued forward, hoping for Tafoya's return and good news, but the scout did not return by the 28th of July. The men and horses had been completely without water for days, and both men and horses were in desperate condition. The hunters decided to go their own way and left the column. Troopers were scattered all along the trail. Eight men well enough to travel took all the canteens and followed Tafoya's trail but found neither him nor the water. They started trying to survive by drinking horse urine and blood. These remedies were not beneficial, but the men were desperate. Their horses were dying anyway, so killing one now and then for its blood and urine was merely hastening its death. The men mixed sugar with the urine to make it palatable. They also resorted to drinking their own urine, if they could produce any. By the afternoon of the 28th, each man was in his own struggle to survive, trying to keep moving, and hoping to find water before he fell down and could go no further. Finally, on the 30th, they straggled in one by one to Double

Lakes, which had water in an extreme drought year. Four men died, and the survivors endured an unbelievable eighty-six hours without water.[8]

All the Buffalo Regiments experienced a great deal of suffering from the harsh climate and fierce enemies, but their most frustrating experiences were the result of racist treatment from local civilians, especially in Texas, a constant enemy that was much more difficult to fight. Life at the Texas forts and outposts was difficult, with little to no recreational opportunity. The posts occasionally had a cantina, which offered beer and wine, cards, and other activities, but many of the men left the posts to pursue other recreation, especially women. Hostility between the soldiers and local civilians often led to trouble. The men at Fort Concho sometimes visited the nearby town of San Angelo, even though the locals made it clear they were not welcome. The Buffalo Soldiers tried to avoid trouble during their visits, but trouble came to them, and violence occurred on more than one occasion. The year 1877 had been an especially difficult one for the men of the Tenth, and the always insulting and often violent Jim Crow treatment the soldiers received from the Texans became too much for some of the soldiers, who decided to defend themselves or even fight back. That fall, several of them decided to relax at Nasworthy's Saloon in San Angelo. Their timing was bad because a group of Texas Rangers under Captain John S. Sparks was also at Nasworthy's. The Rangers objected to the presence of the soldiers and attacked them. After an investigation, Grierson requested that the Rangers apologize, which of course they refused to do. The soldiers decided to stand up for themselves, headed back to town, and fired shots into the saloon. A few months later, in Morris's Saloon, locals stripped a Buffalo Soldier and destroyed his uniform. Once again, the soldiers decided to stand up for themselves and headed back to town with loaded guns. After the shooting stopped, two people were dead. Soldiers were charged with the murder of the two civilians, but the trouble did not end there. In 1881, a civilian named Tom McCarthy killed Private William Watkins in McDonald's Saloon. Watkins often earned drinks in the saloon with his singing, and McCarthy objected when Watkins wanted to stop for the night. Soldiers captured McCarthy and turned him over to local law enforcement officials, who set McCarthy free after members of a pretrial held him over for trial, with no bail. Unfortunately, he had a nearly identical brother whose presence on the streets of San Angelo led soldiers to think McCarthy was once again free. The men of the Tenth had had enough. They had endured years of abuse and insult from the civilians they risked their lives to protect. The perpetrators always went unpunished. After they believed McCarthy had been released again, they posted a notice in town that read: "We, the soldiers of the U.S. Army, do hereby warn the first and last time all citizens and cowboys, etc., of San Angelo and vicinity to recognize our right of war as just and peaceable men. If we do not receive justice and fair play, which we must have, some one will suffer—if not the guilty the innocent. 'It has gone too far, just or death.' Signed U.S. Soldiers." Then, in a very orderly manner, they entered the town and fired weapons into several businesses. They reformed and marched back to the post. The jury at McCarthy's trial found him not guilty in a matter of minutes. The men of the Tenth were confined to the post for the next few months.

Soon, no one had as much time to worry about the conflict between the soldiers and local civilians. With the new year came the usual increase in trouble from Indians, Mexicans, and whites. Mexicans and whites resumed raids to steal cattle and horses from settlers and ranchers, always using the border to evade capture. The Indians became restless for the same reasons they had before. They were starving, and the government was not supplying enough food. The United States gave permission for Indians to leave the reservation to hunt game, but by 1878 the buffalo were essentially gone. With no game to hunt, the Indians, too, found the cattle and horses of the settlers attractive—for food. All this activity kept the Buffalo Soldiers in the field and out of San Angelo. They protected Indians out on hunting permits from bands of whites and Texas Rangers, some of the same Rangers they had clashed with before. They endlessly chased white cattle rustlers, Mexican bandits, and Indian raiders, with unsatisfactory results. Grierson changed tactics and stationed men at all known water holes to force the enemies out of the area. He also set up smaller posts and stations to decrease response time and increase the effectiveness of his troops. This took soldiers away from the barracks, and they usually welcomed such breaks, but endless months in the field were hard on men and horses, physically and mentally, even the men who had spent decades serving in such harsh conditions. During this time, the men continued their tasks of mapping land characteristics and water resources, information that proved invaluable to the men of the Tenth and to settlers. The knowledge they gained also helped them clear the area of Indians and relocate them onto reservations.

General Orders No. 1, issued in February 1881, abolished all military districts in the Department of Texas. Grierson took note of the service of the black soldiers from 1878–1880 of the Tenth, Twenty-Fourth, and Twenty-Fifth from his headquarters at Fort Concho in the District of the Pecos. They had constructed and maintained three hundred miles of telegraph lines, guarded over one thousand miles of wagon roads, and marched 135,710 miles. They had conducted the successful campaign against Victorio and the Mimbres Apaches. They had made the district so safe that settlers flocked to western Texas.[9]

When trouble from Indians, Mexicans, and whites subsided, especially after the Victorio War, the Tenth was transferred to Fort Davis in July 1882, where they served for three years.[10] In 1885, they transferred to the Department of Arizona. A number of Apache bands refused to settle on the dreadful and deadly San Carlos and Fort Apache Reservations and, under the leadership of men such as Geronimo, Mangus, Nana, and Cochise, were leaving death and destruction in their wake. They witnessed what happened to Victorio and his Warm Springs Apaches. They even agreed to settle on the reservations for a time in 1884, but they could not tolerate their families starving, and they determined that fighting for their freedom was far preferable to reservation life. Department of Arizona commander General George Crook needed the Tenth. Headquarters was located at Whipple Barracks, with Troops stationed at Fort Apache, Fort Grant, Fort Thomas, and Fort Verde. They arrived just in time to take part in the campaign to force Geronimo and his Chiricahua Apaches back on to the reservation. The Chiricahua killed four soldiers from the Fourth Cavalry and fled across the border into Mexico. Crook put every available man into the field. The soldiers scouted hundreds of miles and guarded every water hole on the American side of the border. The soldiers spent weeks and months either in the saddle or killing time at water holes, with no success. Sheridan lost patience with General Crook and replaced him with General Nelson A. Miles in April 1886. Only days after Miles took command, Geronimo struck a ranch and committed unspeakable acts on the family there. They killed a mother and daughter and took captive the father and other daughter. This time, the Buffalo Soldiers were in the saddle. Captain Thomas C. Lebo and the men of Troop K were veterans used to chasing the enemy in a harsh environment. Many of them had served on the front line in the Victorio War. Miles continued the relentless pursuit for months, rotating fresh soldiers from the Fourth Cavalry and the Sixth Cavalry. Finally, in August 1886, Geronimo surrendered. Troop H of the Tenth tracked down Mangus leading a separate band and forced his surrender in October. The Buffalo Soldiers had one final distasteful and thankless assignment regarding the Apaches in Arizona. Miles decided to punish the ones who had remained on the reservation along with the renegades. The Tenth received orders to escort the Indians to the train that would take them to Fort Marion in Florida, a place the Apaches considered even worse than the reservations in Arizona, worse than San Carlos.

Reproduction of drawing by Frederic Remington, 1889–1906, Tenth Cavalry, single file in the desert. (Library of Congress)

In July 1886, Grierson's headquarters moved to Camp Grant, then to Santa Fe, New Mexico, in November. The next month, the regiment received sad news. Colonel Grierson, who had commanded the Tenth since 1866, was leaving the regiment to replace General Miles as commander of the Department of Arizona. Grierson was promoted to brigadier general in April 1890, and retired July 8, 1890.[11] The regiment would have to follow their motto of "ready and forward" under a new commander, Colonel J. K. Mizner. Late in 1891, the regiment moved to the Department of Dakota, with headquarters at Fort Custer and troops (beginning in January 1881, companies were called troops) stationed at Fort Custer, Fort Keogh, and Fort Assinniboine in Montana; Fort Buford in North Dakota; and one troop stationed at Fort Leavenworth in Kansas. This was surprising for a number of reasons. The Tenth had always served in hot, dry, harsh, isolated regions of the American West and Southwest. These assignments kept them away from populated areas. A popular myth about the Buffalo Soldiers was that they physically thrived in such a climate and were naturally immune to diseases and maladies found there. Another popular belief was that they would certainly not be able to handle a cold climate. Those and other myths would be shattered in both the Department of Dakota and later when the Buffalo regiments served in Cuba and the Philippines. The Twenty-Fifth Infantry had been in Montana and Dakota since 1880 and had served well.

After their many years in the desert climate of the Southwest, the men welcomed the change and enjoyed most of their time at these posts. The men did well enduring the extreme cold and occasional blizzard conditions. The years were relatively quiet. In April 1894, they were called to maintain the peace along the railroad as unemployed men of Coxey's Army travelled through the region by rail on their way to Washington, DC to protest economic conditions. No trouble occurred. In 1877, Canada's Cree Indians had left the reservation, crossed the border, and caused trouble. In the summer of 1896, the Tenth was ordered to apprehend the Cree Indians and see them safely returned to Canadian authorities. In 1897, Cheyenne warriors from the Tongue River Agency left the reservation and caused trouble. The Tenth apprehended them and arrested them with little trouble. Headquarters moved to Assinniboine in 1894, and Fort Custer was closed in 1897. The Tenth did experience sadness during these years. Lieutenant Powhatan Henry Clarke drowned in the Little Big Horn River in 1893. He was awarded the Medal of Honor for actions in a battle against Geronimo on May 3, 1886. He ran out under enemy fire to save Corporal Edward Scott, who was wounded and unable to move. In 1894, Lieutenant Leighton Finley fell from a horse and died of his injuries a few months later. First Sergeant James Brown, a long-time member of the Tenth, froze to death in 1895. In 1897, Colonel Mizner was promoted to Brigadier General and left the Tenth. Their next commander was Colonel Guy V. Henry. Overall, these years were a pleasant change from Texas and Arizona, where the troops had spent much of their time apprehending various foes. These years were so quiet that Congress contemplated calls for the disbandment of the Buffalo Regiments. The quiet years were about to end, however, not with discharge from the military but with the biggest changes of their careers so far, the Spanish-American War in Cuba.[12]

The sinking of the U.S.S. *Maine* in Havana Harbor on February 15, 1898 signaled a temporary end of isolated service in the American West. By mid-April, the Tenth was on its way to Chickamauga Park, Georgia, and to Tampa, Florida from there. The Tenth received disheartening news when they learned they would leave their horses behind and fight as infantry, but they were still anxious to join in the "Big Show."[13] They served well and received accolades from their commanders and the white soldiers serving with them. The Tenth boasted a unique accomplishment during the battle of San Juan Hill. The color bearer of the Third Cavalry was wounded and fell. The color bearer of the Tenth, Sergeant George Berry, saw the soldier fall and picked up the fallen flag. When he reached the top of the hill, he planted both flags. After the war, the

Tenth Cavalry reported to San Antonio, Texas, and to Huntsville, Alabama, to patrol the border with Mexico. Trouble soon called them away from these posts, and in June 1899, all the Buffalo regiments deployed to the Philippines. The Filipinos the United States had assisted in overthrowing the Spanish declared their independence on June 12, 1948, and demanded an end to American occupation, but the 1948 Treaty of Paris had granted the Philippines to the United States, and President William McKinley made it clear the United States would not grant Philippine independence. The Black Regulars were part of the seventy thousand troops sent to the Philippines from 1899 to 1902. Fighting erupted and dragged on for three long years. American forces captured the rebel leader, Emilio Aguinaldo, on February 4, 1901, ending the war. Over the next several years, portions of the black regiments rotated to the Philippines for occupation duty, but they spent most of their time patrolling the U.S.-Mexican border, relegated back to the isolated posts at which they had served since 1866. Additional details of their service in Cuba and the Philippines are in Chapter 8. When not in the Philippines, they returned to posts in Wyoming and Nebraska, where they spent much of their time with drill, target practice, athletics, and polo, participating in competitions with other regiments.

The Tenth moved to Fort Huachuca, Arizona, in 1914. In March 1916, they joined the command of Brigadier General John J. Pershing in what became known as the Punitive Expedition. On June 21, the Tenth experienced one of the worst days of its history at the village of Carrizal. The story of Carrizal and the Punitive Expedition is in Chapter 8. With the war continuing in Europe and the threat of American involvement growing, The United States shifted focus from Mexico to overseas. The Buffalo Regiments represented some of their most experienced soldiers, but they would not be called to serve in Europe. That story is in Chapter 9.

CHAPTER 6

" 'Neath the Coat of Army Blue"[1]: The Twenty-Fourth Infantry

The searing sun was finally setting on men who thought this day might be their last. For more than two days, they had wandered over the dry, brittle land of the Llano Estacado in West Texas and eastern New Mexico, hoping to make it to the Pecos River before they completely gave out. These Buffalo Soldiers and their white officers had experienced the hardship of a march without water before, but none had endured for this long. Those whose horses still stood tried to stay in the saddle. Those who could not were tied onto their mounts. Those without horses stumbled along the best they could. Horses and men alike concentrated on placing one foot in front of the other. If the men could speak, they would tell a harrowing tale, but their swollen tongues made speaking impossible. Some had letters in their pockets, composed during the last three days for their loved ones, in case they did not survive this time. Mile after mile they trudged, some wanting to just give up and quit, only continuing when forced at gunpoint. Two hundred suffering men for as far back as ten miles were thinking of one thing, water.

Now, at sunset on August 14, 1875, a few at a time, they reached the river, falling from their horses or simply stumbling into the water. Though they drank and drank, they were still thirsty. Many, however, started setting up camp in preparation for more arrivals. Others filled canteens and, after only a short rest, headed back up the trail to the others. Well after dark, the last of the men reached the river. Many knew their arrival was largely the result of the determination of one man, Lieutenant Colonel William R. Shafter.

Shafter was not new to leading black troops. His experience dated back to the Civil War. In September 1863, because of his Civil War service with the Nineteenth Michigan Regiment, Shafter received orders to recruit and organize the Seventeenth Infantry United States Colored Troops. On April 19, 1864, he was promoted to Colonel of the Seventeenth. Shafter and his Seventeenth USCT manned the left flank alongside Colonel Thomas J. Morgan's four black regiments at the Battle of Nashville in December 1864 against General John B. Hood's Confederates. In April 1866, the Seventeenth was discharged, after serving well, and Shafter went home. His hope was to rejoin the army. He cut wood while he waited for orders. In January 1867, he was surprised to receive and happy to accept the position of Lieutenant Colonel of the all-black Forty-First United States Infantry, with Ranald Slidell Mackenzie as the regiment's colonel. The regiment moved to Texas in June 1867, with 577 officers and enlisted men in eight companies, and headquarters at Brownsville, Texas. Shafter was stationed at one of the sub-posts, Ringgold Barracks.[2] Here, he and his men encountered a long list of foes. A persistent enemy was disease, especially yellow fever, which wiped out a number of soldiers, two assistant surgeons, and many of the citizens of the nearby town of Rio Grande City. The proximity of Ringgold Barracks to the border with Mexico meant constant conflict with Indian, Mexican, and American cattle rustlers and murderers. The border provided refuge to all alike, since all the culprits had to do to avoid capture was cross into Mexico. The most persistent enemy, however, was the racist views of the white and Mexican citizens of Rio Grande City, who resented the presence of black troops and manifested that resentment through violence and intimidation.

Other problems added to the challenges they faced. Quarters and barracks in the West and Southwest were abysmal and woefully inadequate for even basic protection from the elements. Duties included mounted scouting on occasion, but mostly tedious labor including barracks and post construction, wagon-road construction, escort duty for payrolls and supply trains, telegraph construction and maintenance, station guard, camp and supply-train guard, and stage remount stations.[3] In 1869, an army reorganization bill reduced overall army numbers to twenty-five thousand and consolidated the Thirty-Eighth and Forty-First into the Twenty-Fourth Infantry. Both Shafter and Mackenzie remained as the Twenty-Fourth's officers, with headquarters at Fort McKavett, Texas, and companies posted at Fort Bliss, Fort Davis, Fort Quitman, Fort

Buffalo Soldier in five-button sack coat, Sturgis, Dakota Territory, 1884–1890, John C. H. Grabill, photographer. (Library of Congress)

Stockton, Fort Clark, and Fort Duncan. The soldiers spent most of their time guarding water holes and crossings, guarding mail and telegraph lines, providing escorts, and serving fatigue duties.

On January 7, 1870, Shafter arrived at Fort Concho in West Texas after a sixty-day leave, in command of companies of the Twenty-Fourth Infantry and the Ninth Cavalry. He took command at Fort McKavett in June 1870, charged with catching cattle thieves, horse thieves, border ruffians, and raiding Indians. This command included the Llano Estacado, also known as the Staked Plains. White men believed this Great American Desert to be completely uninhabitable and a place civilization would not tame. The Buffalo Soldiers shattered this myth. Between 1870 and 1875, Lieutenant William R. Shafter and Buffalo Soldiers from all four regiments made numerous and extensive expeditions across this forbidding land. Lieutenant John L. Bullis and the Black Seminole Indian scouts often accompanied the Buffalo Soldiers on the expeditions across the Staked Plains. The Black Seminole Indian scouts were former runaway slaves who had fled to Mexico rather than settle on Indian Territory as part of the Indian removal. In 1870, the U.S. military persuaded their leader, Chief Wild Cat, and his followers to enlist as army scouts on the western frontier. The U.S. government promised pay, land, and food in return for their service. They brought their families from Mexico to a four-thousand-acre plot of land near Fort Clark. They served honestly and faithfully for eleven years, contributing a wealth of information about the western lands and its peoples and providing critical scouting skills.

Probably the first Buffalo Soldiers on the Llano Estacado were part of the Ninth Cavalry, when Colonel Edward Hatch sent them in the fall of 1869 to capture a raiding party of Kiowa and Comanche. Captain Henry Carroll and his men located some of the warriors in a village

Buffalo Soldier, 1870–1880. (Library of Congress)

of two hundred lodges on the Brazos River. They fought the Indians and destroyed their camp. Company G under Captain John Bacon came under attack by as many as five hundred Kiowa and Comanche warriors. The Buffalo Soldiers killed as many as forty warriors and suffered eight wounded. These columns were in pursuit of raiders and did not map land features. When the Indians fled deeper into the Llano Estacado, the Buffalo Soldiers did not follow them, partly because they did not know the region. Reports of raids were frequent, with the raiders usually making their escape into the mysterious Llano Estacado. Shafter decided to change that and track the Indians down where they thought they were out of reach. Shafter and men from the Ninth, the Twenty-Fourth, and the Twenty-Fifth followed raiders into the area instead of turning back. While they rarely caught the raiders, each pursuit resulted in more information about the area, including available water, fuel, and food. Each pursuit sent a clear message to the Indians who used it as a refuge. The Buffalo Soldiers would follow them anywhere.

On August 22, 1870, Shafter led his first campaign in West Texas, the Pecos River campaign, to catch cattle rustlers. He had with him two officers of the Twenty-Fourth, two surgeons, and 128 men from the Ninth Cavalry. He did not catch the thieves. He covered 473 miles before his return to the post in late September. He discovered that no Indians were present in the entire area of the Pecos River where he scouted, but he had discovered favorite watering and camping places. He also demonstrated that black troops could indeed perform successfully in places the Indians thought the army could not find them. The scout provided valuable information regarding water and other resources, so Shafter decided to send as many scouting expeditions as possible, with the next beginning in November 1870 and ending in January 1871. When the regiment's Colonel Mackenzie was transferred to the Fourth Cavalry in early spring, Shafter commanded until Colonel Abner Doubleday arrived at Fort McKavett in April to take command of the Twenty-Fourth. When Doubleday took command of the regiment at Fort McKavett, Shafter took command at Fort Davis in May. Black troopers there guarded stage lines. When Shafter discovered that stage officials were refusing transportation and food to those troopers, he threatened to discontinue the service unless the abuse stopped. The abuse stopped.

More urgent business soon kept Shafter busy. On June 17, Comanche warriors attacked the Barilla Springs station and took dozens of horses and mules. On June 18, he mounted a pursuit with his black troops, returning to Fort Davis on July 9. He did not capture the warriors, but he did consider the scout successful in finding water, learning the land, and sending a clear signal to the Indians that they were not safe anywhere. He started routine scouts in the Big Ben region of Texas, in Apache country. When winter weather made scouting too dangerous, he turned his attention to post improvements.

Shafter laid more plans for exploration of the Staked Plains, but in June 1872, Colonel Ranald S. Mackenzie, with whom Shafter and the Twenty-Fourth had worked closely, called upon Shafter and the black troops because he knew they were tough and reliable. He wanted them to form a column as part of a larger expedition to track and capture Indians in the Llano Estacado.

Shafter and Companies E, H, and I of the Twenty-Fourth joined Mackenzie on the Brazos in July. Mackenzie relied on the troops to clear certain parts of the area of hostile Indians. Once that mission was complete, Mackenzie took Company E of the Twenty-Fourth straight across the Staked Plains in July, scouting Indians and mapping the region. He went out again in September. Not only did they construct the only accurate maps of the region to date, they located and destroyed Indian camps and refuges. Mackenzie's troops discovered trails, located water and resources, and penetrated Indian sanctuaries. He and men from the Twenty-Fourth Infantry and Fourth Cavalry fought warriors from a large Comanche village of 262 lodges. They took the village, killed around thirty warriors, captured 120 women and children, and completely destroyed the village and its contents. The Mackenzie-Shafter expedition extended into October 1872 and changed Indian behavior. Deprived of previously safe campsites and dependable resources, the Indians had to find other sanctuaries they hoped the soldiers could not locate.

Shafter headed to his next post at Fort Duncan, arriving in December 1872, where Indian raids and cattle rustling were on the rise, with the Indians and rustlers using the border to evade capture. As was his usual practice, Shafter immediately started sending out scouting patrols. Depredations were getting so bad that Mackenzie was ordered to join Shafter at Fort Clark and plan a campaign, beginning with the Kickapoo and Lipan. The campaign started on May 17, 1873. Shafter's knowledge and experience in the area provided Mackenzie with valuable preparation and information for a successful campaign. Mackenzie crossed the Rio Grande and destroyed three enemy villages. The Mackenzie raid angered the Mexican government. Mexican officials either did not desire to or were not capable of stopping raiders from crossing the border. After the Mackenzie expedition, enemy raids into American territory did become less frequent, but the raids did not stop completely. Shafter continued to send scouts and also established outposts along the border. Before he could successfully stop all the raids, Mackenzie left for a furlough, and Shafter was transferred to Fort Leavenworth, Kansas, in June, to lead a committee to determine proper uniforms and equipment for soldiers in the western districts. He remained in Kansas through December and returned to his Texas post in February 1875. His next assignment would test his command skills in new ways. He was to scout the entire Llano Estacado.

The Mackenzie-Shafter expedition forced Indians to return to the reservations in Texas by October 1872. Some still refused and simply moved into New Mexico. In only a matter of months, Kiowa, Comanche, and Cheyenne returned to their haunts on the Staked Plains. Joining them were Comancheros, bootleggers, and whiskey peddlers. Depredations resumed. In spite of the Peace Policy implemented in 1869, by the mid-1870s, many believed the policy to be a failure. Lack of effective Indian agents, orders for the military to stay away from the reservations, and the usual failure of the U.S. government to provide promised annuities led to the outbreak of violence. After the government's continued failure to provide promised annuities, Comanche, Kiowa, and Cheyenne ran out of patience. Their families were starving, and all their cooperation had not brought resolution. They fulfilled their treaty obligations and expected the United States to do the same. Sometimes, simple transportation issues or shortages delayed the arrival of supplies, but at other times, lack of supplies was the result of more insidious behavior, such as corruption on the part of the government, the suppliers, or the reservation agents and traders, who could sell the supplies and pocket nice profits. Others simply did not care or believed the Indians were a menace to be eliminated. One incident in 1862 demonstrated the latter. The United States had entered into the Treaty of Traverse de Sioux in 1851, promising annuities in the form of cash that they could use to purchase supplies from officials at the agencies in exchange for land cessions. In the summer of 1862, the annuity to the Lower Sioux Agency, also called the Redwood Agency, was late, and the Sioux were literally starving. Their chief, Little Crow, made every effort to resolve the problem peacefully. The reservation agent, Thomas Galbraith, refused to release what slim supplies he still had without payment. A trader, Andrew Myrick, was at the agency with fresh supplies. He refused to release food to the starving families without payment, replying, "So far as I am concerned, if they are hungry, let them eat grass." Finally, the desperate Sioux decided to take the food by force. When Myrick's body was discovered after the attack, he had grass in his mouth.[4] These same problems persisted for all reservation Indians. Annuities based on the Medicine Lodge Treaty of 1867 did not arrive, and families starved. The Indians were not allowed off the reservation to hunt to feed their families, or if they were, white buffalo hunters had slaughtered much of the once-enormous herds, and not enough buffalo remained to provide food for the Indians. On June 27, 1874, nearly three hundred warriors attacked a buffalo hunter camp at Adobe Walls. Buffalo hunters were especially hated, since they were wantonly destroying a resource on which the Indians depended for their very survival. Before whites started harvesting buffalo commercially, the plains were teeming with enormous herds. Herds estimated at fifty miles across and twenty-five miles deep were common, with as many as one hundred million head in one herd alone. Indians who subsisted off the herds did not know hunger or want. The Comanche were especially skilled at harvesting from the herds within Comancheria. Mastery of the horse provided an easier means of harvest, plenty of food and resources for the people, and prestige for the hunters. The pace of commercial harvests increased in the 1860s and 1870s, killing millions of buffalo in a brief time period and threatening the livelihood of the tribes who depended on the herds. Approximately thirty-one million were killed in Kansas and sold for fertilizer between 1868 and 1881.[5] By the time of the attack on Adobe Walls in 1874, the once plentiful buffalo were so scarce that warriors could not feed their people. Loss of the buffalo meant destruction of their very way of life as well as starvation. In addition to food, the buffalo provided hides for clothing and shelter, horns for utensils, and other everyday items. Groups planned their yearly activities around the migration of the herds and the annual hunts. Larger yearly gatherings for trade and festivals for building kinship relationships also revolved around the herds. The Comanche hated the twenty-eight men inside Adobe Walls for their part in this destruction. The buffalo hunters held off the original raiders and a larger group who arrived from the reservations to join the attack. The Indians abandoned the attack to conduct a terror campaign in the area, killing dozens of settlers and stealing hundreds of horses. Even though the Indians were raiding in part for survival and in part for revenge, the ranchers, settlers, and military had had enough. All Indians were ordered to register at their agencies by August or be considered hostile and pursued for punishment in what became known as the Red River Campaign, a war that involved as many as twenty engagements between the Indians and the United States. Five columns of troops marched out in pursuit beginning in late August 1874. Colonel Mackenzie left from Fort Concho with Jose Tafoya and Tonkawa scouts as guides, who led the troops to the Indian camp in Palo Duro Canyon. On September 28, Mackenzie defeated the Indians, captured 1,424 horses, and killed a thousand more to prevent losing them in a reprisal raid. The destruction of so many horses at this time was a major blow to the Indians, whose once vast herds of thousands had dwindled.

The Twenty-Fifth Infantry and the Ninth and Tenth Cavalry spent the months between August 1874 and January 1875 in a series of engagements. The first resulted from Indian refusal to comply with reservation enrollment at the Wichita Indian Agency in Indian Territory at Anadarko. The second incident involved the Ninth and Tenth Cavalry at Elk Creek in September. In November, the Tenth Cavalry encountered Cheyenne who had left the reservation and battled them in freezing conditions until they finally gained the advantage. Mackenzie continued to scout the Staked Plains but found no more Indians. By June of 1875, the Indians, including the mighty Comanche, were back on the reservations.

Once the war ended, Shafter and the Twenty-Fourth received orders to return to the Llano Estacado, to sweep it clear of remaining Indians. Shafter used this opportunity to continue scouting and mapping the region. He and Companies A, C, F, G, I, and L from the Tenth, Company A from the Twenty-Fifth, Companies D and F from the Twenty-Fourth, and Lieutenant Bullis and a company of his Black Seminole scouts spent six months in 1875 completing a thorough exploration. The Buffalo Soldiers played a significant role in taming the West, and especially forbidding places like the Llano Estacado, for American expansion. In fact, in 1876, legendary rancher Charles Goodnight pushed a cattle herd into the Llano Estacado, into the Palo Duro Canyon, opening the way for cowboys, trail bosses, and herds by the thousands after him. Thanks to the Buffalo Soldiers, the Llano Estacado, the Great American Desert, was no longer what Randolph B. Marcy had called a "natural barrier between civilized man and the savage."[6]

The Staked Plains, or Llano Estacado, was a region many feared and few entered. Even most Indians only traversed the fringes, but one tribe had a special connection. The Comanche were largely unknown in the Southwest until roughly the beginning of the eighteenth century, with some of their earliest raids in the region.[7] When they first arrived, they had few horses and were not the skilled horsemen they would become, but they soon realized the advantages and benefits of mastering the horse, and they were one of the first tribes to do so. By the mid-eighteenth century, they had more horses than any other tribe. They captured wild horses in various ways, but their favorite way of acquiring horses was to raid for tame horses. They initially sought trade for horses, cattle, and weapons, but by the middle of the century, they possessed thousands of horses and cattle for sale, and they soon made their reputation as formidable traders and fearsome raiders. Along with their mobility from horses, their discipline and their intimate familiarity with the Llano Estacado made them the most feared Indians in the Southwest and a serious military foe. Long before white men arrived, most people knew stories and legends about the Great Comanche War Trail down the length of the Llano Estacado, in part of the area known as Comancheria, and they avoided the region as a place of violence and danger. Those who did travel the thousand-mile trail were mostly Comanche warriors and their captives. Their reputation surpassed even that of the Apache, whose numbers had dwindled by midcentury as a result of Comanche presence in the region. Once the Comanche dominated the region, Mexicans and Comanche both anxiously awaited the annual raiding time, which the Mexicans called Comanche Moon and the warriors called Mexican Moon. Mexican villages braced themselves for the raids they knew would arrive with frightening regularity. From as early as the eighteenth century, Comanche warriors traveled south on the trail and crossed the Red River, the Brazos River, or the Colorado River to raid Mexican villages and haciendas to steal, to kill, and to take captives. They were mostly interested in horses, but they also took "mules and cattle, and many Mexican children."[8] The arrival of white settlers only provided more horses, cattle, and captives for the Comanche. Few had not heard of perhaps the most famous raid of all, the raid on Parker's Fort, on a beautiful spring morning in May 1836. The fort was home to sixteen men, eight women, and nine children. By the end of the gruesome ordeal, five men were killed and mutilated in front of their families. Two women were tortured and wounded. Five others, two women and three children, were beaten and taken captive. Rachel Parker Plummer, seventeen at the time, and her fourteen-month-old son, James, were two of the captives, and her description illustrates typical events on the Comanche War Trail. The other captives were Rachel's aunt, Elizabeth Kellogg, and two Parker children, Cynthia Ann, aged nine, and her brother, John Richard, aged seven. All, bleeding from wounds and in fear and shock, found themselves thrown upon horses and riding at breakneck speed to the north. This part of the journey lasted for ten or twelve hours, with no breaks for rest, food, or water. Finally, they stopped. Rachel and Elizabeth, both naked, bound, and face down, were beaten, kicked, and raped, in front of the children, who were beaten as well. At sunrise, the brutal ride north began again. This was the routine for five days, with no food, scant amounts of water, and continued beatings. Rachel was four months pregnant at the time of the raid. When they arrived at the village, her captors gave her over to an old woman and her daughter, both of whom delighted in making her work long hard hours at difficult tasks, with little food, and the ever-present beatings. Miraculously, she delivered a healthy baby boy. When he was seven weeks old, elders decided he was too much trouble for the tribe and that he diminished Rachel's work productivity, so they strangled him in front of her. He revived, so they tied a rope around his neck and dragged him behind a horse through thistle and cactus until he was in pieces. Rachel snapped and defied orders from both the old woman and her daughter, which led to a physical confrontation with each of them. Rachel won both contests and enjoyed better treatment as a result. However, seeing the death of her son and believing James to be dead, she suffered severe depression and died eighteen months after the raid, never knowing that James had survived. The other children taken in the raid suffered a variety of outcomes, but Cynthia Ann was adopted and assimilated, as was frequently the case with young children. This incident and many others like it made the Comanche the most feared of the tribes of the Southwest.[9]

After the arrival of the Buffalo Soldiers in the years immediately following the Civil War, continued raids from Comanche and other tribes

Buffalo Soldier, 1866–1890, Mosser & Snell, photographer. (Library of Congress)

in the Southwest kept them busy in rugged, dry, inhospitable country. By 1875, changes had occurred. Grant's Peace Policy had failed, Indian affairs had transferred from the Department of the Interior to the War Department, Sheridan had completed a successful offensive with the Red River War to return Indians to the reservations, and Shafter's next assignment, received at the end of May 1875, was to take Buffalo Soldiers to scout the Llano Estacado for remaining hostiles. Shafter was the right commander for the job. The Buffalo Soldiers were the right troops. He had five companies of the Tenth Cavalry, two from the Twenty-Fourth Infantry, and one from the Twenty-Fifth Infantry. He had a number of Black Seminole scouts. Others on the expedition included medical officers, Tonkawa scouts, packers, teamsters, blacksmiths with twenty-five six-mule team wagons, and a pack train of around one hundred mules. The expedition also had its own cattle herd. The approximately 450 men rendezvoused at Fort Concho on June 20 and took the field July 14. Many believed the Llano Estacado was uninhabitable to all but the toughest of the Indians, who only rarely went there themselves. Common thought was that it was an unending ocean of grass with no trees and very little water. Most of the rivers that did meander across it were dry beds much of the year and so full of gypsum and other minerals most other times that the water was not fit for drinking. The Comanche knew where springs provided good water and where fruits, nuts, and persimmons grew. It provided for all their needs, except horses and captives, and it provided escape and refuge from pursuers when they ventured from it to conduct lucrative raids into Mexico, New Mexico, and Texas. Few whites had crossed it, and those who did warned others of the hazards. Captain Randolph B. Marcy was part of the Texan-Santa Fe Expedition that crossed it in 1841. He travelled through it more than once in 1849 and 1852. He described it as a "natural barrier between civilized man and the savage, as, upon the east side are numerous spring-brooks, flowing over a highly prolific soil … while on the other side commence those barren and desolate wastes, where but few small streams greet the eye of the traveler, and these are soon swallowed up by the thirsty sands over which they flow."[10] Most travelers took longer routes to avoid it. Shafter and the Buffalo Soldiers were headed directly into it, and he planned to continue his practice of thoroughly scouting and mapping all trails, land features, and water sources, whether he found Indians or not.

A few days into the expedition, under Shafter's orders, Captain Nicholas Nolan took two companies of the Tenth to scout the area around Rendlebrock Springs. Nolan discovered a large Apache village. The Indians fled before Nolan could attack, but he completely destroyed the village and reunited with the main column in Blanco Canyon in August. Shafter was furious that the Indians had escaped and sent Nolan back to Fort Concho to await court-martial proceedings. Only the intervention of Nolan's commander, Colonel Benjamin H. Grierson, reduced the court-martial to a reprimand.

Shortly after Nolan's return, Shafter, 320 men, and twenty Black Seminole scouts under the command of Bullis, left the supply camp for an extended scout. They soon encountered severe water shortages. Rather than head back to the supply camp, Shafter decided to try to make it to the Pecos River, fifty miles away. Thus began the trek that earned him the name of "Pecos Bill" from his troops, who endured some thirty to forty hours without water.[11] Shafter drove his men beyond what they thought they could endure, until they reached the Pecos River and realized they were alive because of their commander.

The same determination that saw his men through to the river caused Shafter personal problems in the future. Shafter cut his right shin on a sharp rock while swimming in the Pecos that evening. His subsequent determination to continue without proper treatment left him with a suppurating wound that hampered him for the rest of his life. In mid-September, after Nolan's Apaches once again escaped, Shafter rested his men at Three Wells. Around thirty of the very Apaches they sought attacked. Shafter gave chase at dawn. While he discovered and marked Monument Spring, he did not find the Indians, and he was two hundred miles from his supply camp. After marching 860 miles in fifty-two days, enduring extreme heat and water shortages, the ragged men reached the base camp on September 25.

After resting and refitting, Shafter sent 120 men of the Tenth Cavalry under Captain Theodore A. Baldwin on an extended scout. They found no Indians but discovered valuable land features and permanent water supplies at Big Springs, Sulphur Springs, and Muchaque Peak. These discoveries meant that ranchers could successfully raise cattle on the Staked Plains. While Baldwin scouted in the south, Shafter once again sought the elusive Apache, finding a camp on October 17. They attacked at dawn the next morning. The Indians escaped, but Shafter and his men completely destroyed the camp and captured a number of horses and mules. Lieutenant Andrew Geddes and two companies of the Tenth followed the trail of the Indians. They did not overtake them but made additional valuable discoveries of water, mesquite, grass, fuel, and large herds of buffalo, strengthening the belief that cattle ranches could thrive there. Other smaller scouts from the expedition experienced similar results. Company A of the Tenth with Lieutenant Thomas C. Lebo found water and grass. Tenth Cavalry troopers with Lieutenant C. R. Ward found an entire series of wells, dug in such a way that horses could actually walk to the edge and drink.

Shafter received orders in late November to end the expedition. He arrived back at Fort Concho on December 9. From there, Shafter returned to his post at Fort Duncan. For five months, the Buffalo Soldiers explored the region, finding and mapping water and other resources and clearing the region of Indians. By demonstrating that soldiers could maintain a force in the area, they were confident the Llano Estacado no longer hid or provided a sanctuary for Indians. In addition, their discoveries dispelled the common belief that the area was inhospitable to man and beast. When the news reached civilians, they flooded the Staked Plains, establishing sheep and cattle ranches and businesses to support those ranches. This of course meant continued and escalated pressure on Indian lands and resources and meant that the Buffalo Soldiers would remain busy in the West.

By the spring of 1876, Shafter again received assignment to scout the Rio Grande near the Pecos, in search of cattle rustlers, Mexican bandits, and hostile Indians. Bullis and the Black Seminole scouts would once again join the Buffalo Soldiers on a campaign slated to begin at the end of March. They got underway in early April, with two companies of the Twenty-Fourth, five companies of cavalry, Bullis and his scouts, and enough supplies for four months for the roughly 350 men. Rustlers, bandits, and hostiles usually crossed into American territory at night, raided and pillaged, and crossed back into Mexico a night or two later. Included in Brigadier General Edward O. C. Ord's instructions for the campaign was permission to cross into Mexico in pursuit. Based on information from Bullis and his scouts, Shafter decided to enter Mexico in early June in pursuit of Indians. On July 30, twenty soldiers of the Tenth Cavalry under Lieutenant George Evans, along with Bullis and his scouts, attacked a Lipan village near Saragosa, killing twelve warriors and capturing four women and dozens of horses. The soldiers destroyed the camp and all its contents and crossed back onto American territory with the captives, horses, and three wounded troopers on August 4. On another scout into Mexico, Captain Thomas C. Lebo and the Tenth found and destroyed a Kickapoo camp. Not long after this incident, Ord ended the campaign.

Ord ended the campaign because of complaints from the Mexican government about American soldiers entering into Mexico. Ord faced a difficult situation. He needed to stop raids and rustling on American soil without angering the Mexican government. His next assignment for Shafter and his Buffalo Soldiers called for getting the job done with discretion, with someone who could strike into Mexico at night and return undetected. Ord and Shafter hatched a plan. Ord created the District of the Nueces and placed the forts in the district, Duncan, Clark, and San Felipe, under Shafter's command. He requested and received permission from Sherman to pursue into Mexico in the case of fresh trails. Shafter stationed small patrols of the Twenty-Fourth at likely targets along the border. On December 30, Indian raids against area ranchers resulted in dozens of stolen horses and as many as three hundred head of cattle. Captain Alexander B. Keyes and his Buffalo Soldiers along with Bullis and his scouts followed the fresh trail into Mexico. In the Santa Rosa Mountains, they detected an Apache camp. As they cautiously approached, they could see the stolen horses. Entering the camp, they found it recently abandoned, for the meat of at least one hundred head of cattle was still drying. The troops destroyed the camp and its contents and returned to Fort Clark with the remaining livestock on January 23, 1877. The raids slowed but only for a time, escalating in the spring. Renewed raiding and Mexico's refusal to stop the raids led to further permission from Sherman for the Buffalo Soldiers to cross into Mexico. Mexican protests carried little weight when Americans discovered ready markets for property stolen north of the border and taken back to Mexico. The United States responded with renewed calls for Mexico to do its part to stop the raiding.

As negotiations between the United States and Mexico continued, the Buffalo Soldiers entered Mexico less frequently, but a July campaign set off a firestorm involving the two governments and Shafter's own men. After destroying a Mescalero and Lipan village, a small Mexican patrol shadowed the Americans until they left Mexico. Some of Shafter's men accused him of running in the face of a smaller and weaker enemy force. They wanted to fight. Shafter knew a fight with Mexican soldiers would only escalate the tension between the two countries. When he angrily responded to the complaints, twenty-three men from the Twenty-Fourth Infantry and the Tenth Cavalry filed court-martial charges against him in October. The charges were dropped for lack of evidence.

Raiding did not stop. In April 1878, as many as forty Mescalero, Lipan, and Kickapoo warriors, along with some Mexican bandits, conducted a six-day crime spree in Texas. Mackenzie and Shafter knew the raids would continue as long as the culprits maintained sanctuaries in the Santa Rosa Mountains and petitioned Ord for permission to go after them. Permission was not long in arriving. Mackenzie and Shafter planned a two-pronged campaign. Mackenzie took one column with troops from the Eighth Cavalry, the Fourth Cavalry, and Black Seminole scouts. Shafter and the Buffalo Soldiers of the Twenty-Fourth, along with two companies of cavalry and two Gatling guns, comprised the other column. Shafter had around seven hundred men and supplies for two months. Before they could find the outlaws, they encountered Mexican troops under Colonel Pedro Valdez, whose orders were to escort the Americans back across the border. The Americans continued their campaign, with Mexican soldiers and cavalry shadowing them. On June 21, Colonel Jesus Nuncio arrived with Mexican reinforcements. The Americans crossed the border out of Mexico without further incident. The campaign had failed to locate the bandits, but the show of force convinced the Mexican government they needed to both prevent bandits from entering the United States from Mexico to steal cattle, horses, and people and safely escape back into Mexico with no fear of apprehension from Mexican forces. On March 4, 1879, Shafter received promotion to colonel and was transferred to command the white First U.S. Infantry at Fort Randall, Dakota Territory, where he arrived in October. His days of leading black troops, however, were not over.

The men of the Twenty-Fourth were seasoned veterans by the end of this campaign, but the regiment had a rocky start, with politicians, army personnel, and civilians opposing their service completely. Ten years earlier, in compliance with the Army Reorganization Act of March 3, 1869, the Twenty-Fourth Infantry was organized on November 1, 1869, from the Thirty-Eighth Infantry, under Colonel William B. Hazen and Colonel Ranald Slidell Mackenzie and Lieutenant Colonel Cuvier Grover, and the Forty-First Infantry, under Lieutenant Colonel William Rufus Shafter, which had both been created as all-black regiments under the 1866 Army Reorganization Act. Both these regiments had seen combat in the three years since their creation. The Thirty-Eighth fought Indians on several occasions and helped defend Fort Wallace, Kansas, against attacks from Chief Roman Nose's Cheyenne. The Thirty-Eighth boasted something the other black regiments could not match. It had the only known black female soldier. Cathay Williams enlisted as William Cathey in St. Louis in 1866 and received assignment in the Thirty-Eighth. As during the Civil War, when numbers of women served, hiding her gender from surgeons both during her enlistment physical and during the remainder of her service would not have been difficult. Enlistment physicals, if performed at all, were frequently not thorough. She was stationed at Jefferson Barracks, Missouri, and in February 1867, assigned to Company A. Company A travelled to Fort Riley, Kansas, in April, where she was hospitalized for illness on several occasions. The Company moved to Fort Harker, Kansas, then to Fort Union, New Mexico, and finally to Fort Cummings, New

Mexico. By January 1868, her illnesses became more frequent. In July, at Fort Bayard, New Mexico, she appeared on the hospital list again. During all her hospital stays, she was able to maintain the secret of her identity. In October 1868, she was medically discharged. Other than the fact of her gender, her service was unremarkable. Even her fellow soldiers in the Thirty-Eighth probably did not know she was a woman.

The Forty-First also had a busy schedule in the years from 1866 to 1869 and completed scouting and escort details with the Ninth Cavalry at Fort Duncan. Officers of the Twenty-Fourth were Colonel Mackenzie, Lieutenant Colonel Shafter, and Major Henry C. Merriam. Grover transferred to a cavalry regiment. All the regiments of the Twenty-Fourth were stationed in Texas, at forts that had been constructed during or right after the war with Mexico. Forts were constructed in patterns, with lines of forts providing layers of connected protection. The Indian Frontier Line was constructed in 1849, with Fort Inge, Fort Worth, Fort Lincoln, Fort Gates, Fort Graham, Fort Croghan, and Fort Martin Scott. The Rio Grande group included Fort Brown, which was built during the war with Mexico, Fort McIntosh, Fort Duncan, and Ringgold Barracks.[12] These forts were located many miles apart, usually at least two hundred miles, and connected only with inadequate roads. After the Mexican War, Americans flooded into the newly won western territories, making the old forts ineffective for protection from Indians in western settlements. The limited manpower meant that none of the forts had sufficient troops to provide protection over the vast areas involved. The United States built a series of new forts further west in the 1850s. These included Fort Belknap, Fort McKavett, Fort Clark, Fort Stockton, Fort Davis, and Fort Bliss. After the Civil War, when the United States decided to man these forts again, they initially sent troops to Fort Brown, Ringgold Barracks, Fort Bliss, and Fort McIntosh, but during the next two years, the army sent troops to many of the other forts as well. The regiments faced the same problems troops had before the Civil War. Critical manpower shortages meant regiments had too few soldiers to protect settlements and mail routes. Lack of roads and communications between forts and outposts exacerbated these difficulties. The Twenty-Fourth, with headquarters at McKavett and companies spread across Fort Bliss, Fort Stockton, Fort Quitman, Fort Concho, Fort Duncan, and Fort Davis, was no different. Two companies of the Twenty-Fifth were also stationed at McKavett, along with at least two troops of cavalry at each post, but that still did not provide enough manpower.

Americans envisioned the army making the West safe for settlement through Indian subjugation, and the Twenty-Fourth took part in that process; however, most of their service involved not fighting Indians but performing tasks that were even more important in the taming and development of the West. They built roads and bridges, initially for military use, but also necessary for transportation, mail service, and delivery of supplies for civilians. They located and mapped water holes. The control of dependable water sources was vital to waging the Indian Wars, but it was also crucial to the survival of the settlers. They improved waterways, enabling easier travel and more efficient transport of goods. They built important communications links, again, initially between military installations. They established and protected mail routes, conducted and recorded scientific experiments and data, developed agricultural practices, guarded railroad workers, and maintained national parks, among many other things. Since cavalry did most of the scouting and patrols, the infantry carried the lion's share of these tasks. More often than not, they had to build their post from the ground up or make major repairs to existing facilities. Years of non-use had left military infrastructure in the West in deplorable condition. In addition to post construction and maintenance, some of the first roads, river crossings, and communications the troops built were those necessary to connect existing forts.

In July of 1868, Colonel Edward Hatch needed a safer and more reliable mail route between Fort Stockton and San Antonio. He charged Lieutenant Robert Neely and men from the Forty-First Infantry to cut away the steep banks at a site on the Pecos River so that wagons could more easily ford the river, a task that took all summer. Throughout all of these efforts during their decades of service, isolation and labor were never-ending burdens, especially for the black regiments.

The Twenty-Fourth remained at their original posts until 1872, when they transferred to Fort Clark, Fort Brown, Fort Duncan, and Ringgold Barracks. In 1871, Mackenzie transferred to the Fourth Cavalry, and Colonel Abner Doubleday became commander of the Twenty-Fourth.[13] In 1872, Doubleday retired, with Colonel Joseph H. Potter taking command. During these years, they participated in several actions. They were with Mackenzie and the Fourth Cavalry in September 1872, when he captured a large Comanche camp and pony herd. He ordered the camp and its contents destroyed. That night, the Comanches attacked and recaptured most of the herd. Destroying herds rather than capturing became standard army practice after this and similar incidents. In 1873, the Twenty-Fourth again joined Mackenzie and the Fourth Cavalry into Mexico in pursuit of Lipan and Kickapoo Indians. When the infantry did participate in campaigns against Indians, they were usually mounted.

Captain William G. Muller describes two major expeditions:

In the spring of 1875 a big scouting expedition was organized to explore the plains under Lieut.-Colonel Shafter, who was considered the most capable and energetic officer of rank in the Department. This expedition consisted of nine troops of the Tenth Cavalry, one company Twenty-fifth Infantry (Capt. John W. French), two companies Twenty-fourth "D" (Capt. Cunningham and Lieut. Markley) "F," (Lieut. Custer and Beacon) and a company of Black Seminole scouts (Lieut. Markley) and Tenkawan scouts (Lieut. Wood, Tenth Cavalry), and had its rendezvous at Fort Concho, the organizations marching from Duncan about 200 miles. About the only thing known of these regions at this time, as shown in the maps, was like that of the great West as shown by the school atlas of two generations ago.

This little army marched out from Concho in July, 1876, with 65 six-mule wagons, a pack train of about 700 mules and a beef herd; went up the North Concho road to the head of running water, then turning to the right, and directed by compass only, struck Catfish creek, in Canon Blanco, head of the north fork of the Brazos, where the supply camp was established and the Cavalry and the Black Seminole scouts crawled thirty miles up out of the canon to the high plateau of the Llano Estacado, and set out to cross them.

The column marched thirty miles a day over country like an ocean of waving grass. Day after day they hiked, the hundreds of thousands of buffalo lumbering off to each side and the antelope fleeing to a safe distance and turning a gaze at us in wonder. This expedition finally reached the Pecos River at Three Rivers, New Mexico, after great hardship and suffering. During the last lap of this trip the offices on the last night out, having lost all hope, had gotten together and written messages to be taken home by any who might survive. In the meantime, the Infantry had sent out detachments to the southwest, and upon the return of the mounted troops, the Indian villages along the eastern edge of the plains were raided and the country mapped by 2nd Lieut. Thaddeus Jones, Tenth Cavalry. This map, when completed, was one of the finest and most important that ever went to the Engineer Officer, and other maps of that part of Texas today are almost copies of it. (Colton's of about 1888.) This scout was the first mortal blow to the Indian domination of that historic region (traversed by the Spanish explorers before), and the destruction of buffalo finished them.

The movement began May Tenth and the troops reached home December 24, 1875. They captured some 500 or 1,000 ponies, and a lot of squaws, who were taken to Fort Duncan, but subsequently escaped. One little Indian maiden about eight years old, was taken into the family of Lieut.-Colonel Shafter; she seemed willing to be civilized, but after having drawn a knife on a servant, was handed over to the Indian school.

The next year, 1876, another big expedition was organized again under Colonel Shafter, with troops of the Eighth and Tenth Cavalry, companies of the Twenty-fifth and companies D and F of the Twenty-fourth Infantry. Colonel Shafter arranged that only younger officers be sent with the troops. Lieut. Markley commanded all the Infantry. This movement was against the Lipaus and Kickapoos, who lived in Mexico, across the Rio Grande, about thirty miles opposite what is now Langtry, Texas, then a wild, rugged country. The Infantry guarded the crossing at Eagle Nest, and the mounted troops made a dash and destroyed a village, but the whole Mexican population rose against them and they had to make good time getting back. The actual object of this expedition was evidently more than what appeared, but after sending a few small scouting parties up the Pecos, on which the main camp had been established, the expedition returned in September, 1876, having been out five months.[14]

What Muller's account does not include is the role of the black soldiers on these expeditions. The enlisted infantry and cavalry, once again, did the heavy lifting. While little to no source material exists from the Buffalo Soldiers themselves, the success of these expeditions rested, to a great extent, on their shoulders. They had a large share in the suffering and deprivations while on these expeditions as well. Muller mentions that the officers doubted they would survive the expedition. The enlisted men held the same fears. They wrote notes or had others write notes for them in case they perished. They wanted to send final words and thoughts to their loved ones. Often, the clothing and equipment of the enlisted men were inferior to that of officers from the start. After enduring the punishment of the desert on an extended campaign, their clothing and equipment, including horses, were far worse for the wear. Many lost their horses to thirst. Often times, men would drink the blood of the dead horse for nourishment and moisture, though they would actually be worse off than before, because the salt content in the blood and urine simply made them thirstier and more dehydrated. Occasionally, they would mix sugar with the horse's urine and drink that, though, once again, they were worse off than before. Nothing remedied the lack of water. Lips cracked, and tongues and throats swelled, leaving men unable to speak and often unable to eat or drink. Boots, blouses, pants, and leggings grew threadbare or wore out completely before the end of the march, leaving men with little or no protection from the burning sun. Even at times like these, the black regiments boasted the lowest desertion rates in the entire army.

The year 1880 marked a decade of frontier service in Texas for the Twenty-Fourth. That service had been extremely isolated. The black regiments had been consistently denied transfer to more populated areas, even though the white Tenth Infantry had been transferred to Louisiana to relieve them from ten years of isolated service in the same area as the black regiments. In the fall of that year, the Twenty-Fourth transferred from border duty along the Rio Grande to Indian Territory at Fort Reno, Fort Supply, and Fort Sill. One company remained for a while at Fort Elliott in the Texas panhandle. By the end of the year, all the regiment was moved, with headquarters at Fort Supply. Their commanding officer, Colonel Joseph H. Potter, served until 1886, when Colonel Zenas R. Bliss took command until 1895, at which time Colonel J. Ford Kent took command. Their charge was to contain the Comanche, Kiowa, Arapahoe, and Southern Cheyenne who were there on the Indian Territory reservation. Another part of their charge was to keep whites out of the reservation. The cavalry, with their speed and mobility, held most of the duty for keeping whites out, while the infantry was placed to keep Indians peaceful. They found better quarters at their new posts. The duties were basically the same: telegraph construction and repair, which meant cutting thousands of cedar poles and long periods of work in isolated areas. They built and repaired wagon roads. They did not have as much stage line and stage depot duty because of the amount of rail in the region. They built a new wagon road from Fort Supply to Kiowa, Kansas. In September 1886 the stage line between Fort Supply and Dodge City was abandoned, so another stage using the new wagon road started operations between Fort Supply and Kiowa in July. It was the garrison's only regular contact with the outside world. The eighteen-hour trip from Kiowa to Fort Supply ran six days a week. They found Indian Territory even more isolated than Texas, since no civilians were allowed within the limits of Indian Territory.

The forts and towns were many miles apart, increasing the isolation. The post trader did operate a canteen, which helped some. At the canteen, they could have beer and wine, could bowl and play pool, could read and write letters. Other on-post activities included debate, acting, music, and athletics, including competition in shooting, riding, polo, baseball, and football. Still, at times, the men alleviated boredom with forbidden activities, such as gambling, whiskey, and women at off-post establishments. They had incidents of drunkenness and venereal disease as a result of these excursions. One civilian they were reluctant to see evicted from the reservation was Jennie Brown, a white prostitute who entered the territory with the help of a black civilian. Jennie helped alleviate the severe lack of women in Indian Territory, but Colonel Bliss had her escorted off the reservation with a warning not to return. When she snuck back in disguised as a man, Bliss arrested her.[15]

In May 1888, the Twenty-Fourth transferred to the Department of Arizona to posts in New Mexico and Arizona to relieve the white Thirteenth Infantry, which had been there since 1880. The move was complete by June of that year, with the regiment spread out at Fort Apache, Fort Grant, Fort Thomas, and the San Carlos Indian Agency, all in Arizona Territory. Headquarters for the regiment was in New Mexico Territory at Fort Bayard. The barracks conditions were worse than in Indian Territory and in desperate need of immediate repair. The climate at some of the posts was inhospitable and unhealthy, with San Carlos so bad that troops were cycled out every six months for health and morale reasons. Summer temperatures often reached 110 to 118 degrees in the shade! Muller described his new post conditions. "The winters were not bad, but the summers were intensely disagreeable, these posts being like the bottom of a box facing the sun. When night came, one wondered if he could live until morning, and when morning came after vain attempts to sleep on the hot sheets, one wondered how he could get through the day with … myriads of flies, warm water and atmosphere which threatened to make the skin crack open."[16] Their duties were similar to those in Indian Territory, to contain the Indians, this time mostly Apache, on the reservation and to keep whites out of the reservation.

At their new posts, the Twenty-Fourth continued to provide escort. One escort in particular drew attention and was later known as the Wham Payroll Robbery. An army paymaster traveling between Fort Grant and Fort Thomas on May 11, 1889, required escort. On this particular day, the escort was comprised of two noncommissioned officers and nine privates from the Tenth Cavalry and the Twenty-Fourth Infantry. As they traveled, they encountered a large boulder in the middle of the road, which some of the troops proceeded to remove, leaving a few troops to guard the wagon. Sergeant Benjamin Brown oversaw the boulder removal. Concealed nearby and watching were highwaymen, intent on robbery. They warned the escort to put up their hands then began firing, immediately hitting the wagon driver and two horses, making it impossible to move the wagon. The robbers then meticulously targeted the members of the escort, catching Sergeant Brown and his men in the open. Sergeant Brown was wounded in the stomach with the first shots. Eight of his men were wounded. They all continued to fight as they headed for cover in a nearby creek bed. As many as twenty robbers descended on the wagon. Though wounded, Corporal Isaiah Mayes made it to the Cottonwood Ranch two miles away. When help arrived, the bandits were gone, with the $28,345.10. Though the money was gone, Major Joseph W. Wham still had only praise for the members of the escort. He recommended nine men for the Medal of Honor. Seven privates received certificates of merit; Brown and Mayes did indeed receive the Medal of Honor.

The years at these posts were relatively uneventful for the Twenty-Fourth. They were still stationed and serving in the Southwest when the Indian Wars ended in 1891. The Twenty-Fourth, along with the Twenty-Fifth Infantry, had the lowest desertion rate of any other regiments in the army from 1880 to 1886, with lower court-martial rates than their white counterparts. Rates of other regiments were much, much higher; in fact, desertion was one of the biggest problems for the military. Isolation, boredom, and low pay contributed to desertion. White soldiers, in particular, deserted to find their fortune in the gold fields further west.

The Twenty-Fourth boasted the full range of service experiences, from actual military conflict to mapping, exploring, building, guarding, and maintaining. They also experienced events they did not foresee. One of those events occurred in 1894 and involved quelling a domestic dispute between labor and owners, specifically the American Labor Union and the Pullman Palace Car Company. The details of this story are contained in Chapter 3, but the Twenty-Fourth was given the task of controlling railroad workers in a dispute against unfair treatment from their bosses. The Pullman Company had cut wages and had refused to cut corresponding housing rents. Wages were low before the cut, but the wage decrease placed families in jeopardy, and many were literally starving. The American Labor Union joined the strike in support of the railroad workers. Violence erupted, government property was threatened, and federal mail delivery was disrupted. The men of the Twenty-Fourth had personal experience with difficulties in providing for their families and could sympathize with the strikers. Army regulations prohibited married men from enlisting or from marrying after enlistment. A few were allowed to marry, if their wives agreed to serve as servants or laundresses for officers and their families or for laundresses for a company. This practice was not widespread but was common in the Twenty-Fourth. A big problem was that the army did not provide housing, food, medical care, transportation from post to post, or anything else for these women and children. These terms were part of a soldier's enlistment agreement. Married men with wives or families could be transferred wherever the army needed them, but their families had to make it to the new post on their own and find housing and support on their own. When the Twenty-Fourth was sent to control the violence resulting from the strike, to protect federal property, and to make sure the federal mail was not disrupted, the men were in essence on the side of the company and against the workers in circumstances all too familiar to the soldiers. They maintained professionalism and completed their assigned tasks. Their service actually broke the strike. Many strikers tried to get their jobs back at even less pay, to no avail. The Buffalo Soldiers had enlisted to fight the enemy, but they did not foresee the enemy being starving families, whether Indians or striking workers. After this assignment, they returned to their posts for regular garrison duty.

They transferred to Fort Douglas, in Utah, in 1897. In preparation for fighting in the Spanish American War, they left for training camp at Chickamauga Park in Georgia in April 1898, then to Tampa, Florida, at the end of the month. They were part of Kent's Division, but the overall commander was someone they knew well, General Shafter. They arrived at Siboney on June 25, marched for six miles and made camp at Las Guasimas on the 27th. The next day, the Twenty-Fourth was in support of the Thirteenth Infantry Regiment in the attack at San Juan Hill. The Twenty-Fourth was fed into the front line to fill gaps as needed. By the end of the day, the American troops had captured San Juan Block House from the Spanish garrison. In the days after the battle, the Twenty-Fourth dug and manned trenches. Perhaps their most difficult assignment of the war came after the surrender, when they reported to Siboney for hospital duty. Since they were considered an "immune regiment," they were a logical choice for helping care for the wounded and those sick with yellow fever, since many of their officers and commanders believed they could not catch the disease. They arrived on July 15, to deplorable conditions. More than six hundred wounded and sick men were crowded into small spaces, with inadequate ventilation and limited water and supplies. The men of the Twenty-Fourth had to camp on filthy ground, with an infested lagoon nearby. Large numbers of surgeons, nurses, officers, and the black enlisted men were stricken with yellow fever. They were not, as many believed, immune, and they suffered with everyone else. According to Muller, only twenty-four of the 456 black enlisted men escaped the disease.[17] Once they returned stateside and recuperated, they traveled to their new stations in late September, to Fort Douglas in Utah and Fort D. A. Russell in Wyoming.

Between June 13 and July 14, eight companies and the regiment's band transferred to the Philippines, to quell insurrection from Filipino guerrillas. The battalions lost eleven men who drowned in a ferry accident. By late 1899, most of the companies were back in the United States and stationed at posts along the Mexican border. By 1907, companies were stationed back in the Philippines. During these years, they performed the usual garrison duties, and they had occasional skirmishes with Mexican bandits and Filipino insurgents, but they also participated in a number of other activities back home, including regimental competitions in military tournaments that involved marksmanship, drill, tent pitching, wall scaling, athletic games, and other activities. In 1908, the regiment was in the Philippines and sent teams back to the states to participate in athletic competitions, which included football, swimming, and baseball. For much of 1910 and 1911, the regiment was stationed at Madison Barracks, New York, and Fort Ontario, New York. During these years, they performed routine barracks duties and participated in annual military tournaments. In November 1911, they left for routine duty in the Philippines, where they remained until the middle of 1915, when they transferred to the Presidio of San Francisco. In February 1916, they transferred for routine duty to Fort D. A. Russell in Wyoming. In March, they left to take part in General John J. "Black Jack" Pershing's Punitive Expedition into Mexico, arriving at Camp Furlong in New Mexico, Gibson's Ranch in Mexico, and Boca Grande in Mexico in late March. From there, they rendezvoused at Dublan, Mexico, the expedition's headquarters, in early April. They remained at various locations in Mexico until February 5, 1917, participating in patrols and performing routine garrison duties. They returned to Camp Furlong in New Mexico, where they remained for several years.

The Buffalo regiments hoped to represent their country on the World War I battlefields in Europe. They were sorely disappointed. While the Buffalo Soldier regiments were denied honorable combat service in Europe during the war, their government still made use of them. The Twenty-Fourth's Third Battalion, with eight officers and 654 enlisted under Lieutenant Colonel William Newman, was transferred in July of 1917 to provide guard duty for workers constructing Camp Logan, near Houston, Texas, a training camp for American servicemen for World War I. Houston had a long-standing animosity toward black Americans, and the white workers at Camp Logan were in full agreement with the Houston civilians. Jim Crow laws led to trouble from the very first day of the battalion's arrival on July 18, 1917. Though the Twenty-Fourth had decades of admirable service, Texans decided to put them in their place and demanded their adherence to Jim Crow. These troops had been out on the western frontier and in the Philippines and were used to much better treatment than they were receiving in Texas. The Buffalo Soldiers disregarded the laws at every possibility, especially the regulations regarding streetcars. White Houstonians literally threw them off streetcars, with passing automobiles sometimes knocking them down. They suffered other kinds of abuse from civilians and the white workers they were obligated to guard. Tensions were strained, to say the least. Added to the difficulty was the absence of many of the battalion's officers, sent to Camp Des Moines for officer training. Details of the only black officer training camp for World War I are in Chapter 9.

On August 23, 1917, Houston police officer Lee Sparks broke up a dice game, entered a home, dragged a black woman out to the street, and beat her. A Twenty-Fourth Infantry soldier named Edwards protested the beating, was beaten himself, and was jailed. Corporal Charles Baltimore, one of the battalion's sixteen military police whose job was to maintain peace between the Buffalo Soldiers and the whites, questioned Houston authorities regarding Edwards's treatment. Sparks began hitting Baltimore with his pistol. Baltimore ran to avoid the blows, with Sparks firing his weapon at him. Sparks followed Baltimore into a house, beat him, and arrested him. Even though Sparks's partner, Officer Rufe Daniels (killed in the violence that night), claimed he heard nothing offensive from Baltimore in the exchange with Sparks regarding the arrest of Edwards, Sparks later claimed Baltimore had used profanity, so he pistol-whipped him, shot at him, and arrested him.

Word of trouble reached the battalion's camp, with rumors that Houston police had shot and killed Baltimore. Battalion adjutant Captain Haig Shekerjian went to town to investigate. He found that Baltimore had been beaten, but he had not been shot or killed. The immediate Houston police investigation found Sparks at fault. Police Superintendent Clarence Brock suspended Sparks, and Shekerjian took Baltimore back to camp. Before he left the police station, he saw Edwards, still bloody and under arrest. Shekerjian told Baltimore not to say anything of the incident when they got back to camp. Major Snow ordered his sergeants to tell their men the story and gave orders for no men to leave camp until further notice. All seemed quite until about 8:00 p.m., when word circulated that several men, mostly from Company K, had stolen ammunition and were planning revenge. A number of the men armed themselves and marched into Houston. Shooting broke out in camp and in town. A two-hour shootout left four soldiers dead (one of whom, Sergeant Vida Henry, had committed suicide), fifteen white civilians killed and twelve wounded, and four Houston police officers dead, with another fatally wounded. Shekerjian ordered a sergeant to record the names of those still in camp. Roll calls taken frequently during the night indicated as many as 156 men had been involved in the melee.

The army acted swiftly and immediately transferred the entire Third Battalion to New Mexico. With the lack of a real investigation and the summary discharge without honor in the earlier Brownsville affair in mind, the military decided to conduct a thorough investigation of the Houston incident. Some soldiers even offered testimony in return for immunity from prosecution. All who had missed roll call that evening were arrested and court-martialed. In November 1917, sixty-four soldiers were charged at Fort Sam Houston with mutiny and premeditated murder. Fifty-nine were convicted, with twenty-nine sentenced to death and others to long prison sentences. Five were acquitted. On December 22, 1917, Charles Baltimore and twelve others were hanged. Of the remaining sixteen sentenced to death, President Wilson commuted the decision for six of them, but the other ten were hanged. In all, nineteen were hanged, fifty-one were imprisoned for life, and forty served lesser prison sentences. The soldiers of the Twenty-Fourth had served with distinction since 1869, and their treatment at the hands of whites who strongly believed in Jim Crow was a shocking reminder that they still had not gained full equality as a result of their service. Worse was the treatment they received from their own government.

A few Buffalo Soldiers made it to Europe as noncommissioned officers in the all-black Ninety-Second Infantry Division and the all-black Ninety-Third Infantry Division (Provisional), but most of their service in Europe entailed work in the Service of Supply (SOS), a labor department that was heavily weighted with black Americans, or as Pioneer Infantry, also mostly manned with black Americans. The Pioneer Infantry was not a combat unit. It was a labor unit that received the most dangerous labor jobs close to the front lines or the most disturbing and thankless job of reburying the dead. Most of the four hundred thousand black Americans who did make it to Europe received assignment in these two units. A few, the Ninety-Second and Ninety-Third, miraculously made it to the battlefield as combat troops. The Ninety-Third was attached to the French Fourth Army and received fair and respectful treatment from the French. The Ninety-Second remained with the American Expeditionary Forces and received the same racist and discriminatory treatment they almost always had from other Americans. The Ninety-Third served so well with the French that France awarded them many individual and unit citations. The Ninety-Second, without the same treatment and opportunities of the Ninety-Third, did not perform as well. Their stories are in Chapter 9.

After the war, some members of Congress and prominent Americans wanted to eliminate the units of black Americans who had enlisted or had been drafted for service in the war. They also called for elimination of the four regular Buffalo Regiments. After a struggle and much debate, the Buffalo Regiments remained and resumed their duties in the Southwest and in the Philippines. Once again, their hopes for full citizenship and equality as a result of their service were dashed. During the interwar years, they rotated between duty on the Mexican border and routine occupation duty in the Philippines, but another chance soon presented itself. When war clouds gathered signaling World War II, the Twenty-Fourth Infantry prepared for duty in Europe. The stories of their service in that war and in the Korean War are contained in the epilogue. In January of 1948, President Harry S. Truman desegregated the military with Executive Order No. 9981, but desegregation came slowly, and troops in Korea were still segregated. Finally, after the Korean War, desegregation became a reality, and the Twenty-Fourth closed the final chapter on its long decades of service.

CHAPTER 7

Honest and Faithful Service:
The Twenty-Fifth Infantry

February 11, 1973, was Dorsie W. Willis's birthday. The date also marked twenty-eight years of marriage to his wife, Ollie. A ceremony that day at Zion Baptist Church was in honor of Dorsie but was not a celebration of his birthday or his wedding anniversary. The church was crowded with friends, family, journalists, and army representatives; they packed the church that day to witness Dorsie's honorable discharge from the army. The ceremony represented the correction of an injustice he had lived with for sixty-seven years.

Dorsie was a former Buffalo Soldier in the Twenty-Fifth Infantry Regiment, a proud regiment with a distinguished service record on the Great Plains, in Cuba, and in the Philippines. He enlisted in the Twenty-Fifth in January 1905. In August of 1906, one hundred and seventy men and five officers in Companies B, C, and D, Dorsie's Company, replaced the white Twenty-Sixth Infantry Regiment at Fort Brown, the oldest of the Rio Grande garrisons, built in 1846, near Brownsville, Texas. Texans did not welcome black Americans, especially black troops, in their midst. Brownsville was no exception in its racism, and local citizens, white and Mexican, determined to make their stay as brief and as unpleasant as possible, at the very least. Trouble started before their arrival, with white soldiers of the Twenty-Sixth, already stationed in Brownsville, overhearing the townspeople making threats against the Buffalo Soldiers. Trouble continued once they arrived. Businesses, including local bars, refused to serve the black soldiers. The Buffalo Soldiers had frequented businesses and bars while at their post at Fort Niobrara in Nebraska and were taken aback when roughly refused in Brownsville. John Tillman, owner of the Ruby Saloon on Elizabeth Street, set up a Jim Crow bar in the back of his business to take advantage of the cash in the soldiers' pockets on pay days. Frequently, townspeople insulted soldiers for perceived offenses, the insults sometimes leading to violence. Citizen Fred Tate struck Private James W. Newton on the head with his revolver. He claimed Newton had jostled his wife as he passed her on the sidewalk. Incidents continued, and tension mounted. On Sunday, August 12, Mrs. Lon Evans reported that a Negro soldier had grabbed her by the hair, pushed her to the ground, and run. The town newspaper did not have to print the story for everyone in town to hear a greatly enhanced version of it by Monday morning. Commanding officer Major Charles W. Penrose ordered officer of the day Captain Edgar A. Macklin to cancel all passes and make sure all the men were in barracks by eight o'clock that night. Two men were still out on

Buffalo Soldier, Twenty-Fifth Infantry, Company A, standing, in uniform, Fort Custer, Montana, 1884–1890, Orlando Scott Goff, photographer. (Library of Congress)

pass, probably across the border in Matamoros. The post was quiet, with the men relaxing, playing cards, reading books, fishing in the lagoon, or playing baseball. Penrose retired at about eleven thirty, and Macklin went to bed a few minutes before midnight.

Dorsie vividly remembered the events of that night and the decisions afterward that changed his life forever. The sound of gunfire awakened him. He quickly joined others outside the barracks of Company D, trying to locate the source of the shooting. Private Charley Hairston of Company B, who was on sentry duty that night, reported that the shooting was coming from town in the direction of the fort. First Sergeant Mingo Sanders of Company B easily recognized the shots from a variety of weapons, mostly Winchester rifles but also Mausers, a Remington, and pistols. He knew none of the shots came from soldiers' weapons. Dorsie joined his company when Captain Samuel P. Lyon and Sergeant Jacob Frazier arrived and ordered the men to fall in for roll call. Aside from the two men still out on pass, all were present. While the shooting continued, Companies B and D grabbed their arms and reassembled.

The shooting lasted for about ten minutes. When it stopped, the soldiers conducted a search to locate Captain Macklin, the only other man still missing. Penrose sent Lyon and Company D into town to find him. The Buffalo Soldiers encountered mobs of armed and angry citizens claiming to be law enforcement officers, but the soldiers did not verify that at the time, since they were anxious to locate Macklin, who was not in town. He had slept through the entire incident. What was in town, however, was trouble for the soldiers. John Tillman's bartender at the Ruby Saloon, Frank Natus, was dead from bullet wounds. A policeman's arm required amputation after bullets shattered the bone. Townspeople were spreading the news of what happened as quickly as they could. All claimed the soldiers shot up the town and killed Natus. Many wanted to storm the fort and start killing soldiers. Cooler heads prevailed and convinced others that a few representatives should call on Major Penrose and demand he relinquish all suspects into the custody of civilian authorities. Mayor Joe Combe and his brother, Dr. Fred Combe, met Penrose at the post's front gate after the shooting. They informed the major that eyewitness evidence pointed to his men. Penrose was not convinced and thought the townspeople had done the shooting. He informed the Combe brothers that he would confine his command to the post for further investigation. During this meeting, Macklin appeared and reported to Penrose that he had been asleep in his room through the entire incident. Penrose ordered the men to their barracks. Civilians and soldiers alike nervously awaited daybreak.

By 5:30 a.m., all three companies were at reveille. A thorough inspection revealed that none of the post's rifles had been fired recently. Penrose inspected the rifles himself, confirmed the report, and took a careful accounting of all the post's ammunition. On an inspection of the outer walls of the post, however, Macklin came across a number of spent shells and clips from the recently issued Springfield Model 1903 rifle, evidence that suggested to Penrose that his men had done the shooting after all. Later that day, Mayor Combe arrived on post with additional spent shells found in an alley in town. Penrose was discouraged and hoped that attorney Rentfro B. Creager of the United States Commissioner's office would conduct a thorough investigation. Much to his dismay, he realized soon after Creager's arrival that the attorney already believed that the soldiers had committed the crime. Creager was only the first of many to stamp his bias on the incident and condemn the Buffalo Soldiers. Penrose knew he and his men were facing a difficult ordeal, one for which they were already pronounced guilty.

Both the civilians and the soldiers started gathering information and evidence the next day. The citizens' committee conducted interviews of the eyewitnesses. All the townspeople interviewed swore they had personally seen black soldiers in town, firing weapons. The night of August 13 had no moon and was one of the darkest of the season, yet people described the soldiers in vivid detail. Subsequent trial testimony revealed that the hastily recorded accounts contained so many errors that some witnesses admitted their initial statements were untrue. Others added extensive and graphic details with each telling. One witness finally admitted he was not even in Brownsville at the time of the incident. Two days after the incident, the Committee sent its findings and conclusions in a telegram to President Theodore Roosevelt. According to the Committee, between twenty and thirty soldiers had entered town and fired two hundred rounds before returning to the fort, resulting in one dead and one injured, both civilians. This telegraph triggered a series of responses. Major General F. C. Ainsworth asked Penrose if he could prevent his men from committing further violence. His wording clearly suggested that he believed the soldiers guilty based only on the report of the Brownsville Citizens' Committee, with no information from Penrose and no official investigation. Ainsworth made arrangements for all the men to be moved from Fort Brown to Fort Ringgold. The Inspector General's office sent Major Augustus P. Blocksom to Brownsville to investigate the incident. He followed Creager's lead in condemning the soldiers. He reported that the black soldiers resented the racial abuse of the townspeople. He stated as fact that a soldier had assaulted Mrs. Evans, and that on the night of August 13 as many as fifteen of the men of the Twenty-Fifth had fired perhaps a hundred rounds into the town in reprisal for the treatment they had received since their arrival at the fort. These rounds had killed one and wounded another. The civilians were victims, not participants. If they returned fire, it was in self-defense. He read the sworn statements of the soldiers and accused them of lying. He interviewed a number of soldiers, all claiming to know nothing. He accused all the soldiers of a conspiracy of silence to protect the guilty. He was sure they knew the identities of the guilty. So far, not enough evidence existed to convict anyone. He planned to change that.

Conditions went from bad to worse with the arrival in Brownsville of Texas Ranger Captain William "Bill" McDonald. He was not a shining example of the Rangers; he was a racist and troublemaker with an agenda that spelled doom for the Buffalo Soldiers. He conducted his own investigation and, based on absolutely no evidence at all, persuaded Judge Stanley Welch to issue arrests warrants for twelve enlisted men. McDonald insisted Penrose turn the men over to him. Penrose refused, but he agreed to keep the men in the post guardhouse. Penrose then

Buffalo Soldier, Twenty-Fifth Infantry, Company A, Fort Custer, Montana, 1884–1890, Orlando Scott Goff, photographer. (Library of Congress)

received orders to transfer his men to Fort Reno in Oklahoma and to escort the twelve accused to Fort Sam Houston in San Antonio on the way. Judge Welch abrogated the warrants for lack of evidence, but instead of releasing the men and returning them to duty, the military brought new charges and kept them in the guardhouse. Many of the accused had solid alibis. The army was determined to find and punish the guilty. No amount of questioning brought forth confessions or evidence.

Meanwhile, the rest of the men at Fort Reno were confined to the post until the matter was resolved. Governmental officials became more and more frustrated with the soldiers' insistence that they knew nothing. In desperation, Inspector General Ernest A. Garlington submitted the following recommendation:

> I recommend that orders be issued as soon as practicable discharging, without honor, every man in Companies B, C, and D of the Twenty-fifth Infantry, serving at Fort Brown, Tex., on the night of August 13, 1906, and forever debarring them from reenlisting in the Army or Navy of the United States, as well as from employment in any civil capacity under the Government. In making this recommendation I recognize the fact that a number of men who have no direct knowledge as to the identity of the men of the Twenty-fifth Infantry who actually fired the shots on the night of the 13th of August, 1906, will incur this extreme penalty.[1]

As absurd as this idea was, President Roosevelt supported it and issued it in the form of an ultimatum in an effort to force the soldiers to either confess or identify the guilty. At no time did government officials or the president seem to consider that the men were innocent and that the people of Brownsville had perpetrated the raid themselves. In October, Garlington gathered the men at Fort Reno to deliver the ultimatum that if they did not come forward with information within twenty-four hours, they would all be discharged without honor.

Much of the controversy in the coming decades centered on the meaning of discharge without honor, which is not the same as dishonorable discharge. Judge Advocate General George B. Davis carefully explained the meaning of a discharge without honor. The explanation is lengthy but important enough to place here in its entirety:

> The separation of an enlisted man from the military service is regulated by the requirements of the Fourth Article of War, which provides that—

Art. 4. No enlisted man, duly sworn, shall be discharged from the service without a discharge in writing, signed by a field officer of the regiment to which he belongs, or by the commanding officer when no field officer is present; and no discharge shall be given to any enlisted man before his term of service has expired except by order of the President, the Secretary of War, the commanding officer of a department, or by sentence of a general court-martial.

It will be noted that the article above cited contemplates at least two classes of discharges: (1) Honorable discharges, which are given when the term prescribed in the enlistment contract has been served honestly and faithfully; (2) dishonorable discharges, which are given in pursuance of a sentence of a general court-martial. Otherwise the classification of discharges has never been assumed by Congress, but has been left by it to the Executive branch of the Government. At present there are three kinds of discharges expressly recognized, to wit: The honorable, the dishonorable, and the discharge without honor. The dishonorable discharge is given only in the case of discharge by sentence of court-martial. The discharge without honor is given in the cases first specified in Circular 15, Headquarters of the Army, 1893, but this circular did not *create* such discharge; it merely gave it a name. Before the issue of the circular and as far back as the rebellion (notwithstanding that it was from time to time theoretically asserted that the only kind of discharges known to the law were the honorable and the dishonorable, and that all discharges except by sentence of court-martial were honorable) a third kind of discharge was out of necessity resorted to. It is now recognized that there is a kind of discharge which is neither honorable nor technically dishonorable, but must be classified by itself. This is the 'discharge without honor.'

There were many soldiers summarily discharged during the rebellion for causes tainting the character of their discharges. In numerous cases the orders were made to read dishonorably discharged, although a dishonorable discharge, in the technical sense of that term, can not be imposed except by sentence of a court-martial. A summary discharge can not be a dishonorable discharge, if the term is used in such technical sense, but it may be for a cause tainting the character of the discharge—a discharge manifestly not honorable. Such a summary discharge is now called a discharge without honor. Its name, however, is only important as a recognition of a discharge, not technically dishonorable, but not honorable in fact. It might not be going too far to say that when soldiers were summarily 'dishonorably discharged' during the rebellion the order was so worded simply because the soldier had done something to disgrace the service, and could not be in fact honorably discharged. Thus where a volunteer soldier under arrest for desertion was 'dishonorably discharged' by order on account primarily of the desertion, it was held that while his discharge was not technically dishonorable it was what is now called a discharge without honor, and therefore not honorable.

It would thus appear that to entitle a soldier to an honorable discharge, his services during his term of enlistment must have been honest and faithful. If during his term of enlistment, the soldier becomes incapable of rendering service on account of disability contracted in the line of duty, he is granted a discharge on a proper surgeon's certificate of disability, and the discharge so granted is honorable. There are a number of other cases in which an honorable discharge is granted prior to the expiration of the term of enlistment, as to a veteran, or to one who obtains his discharge by purchase, or is discharged on his own application for reasons deemed sufficient by the Department to warrant his separation from the military service. If a soldier commits an offense of so serious a character as to warrant his discharge, by way of punishment, charges are preferred, and the case is tried by general court-martial. Upon conviction by such a court, a dishonorable discharge may be lawfully imposed under the authority conferred by the Fourth Article of War. The particular offenses for which this punishment may be awarded are described in the Articles of War.

Although not having committed an offense of sufficient gravity to warrant his trial by court-martial, the conduct of a soldier may be such as to warrant the termination of his enlistment contract because he has not served the Government honestly and faithfully, as he is required to do by the engagement which is embodied in his oath of enlistment. In such a case, when reasonable efforts have been put forth with a view to the correction of his faults, his enlistment contract may be annulled in the manner prescribed in the Fourth Article of War. The issue of discharge without honor is regulated by paragraph 148 of the Army Regulations, which prescribes, *inter alia*, that the form for discharge without honor will be used in the following cases:

2. The blank for discharge without honor when a soldier is discharged:
   (a) Without trial, on account of fraudulent enlistment.

(b) Without trial, on account of having become disqualified for service, physically or in character, through his own misconduct.

(c) On account of imprisonment under sentence of a civil court.

(d) Where the service has not been honest and faithful; that is, where the service does not warrant his reenlistment.

(e) When discharge without honor is specially ordered by the Secretary of War for any other reason.

3. The blank for dishonorable discharge, for dishonorable discharge by sentence of a court-martial or military commission.

Paragraph 146 of the Army Regulations contains certain provisions which, if carefully read, will be found to be in entire harmony with the requirements of paragraph 148, above cited. Paragraph 146 applies *exclusively* to the case of a discharge at expiration of the soldier's term of enlistment and to the form of discharge which shall be used in that case, and provides that:

146. The character given on a discharge will be signed by the company or detachment commander, and great care will be taken that no injustice is done the soldier. If the soldier's service has been honest and faithful, he will be entitled to such character as will warrant his reenlistment—that is, to character at least "good." Where the company commander deems the service not honest and faithful, he shall, if practicable, so notify the soldier at least thirty days prior to discharge, and shall at the same time notify the commanding officer, who will in every such case convene a board of officers, three if practicable, to determine whether the soldier's service has been honest and faithful. The soldier will in every case be given a hearing before the board.

If the company commander is the commanding officer, he will report the facts to the next higher commander, who will convene the board. The finding of the board, when approved by the convening authority, shall be final. Discharge without honor on account of 'service not honest and faithful' will be given only on the approved finding of a board of officers as herein described.

When an honorable discharge is given following the action of the board, the fact will be noted on the discharge and on the muster rolls.

The proceedings of boards convened under this paragraph, showing all the facts pertinent to the inquiry, will be forwarded by the reviewing authority direct to The Military Secretary of the Army.

As has been said, the requirements of the paragraph last above cited are only applicable in determining the character of discharge to be given an enlisted man at the expiration of his term of enlistment. It has never been regarded as restricting the authority vested in the President and the Secretary of War in the Fourth Article of War.

It would thus appear that the last clause of the Fourth Article of War vests a discretion in the President to annul an enlistment contract whenever, in his opinion, that course is dictated by the public interest. The English practice, upon which our military administration is to a considerable extent based, is substantially similar to that prescribed in the Articles of War. Clode, in his Military Forces of the Crown, says in speaking of the soldier's enlistment:

Though an engagement is made for a term certain, the Crown is under no obligation to retain the soldier, either in pay or in arms, for that period, but may discharge him at any time. The safety of the realm may depend in some measure on the immediate discharge or dismissal of any man or regiment in arms, and, equally, that the cause of such dismissal should not at the time be disclosed by the responsible ministers of the Crown. (II Code, Military Forces of the Crown p. 40.)

The provision of a suitable agency for the investigation of charges of wrongdoing on the part of enlisted men, in the operation of which questions of fact may be investigated, findings reached, and, in case of conviction, adequate sentences imposed, restricts the exercise of the power of summary discharge which is vested in the President in the article above cited, to cases in which the conduct of the soldier and the character of the services rendered can not be investigated by a military tribunal. In the case under discussion it is an essential incident of a judicial investigation that those who are aware of the wrongful acts committed should testify, under oath, as to facts within their knowledge. To defeat such an inquiry, a considerable number of enlisted men have entered into a criminal combination, in the execution of which they decline to disclose facts which are known to them touching the very serious offenses against public order which were committed at Brownsville, Tex., in August last. In that view of the case, the question presented is, are men who enter into such a combination rendering honest and faithful service within the meaning of their enlistment contracts? In other words, can men admittedly so disregardful of public authority be trusted and relied upon when upon an occasion of public emergency they are called upon to support it?

Very respectfully,
Geo. B. Davis,
Judge Advocate General[2]

The men of the Twenty-Fifth were shocked. They were accused of crimes they did not commit. They were accused of withholding evidence they did not have. They were threatened with discharge without honor, a punishment they did not deserve that would ruin their lives and destroy the careers they had built. Company B's First Sergeant Mingo Sanders went to talk to Garlington. He was not there to provide evidence, however. As senior noncommissioned officer of the regiment, he was there to appeal to the General and convince him that he had no evidence to

Buffalo Soldiers, Twenty-Fifth Infantry, some wearing buffalo robes, Fort Keogh, Montana, December 14, 1890, Chr. Barthelmess, photographer. (Library of Congress)

offer, and neither did his men. He simply could not understand why this was happening to him and his men—and why no one would believe them when they told the truth that they had no information about that night that they had not already reported. He and his wife, Luella, were counting on his retirement, and losing it through no fault of his own was unthinkable. Sanders's service record was impressive. He enlisted in May 1881, and had provided loyal and dedicated service for twenty-six years, including time in the Dakotas, in Cuba, and in the Philippines. He was part of the bicycle unit under Lieutenant James Moss when the regiment was stationed in Missoula, Montana. Brigadier General Andrew Sheridan Burt, who commanded Sanders in the Philippines, wrote that, "Mingo Sanders is the best non-commissioned officer I have ever known." Burt had confidence in the entire regiment, stating, "Will they fight? Why they would charge into hell, fight their way out and drag the devil out by the tail."[3] Sanders reenlisted in 1886, 1891, 1896, 1899, 1902, and 1905, each time with a rating of excellent character.[4] At the time of his discharge without honor, he had less than two years to serve before he could retire and receive a pension of three-quarters of his pay. He appealed to Garlington to reconsider the decision to discharge all 167 men at Fort Brown that night. Sanders's appeal did not move Garlington, who filed his recommendation for the discharge order the next day.

Roosevelt fully supported the recommendation, but he hesitated to issue the order immediately. He decided to wait until after the 1906 midterm elections, so that the news would not hurt his party in the elections. Roosevelt had previously shown appreciation for black soldiers. He showered the Buffalo Soldiers with praise for their performance next to his Rough Riders on San Juan Hill and Kettle Hill during the Spanish American War in July 1898. Some of the men he praised, such as Mingo Sanders, were now members of the group he would soon condemn. Many Americans knew that the Buffalo Soldiers played a critical role in that military success, yet, after the war, when he was campaigning for the office of president of the United States, he eschewed the black soldiers. During his campaign for president, he relied heavily on the actions of the Rough Riders under his command at San Juan Hill, but he did not mention that the Buffalo Soldiers were even present. His support of Garlington's recommendation was probably more politically motivated than racially driven. He needed to court certain groups to win the office. Roosevelt directed the War Department to issue Special Orders No. 266, based on Garlington's recommendation, on November 9, right after the election, to discharge all 167 men without honor. The men of Companies B, C, and D were summarily dismissed in a humiliating ceremony on November 12, 1906. Order No. 266 stated: "By direction of the President, the following-named enlisted men who, on August 13, 1906, were members of Companies B, C, and D, Twenty-fifth Infantry, certain members of which organizations participated in the riotous disturbances which occurred in Brownsville, Tex., on the night of August 13, 1906, will be discharged without honor from the Army by their respective commanding officers and forever debarred from reenlisting in the Army or Navy of the United States, as well as from employment in any civil capacity under the Government."[5]

The outcry from black Americans was widespread and immediate. Many called for a formal investigation and trial, which had not occurred. One man, Senator Joseph B. Foraker, senator from Ohio, heeded the call and began a campaign to correct the wrongs done to these men. Foraker had served on the Senate Committee on Military Affairs that investigated the Brownsville Affray, as the committee termed it. The majority report of that committee had fully concurred that the men were clearly guilty and supported the discharge without honor. The minority report of the committee, of which Foraker was a member, indicated the lack of evidence and contradictions in civilian testimony. The minority report concluded that punishing all the men was not correct or fair. Foraker conducted thorough investigations and interviews. For example, he discovered that the shell casings found outside the fort and in an alley in town had been fired on the target range at Fort Niobrara in Nebraska, before the Twenty-Fifth even arrived at Fort Brown. They were stored in an unlocked box in an open area, accessible to anyone in town. Soldiers testified that children routinely took some of the casings to sell. Foraker also noted that the civilians' weapons had not been checked for firing at the time of the raid. He proved that the eyewitness statements could not be true, and that their claims were humanly impossible under the conditions of that night. None of the government's investigators had considered the possibility that the soldiers were innocent and had not looked for evidence that might incriminate the townspeople. Some, such as McDonald, Blocksom, and Garlington, manipulated evidence as part of their personal agendas to prove the soldiers guilty.

Foraker's efforts were putting pressure on the president. Accusations surfaced that Roosevelt's actions were the result of racism. Foraker continued his call for Congress to open a formal investigation into the matter. On December 14, the War Department announced charges against Penrose and Macklin. Both officers received a trial and were acquitted. In February 1907, the Senate Committee on Military Affairs met to begin hearings on the Brownsville affair.[6] Foraker was confident the evidence would gain a reversal for the soldiers. He was wrong. The Senate Committee completely ignored such evidence as the shells, which clearly were not part of the shooting that night, in favor of the political needs of the Republican administration in an election year. In March 1908, they filed the results of their findings. They noted that the evidence against the soldiers was abundant and conclusive, and they found them all guilty.

Public outrage continued after the committee verdict, and so did Foraker in his investigation. So did the administration, but not for the same reason as Foraker. On the eve of the election, the administration wanted to eliminate the last traces of the Brownsville affair, so when a private investigator named William G. Baldwin and a journalist named Herbert J. Browne approached Secretary of War William Howard Taft with supposed proof of the soldiers' guilt, Taft offered them a contract for a fee in return for the names of the guilty. Taft hoped identifying the guilty soldiers would clear the innocent ones and reflect favorably on him and his election hopes. Baldwin and Browne promised the names by June 15. Unbeknownst to Taft, Baldwin and Browne had also approached Foraker, who had paid them five hundred dollars before he realized they were swindlers. The two men visited the homes of some of the discharged soldiers and used bribes and intimidation in an effort to get any information. Their efforts failed. Foraker was amused that the administration was paying the same men thousands of dollars, twenty thousand total. Browne and Baldwin claimed to have a solid statement from a witness named Boyd Conyers. Foraker obtained letters from Conyers revealing that he not spoken at length to Baldwin and Browne and that they had produced a false confession in his name. Foraker brought his evidence before Congress and proved Browne and Baldwin to be swindlers, but in the process, he became the target of political backlash and lost his Senate seat in the fallout.

One final hearing in 1910 raised the hopes of men like Dorsie Willis and Mingo Sanders, but on April 9, five generals unanimously upheld the 1907 decision of the Senate Committee. In a strange twist, they listed fourteen men who would be eligible to reenlist. Willis and Sanders were not among the fourteen. Sanders wept at the discharge ceremony, hired a lawyer, and fought the decision, to no avail. Years later, he and his wife Luella were living in Washington, DC, when Mingo's leg had to be amputated from diabetic complications. He died at Freedmen's Hospital on August 15, 1929, and was buried at Arlington National Cemetery.[7] Dorsie Willis got a job at a barbershop shining shoes and cleaning. He had just retired from that job a few months before the government contacted him in 1872 about his honorable discharge.

Willis might have died like the other soldiers, taking the dishonor with him to the grave, but a journalist named John D. Weaver became interested in the story after he discovered that his father, Henry B. Weaver, was the court reporter for the final hearing in 1909 and 1910. What he found shocked him, and he was determined to find the truth. His first book on the subject was entitled *The Brownsville Raid*. It gained a great deal of attention for the case. Soon, Weaver was one of a group of people dedicated to clearing the men. In 1962, Gus Hawkins, elected to the House of Representatives, introduced a bill, H. R. 6866, requesting the government to rescind Special Orders No. 266. The army was staunchly against the bill and in 1972 reconfirmed the original findings of 1910. They refused to reopen the case. Fortunately, the bill did not die but reached the desk of Acting Attorney General Richard G. Kleindienst, who believed correcting the injustice committed on 167 men worthy of time and attention. He recommended the army simply set aside the discharges without honor, making H. R. 6866 unnecessary. On September 28, 1972, the army announced that it was clearing all 167 men of all charges and reversing their discharges without honor to honorable discharges. They would not receive back pay, but their names would be cleared. Weaver later learned that his book, *The Brownsville Raid*, had served an influential role in the decision. At long last, the government reversed its decision. Dorsie's former boss from the barbershop called him with the news. Dorsie was eighty-six years old and one of two Buffalo Soldiers from these companies still alive. The other was Edward Warfield of Company B. Their lives had taken very different paths because of the Brownsville Raid, but the April 9, 1910, decision separated their paths even more. Warfield was one of the fourteen eligible for reenlistment. He reenlisted, served in France in World War I, received an honorable discharge, and had been on a military pension since his retirement as a security guard for the government. Dorsie was the only court-martialed Buffalo Soldier who lived to see exoneration. He also finally received $25,000 in compensation. On August 24, 1977, Dorsie died. He was ninety-one years old. He was buried at Fort Snelling, Minnesota, with full military honors.[8]

Quintard Taylor Jr. stated in the introduction to John H. Nankivell's *Buffalo Soldier Regiment: History of the Twenty-Fifth United States Infantry, 1869–1926*, "Few groups in African-American history have been more revered and reviled than the 'buffalo soldiers.'"[9] The Twenty-Fifth received more than its share of revilement. To make matters worse, as happened in Brownsville, they did not deserve such treatment or reputation. Their story is one of continued effort to serve honorably in the face of unfair and racist treatment. Throughout their decades of service in Texas, New Mexico, Arizona, Montana, the Dakotas, Cuba, and the Philippines, the Buffalo Soldiers did more than fight Indians and patrol the border during the years after the Civil War. They helped build the West economically and physically.

The Thirty-Ninth was organized on August 22, 1866, in General Sheridan's Department of the Gulf, with headquarters at Greenville, Louisiana, until March 25, 1867. At that time, its ten companies left for other stations in Louisiana and Mississippi, where they served until the regiment was discontinued on April 20, 1869, to become part of the Twenty-Fifth. Colonel Joseph A. Mower commanded the Thirty-Ninth, along with Lieutenant Colonel Frank Wheaton and Major Alexander Von Schrader. The Fortieth was first stationed with the Department of Washington, then in 1867 with the Department of the South. Colonel Nelson A. Miles commanded the Fortieth, along with Lieutenant Colonel E. W. Hicks and Major Charles E. Compton. In April 1869, they went to New Orleans for consolidation with the Thirty-Ninth to form the Twenty-Fifth, organized April 20, 1869. The officers of the Twenty-Fifth were Colonel Joseph A. Mower, commander of the Department of Louisiana, Lieutenant Colonel Edward W. Hinks, Major Zenas R. Bliss, Chaplain D. Eglinton Barr, First Lieutenant and Adjutant J. M. Lee, and First Lieutenant and Quartermaster H. B. Quimby. Headquarters was at New Orleans. The Twenty-Fifth served in Louisiana and Mississippi from April 1869 until May 1870. Colonel Mower died on January 6, 1879, and Colonel Joseph J. Reynolds, commander of the Department of Texas, took command of the regiment. By May 1870, when the Twenty-Fifth transferred from Louisiana to Texas, where it would serve for the remainder of the decade, the regiment had dropped to 507 enlisted. Attached to them at this time were fifty Seminole Negro Indian Scouts that Major Bliss recruited. They served with the four Buffalo regiments for a number of years and received four Medals of Honor. In Texas, the Twenty-Fifth was headquartered at Fort Davis under the command of Lieutenant Colonel George L. Andrews, with the following stations: Headquarters, Band, Company D, and Company F at Fort Clark; Companies A and G at Fort Davis; Company B at Fort Quitman; Companies C and H at Fort McKavett; Companies E and I at Fort Duncan; and Company K at Fort Stockton. On December 15, 1870, Colonel Reynolds transferred to the Third Cavalry. The Twenty-Fifth experienced a succession of officers, until Colonel George L. Andrews took command on June 19, 1871. During 1871 and the first part of 1872, the regiment built and repaired telegraph lines and roads, scouted for Indians, maintained the garrison, and provided escort duty for the Butterfield Stage line. During the 1870s, the Twenty-Fifth served with other regiments, including the other Buffalo regiments.

On July 8, 1874, Company I, stationed at Fort Sill, Indian Territory since April 1873, received a break from garrison boredom. They marched thirty-five miles to the northeast, to the Wichita Agency on the Washita River, in response to trouble involving the Kiowa and Noconees Comanche under Red Food at the agency. Fighting broke out on August 22 and 23 between the Indians, I Company, and four companies of the Tenth Cavalry under the command of Lieutenant Colonel J. W. Davidson, who provided a detailed report to the Assistant Adjutant General of the Department of Texas. According to Davidson's report, hostile Comanche and Kiowa had taken refuge at the agency after a series of raids in the area. Noting that these Indians had disregarded orders to enroll as friendly on August 3, Captain Gaines Lawson of the Twenty-Fifth, in command at the agency, requested assistance on the 21st. Davidson informed Red Food that if he and his people wanted to stay and receive the benefits of the agency, they needed to surrender their arms and enroll, to which Red Food agreed. Lieutenant Woodward of the Tenth took forty men to assist Red Food with their surrender of arms. It quickly became clear that Red Food had no intention of surrendering, and fighting broke out. Captain Lawson deployed his infantry to a pre-designated place on the Washita to prevent Indian escape. Enrolled Indians joined in the fight against the Buffalo Soldiers. During the two-day fight, Lawson's men successfully prevented Indian escape up the Washita, helped to guard buildings on the agency grounds, and put out fires Indians started to burn out the soldiers. Uneasy peace returned, with Davidson taking the prisoners back to Fort Sill and Lawson remaining at the agency to maintain the peace.[10]

In 1875, the Twenty-Fifth was part of the attempt to clear the Llano Estacado of Indians. The Twenty-Fourth, under Col. William Shafter, along with men from the Tenth and Twenty-Fifth, spent six months finding and destroying camps of Apache, Comanche, and Comancheros in the region. During the years from 1875 to 1880, they crossed over into Mexico on several occasions, pursuing Indians and Mexican bandits. The Rio Grande border between the U.S. and Mexico ran for sixteen hundred miles. The frequent raids of Mexican bandits and hostile Indians into Texas necessitated protection from the army, but the nature and size of the border made escape for the culprits easy and apprehension nearly impossible. Sheridan and others made requests for laws authorizing

American pursuit across the Rio Grande into Mexico, overriding Mexican opposition to such action. American forces occasionally crossed the border anyway, partly to catch bandits and hostiles and partly to send a message to Mexican authorities that if they could not prevent these forays into Texas, the United States would. On June 12, 1878, Company B under Captain Charles Bentzoni crossed the Rio Grande with Colonel Ranald S. Mackenzie and the Fourth Cavalry, in search of cattle thieves. They returned to the United States on June 21. According to Mackenzie's report, travel went well for the first couple of days, when poor scouting exacerbated a water shortage. Mackenzie considered turning back but changed his mind when the water situation improved. Colonel Shafter and Captain Young joined the column on the San Diego River on the 17th. On the 19th, they encountered Colonel Pedro Valdez and a number of Mexican soldiers, who sympathized with the column's mission but informed Mackenzie that Valdez had orders to get the Americans back across the border and out of Mexico. Colonel Valdez did not have enough men to attack the American forces, but Colonel Nunzio arrived with reinforcements and requested American withdrawal. Even with Nunzio's reinforcements, the Mexicans did not have adequate forces. The Americans ignored their request. On the morning of the 21st, Mackenzie sent Lieutenant Crews to reassure the citizens of the Mexican village of Montelova Viego that they would not be harmed in the American pursuit against the cattle thieves in the area. The situation became such that Mackenzie ordered American troops back across the border rather than risk a fight with Mexican troops. This incident, however, resulted in more stringent control of the border on the part of Mexico.

During these years, the companies were chronically understrength, making their tasks even more difficult. On November 25, 1878, commander of the regiment, Colonel George L. Andrews, requested replacements of enlisted men, noting that some companies had only five or six men rather than the fifty outlined in the March 1869 reorganization plan. Even without the men they needed, they gave every effort to do their duty to the best of their abilities, ranging from garrison duty to scouting for Indians with the cavalry. On July 23, 1879, Captain Courtney and Company H joined Company H of the Tenth Cavalry to track hostile Indians. They discovered and fought the Indians near Sulphur Springs, Texas. Courtney and Company H accompanied men from Company H of the Tenth Cavalry again on September 12, 1879, to scout Carrizo, Capote, Van Horne, and Eagle Mountains. They fought protecting a water tank in the Van Horne Mountains. During their service in the Department of Texas, they, along with other Buffalo regiments, constructed and maintained three hundred miles of telegraph lines, guarded over one thousand miles of wagon roads, and marched nearly one hundred and forty thousand miles in one of the harshest climates on earth. They participated in the campaign against Victorio and the Mimbres Apaches. They made the district so safe that settlers flocked to western Texas and the military contemplated where next to send the regiments.

Several factors played a role in the debate about their next assignment. Some of the suggestions clearly showed concern for the regiment's white officers and families rather than the noncommissioned officers and enlisted men. Officers had resigned because they objected to the harsh, hot, dry climate as well as to the extreme isolation. General C. C Auger, commander of the Department of the South, suggested Louisiana and Arkansas, which would have provided a change in climate but also would have placed the men in the midst of hostile Southerners. Another objection was that the regiments would be too close to whites. General William T. Sherman favored Louisiana because he felt the black regiments should be rotated out of the West as white regiments already were. General E. O. C. Ord, commander of the Department of Texas, thought it only fair the black regiments receive rotation to more favorable locations and stated so in an annual report:

> I would like to impress upon the government, that the officers and men who stay and scout with their commands, out in the desert districts of Texas, and perform their full duties, are entitled to something more than commendation.
>
> The climate of these deserts, is, for the most part, rigorous, and the troops are subject to extremes of heat in summer and cold in winter, with frequent privations, such as hunger and thirst. It would not be regarded by them as a hardship, and would redound to the advantage of all concerned, if the regiments that have, for so many years endured such service, could take their turn for duty in the vicinity of civilization. I refer especially to the Tenth Infantry and the colored troops.[11]

The most surprising idea was the suggestion to transfer the Buffalo regiments to the Department of Dakota. White Americans had long held the belief that black soldiers would die in the extreme cold of northern regions. However, in April 1880, the Twenty-Fifth was ordered from Texas to Dakota Territory. The regiment made the move between May and August, with headquarters at Fort Randall and companies stationed at Fort Meade and Fort Hale. They still constructed telegraph lines and guarded crews of the Northern Pacific Railroad, but they did not scout or provide stage escorts in the Dakota Territory. One new duty was woodcutting. They also occasionally encountered other duties, such as in 1881, when spring flooding on the Keya Paha River stranded eight hundred settlers, and Company F came to their rescue. The flood washed out homes and destroyed belongings. The men of the Twenty-Fifth risked their lives to save a cattle herd. They took a collection from their personal funds to provide food, shelter, and clothing for the families they rescued.

One of the most notable of their duties during their service in the Dakotas involved the Sioux leader, Sitting Bull. After the Sioux defeat of Custer at Little Big Horn, Sitting Bull and a number of his people fled to Canada. In the coming years, survival became more difficult. They returned to the United States and surrendered in 1881. Sitting Bull and more than one hundred and fifty of his people arrived at Fort Randall as prisoners, turned over to the charge of the Twenty-Fifth, who watched over them until his transfer to Fort Yates in 1883.

The Twenty-Fifth served in Dakota Territory from 1880 to 1888, at which time they served in Montana from 1888 to 1898, with headquarters at Fort Missoula and companies at Fort Harrison, Fort Custer, Fort Shaw, and Fort Assiniboine. While stationed in Montana, the Twenty-Fifth did something no other regiments, black or white, had done. It was during this time that they conducted trials using bicycles. Soldiers from the Twenty-Fifth Infantry comprised the Bicycle Unit, and while they were not the first choice for the study, they were the most successful. In 1891, General Nelson A. Miles, commander of the Department of the Missouri, decided that the military could make good use of bicycles, in a variety of ways. Troops on bicycles could act as couriers. Bicycles did not require food and water, and they were quiet and more versatile than horses. The first group to conduct experiments with bicycles was the Fifteenth Infantry stationed at Fort Sheridan in Illinois, but their activities were limited and did not involve any cross-country travel. The Secretary of War did not approve an extension of the plan. Miles did not give up on his idea, and his promotion to major general of the army in 1895 provided the opportunity he needed. In 1896 and 1897, Lieutenant James A. Moss used men he selected from his Twenty-Fifth Infantry troops stationed at Fort Missoula, Montana, to form the Twenty-Fifth Infantry Bicycle Corps and to conduct long-distance experiments with bicycles. The corps first bicycled 126 miles to Lake McDonald and back. The trip was hard on both men and bikes because of bad roads, rain, wind, mud, and hills, and the bikes needed frequent repair. Moss revised their tactics before their next trip, an eight-hundred-mile journey to Yellowstone Park and Fort Assiniboine and back to Fort Missoula. He procured a few puncture-proof tires, increased the rations the men carried from two days to four, and arranged for rations to be available every 150 miles along the route. One of the biggest problems continued to be tire punctures and delays to make repairs. The trip lasted twenty-four days, from August 15 to September 8. Moss and his men resumed the experiment on a much longer trip the following summer. Moss made some changes. He handpicked twenty men from those stationed at Fort Missoula, including Sergeant Mingo Sanders as acting first sergeant for the corps. He planned to ride nineteen hundred miles, to St. Louis and back, with rations, arms, and ammunition. He arranged for a surgeon to accompany them. Secretary of War Russell Alger finally approved the plan when the Spalding Bicycle Company agreed to provide military-grade bicycles with puncture-proof tires at no expense to the military. They would carry camping gear, cooking utensils, arms and ammunition, and food for two days. Rations were stationed along the route at about every hundred miles. Moss planned to cover fifty miles a day.

They departed Fort Missoula on June 14, 1897, and rolled into St. Louis on July 24, averaging nearly the fifty miles a day Moss planned. The ride was tough, with snow, sleet, and mud making things difficult from the second day. After they left the mountains, the heat was sweltering. The men suffered from dehydration from the heat and from the alkali water along the route, causing suffering the men had known all too often. Along with poor weather conditions and lack of water and adequate food, the road conditions made the journey difficult, with the men having to walk their bicycles for at least several hundred miles. Even walking the bicycles was difficult, as the wheels became caked with thick mud every few feet that had to be cut off the tires. The men, also caked with mud and often short on water and rations, still made good progress and demonstrated the usefulness of troops on bicycles. When they entered Crawford, Nebraska, on July 3, the Ninth Cavalry band was there playing for the July 4th celebration and greeted their fellow Buffalo Soldiers with special music in their honor. When they arrived in St. Louis, a crowd greeted them. They rested and received orders to return to Fort Missoula by train. They arrived on August 19. Moss and his men had conducted successful trials using bicycles, but his requests for further trials ended in rejection. Disappointment did not diminish their accomplishment.

During their time in Dakota Territory, they saw little action against Indians. Much of their time in Dakota was not pleasant. Some of the men from Fort Meade were accused of the murder of Dr. Lynch in nearby Sturgis City. Locals in the town lynched a corporal in retaliation. Some of the men formed a detail, marched into town, and shot up a home and a saloon, killing a man. In the early months of 1888, they transferred to Montana Territory. Here as well, a soldier was lynched after murdering a citizen. Townspeople had attempted to arrest the soldier after an altercation with a white soldier. Realizing he was in peril, he panicked and killed a citizen during his escape. He was found dead in an alley the next morning. Other problems were not as serious, but they still presented difficulties for the men and their officers. To alleviate boredom and reduce chances of soldiers getting into trouble in local towns, the post trader was authorized to keep a cantina near the base for the men. They bowled, had beer, played games, and read. Some of the men still occasionally went into the local towns. In November 1889, Sam Griswold was fined forty dollars and trial costs for drunkenness on Sunday during which he had fired his weapon within the city limits. About a month later, Private Jacob Jones was charged twenty-five dollars and court costs for getting drunk and trying to use a razor on Lizzie Maroney of the "Four-Mile" house when she refused her services.

The Twenty-Fifth did have to attend to some problems with Indians on the reservations, but one incident was the fault of the local sheriff rather than the Indians. On June 11, 1889, the local sheriff asked Colonel Andrews for assistance extracting Flathead Indians accused of murder from the Flathead Indian Reservation at Ravalli in Montana Territory. Andrews refused, since any request for military assistance needed to come from the Indian agent. The next day, the Indian agent, Peter Ronan, did indeed ask for help immediately. Apparently, the sheriff had decided to enter the reservation on his own to apprehend the suspects. In the event, an Indian ended up shot, which of course upset the Flatheads. Later that afternoon, Captain Gaines Lawson arrived with three companies. No more violence occurred, and two companies left the reservation on July 9, with one staying until July 12, just to be sure there was no more violence.

In April 1890, the Twenty-Fifth answered the call of settlers north of Flathead Lake in northwestern Montana for protection against reservation Indians and some Canadian Indians. The Twenty-Fifth patrolled from their base at Demersville and went back to Fort Missoula in September. In November 1890, they were sent to the Pine Ridge Agency as a reserve force related to the Ghost Dance incident. The Indians at the Pine Ridge and Rosebud reservations were converting by the thousands to the Ghost Dance movement, which agents feared would lead to trouble.

Major General Nelson A. Miles, commander of the Division of the Missouri, commanded the campaign against the Sioux Ghost Dancers. Four companies of the Twenty-Fifth were sent to Fort Keogh on November 29. They camped in tents in weather reaching nineteen degrees below zero. The Ghost Dance campaign led to the Wounded Knee massacre and the final chapter in the Indian Wars. The end of conflict in the West was not the end of action for the Buffalo regiments.

The Twenty-Fifth was the first of the black regiments ordered east at the outbreak of the Spanish-American War I in 1898, with the others soon following. The United States declared war on April 25, but the Twenty-Fifth headed to Florida on April 10, arriving on May 7. They encountered disturbing racist behavior on June 6, when they observed men from a white regiment shooting at a two-year-old black child, bullets actually tearing the baby's clothes. Violence erupted when the Twenty-Fifth intervened to rescue the child. Fortunately, the Twenty-Fifth was slated to leave on the 14th for Cuba, where they spent fifty-three days fighting the climate, malaria, supply shortages, the Spanish enemy, and their oldest enemy, racism.

On July 1, the Twenty-Fifth comprised part of the six-thousand-man assault to take the Spanish fort at El Caney. The Twenty-Fifth claimed to be the first to enter the fort. Two of the Twenty-Fifth's soldiers kept a piece of the enemy flag they tore off when officers from the white Twelfth Infantry demanded they relinquish it and laid claim to taking the fort themselves. The Twenty-Fifth lost one officer and six enlisted men in the battle. They returned home in August, with headquarters and four companies stationed at Fort Logan, Colorado, and seven companies at various posts in New Mexico and Arizona.

In early 1899, they were reassigned to the newly annexed Philippine Islands to control the insurrection of the Filipinos protesting American occupation, a guerrilla war that would last for three years in the provinces of Bataan and Zambales. On January 5, 1900, they captured General Servillano Aquino's stronghold. During the years 1899–1902, the Twenty-Fifth lost one officer and nine enlisted. They were withdrawn in June of 1902, even though the rebels had not been clearly defeated. One possible reason for the early withdrawal of black troops from the Philippines was the relationship between black Americans and the Filipinos. As many as five hundred black soldiers married while on duty there and remained in the islands after the troop withdrawal.

Their new assignments were once again out West, with the First and Third Battalions at Fort Niobrara in Nebraska, and the Second Battalion at Fort Reno in Oklahoma Territory. Trouble came with the May 1906 transfer of the regiment to Texas, with headquarters and the Second Battalion to Fort Bliss near El Paso, the Third Battalion to Fort McIntosh, and the First Battalion to Fort Brown, near Brownsville. That story opened this chapter. In August 1907, the once-again full strength Twenty-Fifth was sent for another tour in the Philippines, then, in 1909, to Fort Lawson near Seattle and Fort George Wright near Spokane in the Pacific Northwest. During their three years in the Northwest, they fought forest fires.

On January 1, 1913, the Twenty-Fifth received transfer to Schofield Barracks in Hawaii Territory, where they remained throughout World War I, denied the opportunity to fight in Europe. Some of the officers and men went to the officer training camp at Fort Des Moines. These were the only members of the Twenty-Fifth to see active duty in Europe. In August 1918, the Twenty-Fifth was transferred to various posts in Arizona. They remained at their last regimental post, Fort Huachuca near Nogales, Arizona, for fourteen years. They saw action in World War II and the Korean War. Details of their service in these wars are in Chapter 9 and the Epilogue.

CHAPTER 8

Cuba, the Philippines, and Mexico

By 1891, the Indian Wars were over, with the last of the tribes subjugated and the continent safe for settlers. The Buffalo Soldier regiments remained in their isolated outposts in the West and Southwest, while calls came from within Congress to disband the regiments and discharge these soldiers who seemed to be no longer needed. Need arose in just a few years, with a series of wars and campaigns that kept these regiments alive and busy. They functioned in critical roles in the Spanish-American War in Cuba in 1898, the Philippine Insurrection from 1899 to 1902, and the Punitive Expedition in Mexico in 1916 and 1917.

The February 15, 1898, sinking of the U.S.S. *Maine* in Havana Harbor was a pivot point in a strained relationship between the United States and Spain that dated back at least ten years. Spain was not the first colonial power to mistreat its subjects in faraway lands—this time in Cuba and the Philippines. Americans supported Cuban rebels fighting against Spain and urged formal intervention. American yellow journalists and Cuban Americans spent years making sure Americans heard stories of atrocity on the part of the Spanish against their subjects in Cuba, whether true or fabricated. At the same time, they made sure that any incidents that would reflect poorly on the rebels remained away from American news sources. Americans immediately suspected that the Spanish had blown up and sunk the *Maine*, killing two hundred and sixty-six sailors, including twenty-two black Americans. Later investigation proved the *Maine* explosion was most likely an unfortunate accident, but at the time Americans believed it was an act of war and demanded that President William McKinley send troops to Cuba in support of the rebel cause. Spain did not want a war with the United States and agreed to every American demand in an effort to prevent war, every demand except granting Cuba independence. The United States declared war on April 21, 1898. Even though the war would of necessity be mostly a naval war, both powers needed boots on the ground. The U.S. Navy was more prepared than the army and far larger and superior to the Spanish Navy, which was not a threat to the Americans and suffered defeat quickly. The U.S. Army, however, which had spent the years after the Civil War in the Indian Wars on the frontier, did not have nearly the numbers it needed to meet the Spanish. The Spanish ground forces numbered around one hundred and fifty thousand men who were already equipped and trained. The U.S. Army had fewer than twenty-eight thousand.[1] Many were new and inexperienced. By the end of May, McKinley had two hundred thousand volunteers. As was so often the case with American military preparedness, the small standing army was insufficient to even begin operations against the enemy, and these volunteers needed sufficient time to organize and train before they could deploy. Logistical problems and shortages of nearly everything slowed the process to a crawl. Unfortunately, the same William R. Shafter, commander of the Twenty-Fourth Infantry who was competent and capable on the frontier, was disorganized and ineffective as the commander of the much larger force to leave Tampa in early June. The sluggish and unorganized preparation of the volunteers placed much of the initial battlefield responsibility directly onto the shoulders of the Ninth, Tenth, Twenty-Fourth, and Twenty-Fifth Regiments of the regular army. In preparation for the possibility of war, some of the regular regiments had already transferred to areas in the South. In March, the Twenty-Fifth Infantry left Montana for Dry Tortugas, an island located between Cuba and Key West. The other regiments followed in early and mid-April. The Ninth and Tenth Cavalry left Nebraska and Montana for Georgia, and the Twenty-Fourth Infantry left Utah for New Orleans. Shafter's mishandling of the process of transporting men and supplies to Cuba made a bad situation worse for the regulars. In addition, ironically and mistakenly, but in line with past thinking, many Americans believed the black regiments were the perfect choice to send into this war because they were better suited to the hot, tropical climate and were immune to tropical diseases. They even came to be known as the immune regiments.

In addition to the regular army immune regiments, the black volunteer units were formed based on the same belief. Large numbers of black Americans enthusiastically volunteered to serve. As in the past, they were only accepted once white volunteers came up short of needed numbers. Four new immune regiments, the Seventh, Eighth, Ninth, and Tenth United States Volunteer Infantry (USVI) were all black. White officers would command them until black officers became available—if any ever did. Black America responded with renewed disappointment and disgust, reacting with cries of "No officers, no fight!" New waves of the same old racism resulted in objections to their service in Cuba altogether, whether that service was part of white units or in segregated units. Once again, offices refused to accept command of black units based on their own racism and fear of career damage. Some state militias responded with appointments of black officers. All this maneuvering mostly came to naught, however, because the war was over before they could train and deploy. They did, however, suffer from outbreaks of typhoid and dysentery while in training camps.

The four regular army Buffalo regiments were ready to go in plenty of time, but many Americans still resented black troops in combat roles, and the Buffalo Soldiers were dismayed and angered at the increased racism and Jim Crow laws they encountered on their journey from their posts to training camps in the South. One incident was particularly telling and tried their patience beyond their control. White American soldiers had selected a black toddler to use for target practice for fun. The goal was to see how close they could come to hitting him without actually hitting him. The little boy was terrified. When soldiers from the Twenty-Fourth and Twenty-Fifth saw what was happening, they immediately stepped in, and the fight was on. More than two-dozen soldiers from the Twenty-Fourth and Twenty-Fifth were injured. Northern newspapers expressed outrage against the white soldiers. Southern newspapers vilified the Buffalo Soldiers.

Things only got worse. The military did not have adequate leadership and organization at this time. The staging areas for troops were undersupplied and lacking in sanitation measures. The port slated for troops to load onto transport ships was woefully inadequate, resulting in bottlenecks. Because of poor management and a shortage of cargo ships, the Ninth and Tenth Cavalry Regiments would fight without their mounts. In addition, they received the worst quarters for the voyage to Cuba, and when departure was delayed for a week, white troops were allowed shore leave, and black troops were not. Once they did reach Cuba, on June 22, stormy seas at the landing zone resulted in the drowning deaths of two soldiers of the Tenth, Corporal Cobb and Private English. Once ashore, they joined the white First Cavalry Regiment and the white First Volunteer Cavalry Regiment, soon to be known as the Rough Riders, under the command of Lieutenant Colonel Theodore Roosevelt. The trains sent to transport them to their camps were too badly damaged to haul the troops and their equipment, so they had to march along narrow paths through the jungle to reach their camps. The next day, they participated in the first of three major engagements of the war: Las Guasimas, El Caney, and San Juan and Kettle Hills.

Roosevelt's Rough Riders were losing ground in an attack against well-fortified Spanish positions at Las Guasimas. They were on the verge of losing the battle, when the Ninth and Tenth Cavalry arrived and turned the tide. They overran the Spanish position and took the important town of Las Guasimas. Captain John J. Pershing, who would later gain the nickname "Black Jack" because of his leadership of black soldiers, credited his men of the Tenth with saving the Rough Riders from a loss and from additional casualties. The Rough Riders and Roosevelt credited both regiments, especially the Tenth. They showered the Buffalo Soldiers with thanks and praise. White accounts of the June 23 battle months later, however, became inaccurate and controversial. After the war, the Rough Riders and especially Roosevelt changed their stories, minimizing or even eliminating the contributions of the Buffalo Soldiers. This reversal was perhaps the result of racist peer pressure. Politics was probably more of a motivator for Roosevelt than racism, however, since showing support of black Americans would offend potential voters and hurt him in his campaign for the presidency. Indeed, many later historical accounts of the battle focused completely on Roosevelt and his Rough Riders, with little or no mention of the black regular army troops, who played such a significant role.

Immediately after the battle, however, and in the next engagements, many fellow white soldiers perceived the Buffalo Soldiers as valued members of the American forces. The Buffalo Soldiers continued to earn that respect at the Battle of El Caney on July 1. The Twenty-Fifth used their sharpshooters to clear approaches to the town and enable other troops to breach the Spanish defenses and take the town. While the Twenty-Fifth was engaged at El Caney, the Ninth, Tenth, and Twenty-Fourth were part of the successful charge up San Juan and Kettle Hills.

A siege brought the surrender of Santiago City on July 17, ending the land phase of the war, but the aftermath was worse for the Buffalo Soldiers than the war itself. Immediately after the war, the black regiments received the worst of the labor assignments. They also received an assignment based on the incorrect belief that they were immune to certain diseases. One irony of the postwar duty was when the Twenty-Fourth, one of the immune regiments, received assignment to serve in yellow-fever hospital wards. They served well, and they came down with yellow fever, disproving the belief of many that they were naturally immune. Troops were also suffering severely from malaria and dysentery.

After the war, the Tenth Cavalry reported to San Antonio, Texas, and to Huntsville, Alabama. The Ninth Cavalry reported to Fort Ringgold, Texas. The Twenty-Fifth Infantry reported to El Paso, Texas. The Twenty-Fourth Infantry also reported to Texas. The four regiments would patrol the border with Mexico. All the regiments experienced extreme racism and violence on the journey to their posts and from the local populations after they arrived. Trouble soon called them away from these posts, and beginning in June 1899 they started deploying to the Philippines, with all four regiments in the Philippines by the end of the summer. The Philippines had been a Spanish possession, and the United States had assisted the Filipinos in ousting the Spanish. Disagreement soon arose between the Americans and the Filipino insurgents. The Buffalo Soldiers' assignment was to fight Filipino rebels demanding independence and the end of American occupation. The Filipinos declared their independence on June 12, 1898, but the 1898 Treaty of Paris had granted the Philippines to the United States, and President William McKinley made it clear the United States would not grant Philippine independence. The black regulars were part of the seventy thousand troops sent to the Philippines from 1899 to 1902. With them were the all-black Forty-Eighth and Forty-Ninth Volunteer Infantry Regiments.[2] Fighting erupted and dragged on for three long years. Most of the fighting involved raids and guerrilla tactics over mountains and in swamps and jungles. The American soldiers suffered from illness and weather conditions, especially during the wet season. Both sides resorted to gruesome methods to gain victory. Filipino guerrillas murdered dozens of men from the Ninth Infantry in 1901 who had surrendered. The Filipinos and the Americans practiced torture, including the water cure. Between four and five gallons of water were poured into a captured enemy soldier, resulting in excruciating agony. The water would be forced out with pressure on the stomach. If the prisoner still refused to talk, another application of the water cure could change his mind.[3]

Slowly but surely, the Americans chipped away at the rebel forces. The Buffalo Soldiers performed routine duties, such as guarding supplies and work teams, scouting, and providing escorts. They helped their chaplain build and establish schools for Filipino children. American forces captured the rebel leader, Emilio Aguinaldo, on February 4, 1901, ending the war.[4] Filipino General Vincent Lukban continued the fight after Aguinaldo's capture. He kept American forces busy until April 1902 when he, too, was captured.

As often happens during wartime, soldiers found ways to get into trouble. Sometimes, the trouble found them. While on duty as part of the American occupation forces in the Philippines, black soldiers experienced the same type of racist treatment as in the States. White Americans practiced discrimination and segregation in the Philippines just like they did at home, barring black soldiers from restaurants and businesses. Much of the time, they received better treatment from the Filipino civilians than from the Americans. Desertion had been somewhat of a problem during the war, with both white and black soldiers deserting. Desertion of black soldiers might have been the result of racist treatment, and desertion carried the death penalty. Death sentences for fifteen soldiers were commuted, but two soldiers were executed for desertion.[5] The two executed men were black; the rest were white. The president who ordered the commutations and approved the executions was Theodore Roosevelt. In the next several years, portions of the black regiments would rotate to the Philippines for occupation duty, but they spent most of their time patrolling the U.S.-Mexican border, relegated back to the isolated posts at which they had served since 1866, training, providing labor and escort, and competing in marksmanship and sporting competitions. The years following the Philippine insurrection had their fill of danger and disappointment for the regiments, most of it at home. Racism frequently erupted into violence and led to incidents such as the Brownsville Tragedy in 1906.

After the Philippine insurrection, their next major engagement was closer to home. The Mexican government of President Victoriano Huerta came under repeated rebel attacks, many under the leadership of Governor Venustiano Carranza, who wanted to establish his own government. This fighting frequently crossed the border into the United States and resulted in the deaths of American civilians and destruction of their property. The culprits would escape back across the border, out of reach of the American military. As these depredations increased, Americans demanded something be done, and the government moved the black regiments closer to the conflict. The Ninth moved to Douglas, Arizona, in 1912, and the Tenth moved to Fort Huachuca, Arizona, in 1914. The Mexican government did not put any effort into stopping these same rebels from raiding into the United States, and they did not grant permission for American troops to pursue the bandits into Mexico. Meanwhile, in 1913, the United States government decided to support the Carranza faction. Within a year, Carranza replaced Huerta as president. Things did not improve, however, when one of Carranza's followers, Francisco "Pancho" Villa, resented American support for Carranza and decided he wanted to be president. Villa thought that instigating a war between Mexico and the United States would help his cause, so he killed sixteen American miners near Santa Ysabel, in what came to be known as the Ysabel massacre, and in March 1916 he conducted a raid against Columbus, New Mexico, killing Americans there. Rather than go to war with Mexico, Americans demanded Villa's apprehension and punishment.

Once again, the United States called on the ever-faithful Buffalo regiments to accomplish this task. Leadership would walk a fine line in apprehending Villa without starting a war with Mexico. President Woodrow Wilson chose Brigadier General John J. Pershing for the job. Pershing's plan was to send two columns into Mexico. The Thirteenth Cavalry, Eleventh Cavalry, and companies of artillery, engineers, and the air squadron would head into Mexico from Columbus, New Mexico. The Buffalo Soldiers of the Tenth Cavalry, the white Seventh Cavalry, and an artillery battery would leave from Hachita, New Mexico. After crossing the border on March 15, 1916, and rendezvousing at Colonia Dublan, which would remain their base camp until they left Mexico in February 1917, they spread out in three columns, two of which were comprised of troops of the Tenth. They patrolled through April with little success. They endured severe privations. The climate was very hot and dusty, and the government was not provisioning them, so they had to live off the land, so to speak, supplying themselves and their horses with what food they could buy with what money they had. In May 1916, the Twenty-Fourth joined the expedition. The campaign developed a routine of patrols from the base camp. Word came of a concentration of enemy forces at Villa Ahumada. Pershing sent Troop C of the Tenth, under Captain Charles Boyd, and Troop K, under Captain Lewis S. Morey, to investigate. On their way, the column encountered Mexican troops at the village of Carrizal on June 21.[6] Boyd requested permission to pass through the town. By this time, the Mexican government and its troops strongly resented the American presence. The Mexican soldiers were under orders to only let Americans travel north toward the American border, and the Mexican soldiers at Carrizal steadfastly denied the American troops safe passage through the town, demanding they go around. Boyd did not like that idea and, though outnumbered against well-fortified defenses, decided to pass straight through the town anyway. Boyd should have gone around. His scouts advised him to return to Pershing or go around. Boyd's decision is puzzling because Pershing's orders were to proceed with care regarding Mexican troops so that strained relations between Mexico and the United States would not escalate to war. Boyd's calculation that the Mexican commander would back down at a show of force was dead wrong. Boyd was among the first killed. As he communicated his intention to ride straight through the town, the Mexican troops moved to completely surround the Americans, placing them in a precarious position. The engagement quickly turned into a melee with black troops, surrounded and out of ammunition, trying to avoid being wounded, killed, or captured. Lieutenant Henry R. Adair of Troop C was killed with Boyd. Morey was wounded in the shoulder. He ordered the men to begin retreating as they could. The American force suffered twenty-four captured and nine to twelve killed. Reports of the numbers killed vary because some of the bodies were never recovered.[7] Americans were incensed, and Mexicans were elated. President Wilson demanded release of the prisoners, who were returned to American officials on June 29.

The Americans remained in Mexico, however, conducting regular patrols until President Wilson called them back to the States because of the threat of war in Europe. They did not apprehend Villa. The Tenth Cavalry and the Twenty-Fourth Infantry returned to border patrol on the American side of the border. Villa continued his harassment at the border. Eventually, in 1923, rival Mexican forces killed him. Since the American forces failed to capture Villa, many historians see the punitive expedition as a failure, but Pershing and his men succeeded in breaking up all of the rebel forces and strongholds, making it nearly impossible for Villa to continue the fight. Indeed, he did not attack Americans after the arrival of U.S. troops in 1916.

The punitive expedition marked the last cavalry charge and the last use of horses in American military campaigns. In addition to closing the door on some traditions, the United States military transitioned to mechanized vehicles and airplanes. The First Aero Squadron, Aviation Section, Signal Corps arrived in Mexico with eight planes. The planes performed reconnaissance from above, increasing the amount of ground Americans forces could patrol and providing valuable mapping information. The planes did not function as well as planners hoped but did provide valuable assistance in delivering messages, in taking aerial photographs, and in finding troops in the field. Within a month, all the planes were non-functioning, but the pilots gained experience they would take with them to Europe in World War I. Commanders in Mexico used trucks and motorcycles with sidecars to become familiar with the terrain and to deliver supplies. American forces continued this practice in Europe. On April 1, 1916, Major Charles Young, West Point's third black graduate, and troops of the Tenth Cavalry approached enemy defenses at Agua Caliente under the covering fire of machine guns, the first but not the last time U.S. troops would use this tactic. While all these things made little difference on the punitive expedition, they prepared American forces for service in World War I Europe. They also added to the record of accomplishments for the Buffalo Soldiers.

One last benefit from the punitive expedition was the experience, training, discipline, and preparation of the soldiers and of Pershing. It would have served the black regiments well in the next war, had they gotten the opportunity to join the American forces in Europe. Alas, most did not get that opportunity. The next chapter will examine that story. Pershing also gained valuable command experience. He had commanded the Tenth in Cuba, and he had commanded the Tenth and the Twenty-Fourth in Mexico. He clearly had confidence in the black troops. His decisions regarding black troops in World War I do not reflect that confidence. The next chapter will tell that story as well.

From the Indian Wars to the years leading to World War I, the black regular army regiments received the call each and every time the United States needed troops. They fought the enemy on the battlefield and civilians in times of domestic violence. They protected white Americans, black Americans, Indians, and civilian and government property. They fought against the elements, putting out forest fires and protecting people and property from natural disasters. They served in Cuba in the Spanish-American War, in the Philippine insurrection, and on the punitive expedition. They served well in each campaign. They received the worst duty assignments between the campaigns and were sent to isolated outposts, mostly along the border with Mexico. At each step, they faced racist abuse and discrimination that often led to violence. They suffered terrible punishment, sometimes death, when they chose to defy racist treatment. Sometimes, they were falsely accused and unable to prove their innocence. Through all this, they served honestly and faithfully. To them, as with those who had fought before them, military service was a path to equality, and they served with that hope. The punitive expedition reflected poorly on Captain Boyd but not on the men themselves. President Wilson did not call the black troops from Mexico because they had failed. He called the Buffalo Soldiers out of Mexico because war clouds were gathering over Europe. The Buffalo Soldiers and other black Americans were once again ready and willing to serve, even though their hope of equality in exchange for service had yet to be realized. World War I would provide another opportunity, but first they had to get to the battlefields, and that would be the most difficult part of their fight. Even with the Buffalo Soldiers' service record, many white Americans remained adamantly opposed to black combat troops, especially overseas. The problem for white Americans was that they wanted black Americans to do their fair share of service and reduce the burden on whites, but calling on them to fight was unacceptable. The solution was to keep the experienced Buffalo Soldiers out of the way at distant posts and accord black volunteers and enlistees labor assignments only. That was the plan in the years before American entry into the war. Black Americans and war demands altered those plans, once again offering the hope of equality in exchange for service. Despite their intentions, white Americans were thwarted in their efforts to sideline both the Buffalo Soldiers and black volunteers and enlistees. Some of the noncommissioned officers of the black regular army served as officers of black regiments in Europe. The story of that service is in Chapter 9.

CHAPTER 9

Black Is Not a Color of the Rainbow: World War I

Henry Johnson was an American hero. He was also a hero in France, the first American soldier to receive the French Croix de Guerre, with palm leaf, no less. Henry was different from other American heroes. Henry Johnson was black. His story hit major papers in the United States and made him a national hero overnight. He was a private in the 369th Infantry Regiment of the Ninety-Third Division (Provisional), originally the Fifteenth New York National Guard, known as the Harlem Rattlers. His actions during the night of May 13–14, 1918, saved fellow soldiers, repulsed a German attack, and gained respect for black soldiers in the eyes of the French, the Germans, and Americans.

Corporal Allen London and four privates, including Henry Johnson and Needham Roberts, headed into no-man's land to man a listening post, a crude and muddy hole in the ground with a duck-board floor and a perimeter of tall grass and barbed wire known as Combat Group No. 29. They were armed with their French Lebel rifles and a box of grenades. Johnson also had the bolo knife that many of the Rattlers had received to use as sidearms. Johnson and Needham were on watch as the others slept in a nearby dugout. He and Needham were soon convinced that a number of German soldiers were approaching the post. Suddenly, German soldiers swarmed their position, and Needham was wounded with the first enemy shots. Though immobilized with wounds, Needham fed Johnson grenades to lob at the enemy. Johnson emptied his rifle into the first of the enemy to reach the post, killing one and wounding two. Out of ammunition, he used his rifle as a club on a fourth German. At about that time, he noticed a German leaning over Needham and strangling him. Johnson drew his bolo knife and plunged it into Needham's attacker, then into another, and another. The Germans just kept coming. When Johnson plunged his knife to the hilt into the head of yet another German, the Germans decided to gather their dead and wounded and retreat. Johnson kept up the fight, tossing grenades at the retreating enemy, squarely hitting at least one. Johnson was hit in the right arm and both legs and was weak with blood loss by the time London and the others reached them and carried them to safety.

Journalist and staunch racist from Kentucky, Irving S. Cobb, was a war correspondent for the *Saturday Evening Post*. He heard black troops were in combat and went in search of a story. He found it when he walked the ground with military officials the morning after the battle. Examination of the path of enemy retreat revealed incredible carnage, leading to estimates that Johnson and Needham had fought off at least twenty-four Germans, killing several. Johnson and Needham were both hospitalized and slowly recovered from their wounds. The Battle of Henry Johnson, as Cobb called it, brought fame to Johnson and Needham, to the Ninety-Third Division, to the Fifteenth New York, and to the black fighting man. It also brought respect from the German enemy, who referred to them as fighters from hell. The 369th became known as the Harlem Hellfighters.

Johnson was not the only hero among the black American troops in World War I; there were many. Sergeant William Butler, on the night of August 17–18, 1918, prevented the capture of some of his fellow soldiers, including First Lieutenant Gorman Jones, from as many as seventeen Germans. He received the American Distinguished Service Cross and the Croix de Guerre. The stories of these heroes reflect admirable service in the face of incredible odds against them. Sadly, the recognition came from the French and the Germans rather than from their own country. The United States discouraged the French from awarding black Americans for battlefield bravery and was more than reluctant to award these men themselves. Indeed, had the United States followed through on its original intentions, there would have been no black heroes because there would have been no black combat troops. White resistance to any black combat service remained stiff.

Earlier events involving black troops in Texas strengthened white resolve against arming blacks in Europe or anywhere else.

When Americans contemplated black service in World War I, neither arming nor exempting blacks from service appealed to Southerners.

Many Northerners agreed. However, blacks saw service as "the most sacred obligation of citizenship." In addition, formal American entrance into the war on April 6, 1917, required mobilization of all financial, human, material, and ideological resources. "The Selective Service Act, passed on May 18, 1917, required all men between the ages of twenty-one and thirty-one to register. The creation of the Selective Service System marked a defining moment in U.S. history ... [and] represented a significant expansion of the state and its incursion on the lives of individual citizens. It also shifted the authority to mobilize military manpower resources from the local and state levels to the national."[1]

With the Brownsville and Texas incidents still fresh in the minds of many Americans, the United States planned to ignore the race issue by establishing separate and segregated regiments and divisions comprised of black National Guard units and black draftees, with white officers in command. Black soldiers in Europe would serve as laborers, support troops, and stevedores only. Secretary of the Navy Josephus Daniels planned to use blacks as cooks, stewards, and mess attendants. This left the problem of what to do with the regular Buffalo regiments. The army decided not to use any of these experienced regiments in Europe. The Ninth Cavalry spent the duration of the war stationed at Stotsenburg Camp in Luzon, Philippines. Most of the Tenth Cavalry spent the war at Fort Huachuca, Arizona, on border patrol. More than sixty officers from the Ninth and Tenth became officers in other units, and nearly six hundred were promoted to noncommissioned rank to serve with other units. The Twenty-Fifth Infantry was stationed at Schofield Barracks in Hawaii when the war broke out but was transferred in late 1918 to join the Tenth Cavalry on border patrol, to free a white regiment for service in Europe. Around eighty noncommissioned officers of the Twenty-Fifth were sent for officer training, received their commissions as lieutenants, and served with labor and training units during the war. The Twenty-Fourth Infantry was initially stationed in Houston, Texas, to guard construction workers at Camp Logan. After the violence in Houston, those members of the Twenty-Fourth not court-martialed, killed, or imprisoned were immediately transferred to the Philippines for the rest of the war. Twenty-five men from the Twenty-Fourth were sent to officer training, and twenty-one received commissions. These officers served with the all-black Ninety-Second Infantry Division in Europe, comprised of draftees.

Black Americans also demanded to see black officers in Europe. None of the fourteen existing officer schools in 1914 admitted blacks. The War Department established Camp Des Moines in Iowa for black officer training. Lieutenant Colonel Charles Young, a West Point graduate holding the highest rank of a black officer to that point and one of two black officers in the military, was stationed at that time with the Tenth Cavalry at Fort Huachuca, Arizona, and was a logical choice for promotion and transfer to Camp Des Moines. He had served as a major with the Tenth in the 1916 punitive expedition, receiving promotion as a result of his outstanding leadership. He was in line for promotion to brigadier general and had received recommendation for that promotion from an examining board. A combination of racism and a suddenly required physical that revealed high blood pressure led to his early retirement, with President Woodrow Wilson's complicity. Young's protests went nowhere. He was forced into early retirement on July 30, 1917. The men at Des Moines and the entire black population were devastated at the news and felt betrayed. Young was forty-three years old and had never taken a sick day in all his years of service. On November 6, 1918, five days before the armistice on November 11, the army reinstated Young and sent him to serve in Liberia, where he contracted a fever and died. The other black officer at the time available for possible combat was Ben Davis Sr., but he was sent in July 1917 with the Ninth Cavalry for duty in the Philippines.

The War Department gave the Des Moines position to white officer General Charles Ballou, a former commander of the Twenty-Fourth, whose racist ideas would not help the black candidates. He made sure the training was limited to infantry, with no artillery instruction. The ninety-day training period came to an end, but no plans were made for the officers to transfer to duty, so they simply extended the training another four weeks to keep the graduates occupied and out of the way. Some gave up and went home. The camp closed on October 14, 1917. Of the 639 officers who successfully completed training at Des Moines, none were permitted rank beyond captain. This way, the military would not have to worry about any black officers commanding whites in the war. Like the men they commanded, these officers would be assigned to labor units.

Since black soldiers were to provide only labor, many men who would not normally pass the physical for enlistment did pass, with enlistment boards believing that since they were performing civilian labor with a variety of disabilities, they could do the same in uniform. All black troops were initially assigned labor duty, but a few lucky ones did gain combat roles. The labor battalions were even issued denim overalls instead of uniforms.

Secretary of War Newton D. Baker had promised an insistent black community that indeed blacks would serve in combat. Not keeping that promise was dangerous. In November 1917, the War Department organized the two black combat divisions, the Ninety-Second Infantry

Charles Young. (Library of Congress)

Division, composed of black draftees and the Camp Des Moines officers and medical officers, and the Ninety-Third Infantry Division, with one regiment of draftees and three regiments of National Guard. The two divisions had about thirty-seven thousand soldiers. They received a fraction of the combat training required for combat units. Racism at training camps and the thinking that they would mostly provide labor led to their early deployment to Europe, where they received labor assignments as soon as they arrived. But for promises and some luck, they might have remained in these assignments throughout the war, as most black American soldiers did.

The Ninety-Second Infantry Division (Colored) was established on October 24, 1917, at Camps Grant, Upton, Dix, Meade, Dodge, Sherman, and Funston, and this division was a draft division. They dubbed themselves the "Buffalo Division" and selected an insignia with a black buffalo on an olive background. The white officers of the division refused to wear the buffalo insignia because of its historical representation of black troops only. Units of the Ninety-Second arrived in France from June 19 through July 18. Its commanders were Major General Charles C. Ballou, Major General Charles H. Martin, and Brigadier

General James B. Erwin. The division was attached to the U.S. Second Army, under General Robert Bullard, who did not have faith in black troops and did not get along with Ballou. In many ways, this division was doomed for failure from the start. The Ninety-Second never trained together as a division before deployment. Ballou got the command because he had served with the Twenty-Fourth and had been on staff at Fort Des Moines, but he was not a good commander for the job. The Ninety-Second was comprised of inexperienced draftees. Unlike the Ninety-Third Division, they remained with American forces for the duration of the war and performed poorly as a result of racism, lack of training and equipment, denial of opportunity, and poor leadership. The Germans were well aware of American racism and tried to use it to their advantage. When the Ninety-Second was deployed to take the village of Frapelle, the Germans dropped leaflets for the black soldiers, asking why they would serve with racists and offering equal treatment if they came over to serve with the Germans. Not one man in the Ninety-Second took the offer, even when Ballou persisted in racist and unfair treatment, such as blaming the soldiers for the division's failures on the battlefield rather than placing the blame where it belonged, with white officers who were incompetent or who intentionally placed black soldiers in situations that denied them the opportunity to perform well. In November 1918, after the regiment's poor performance in the Meuse-Argonne Offensive, which was due to Ballou's poor command, Ballou even went so far as to court-martial black officers for cowardice leading to battlefield failures. Five were actually convicted and sentenced to death, their sentences later reduced to lengthy prison terms. Fortunately, Lieutenant General Robert L. Bullard took command and implemented steps to improve training and raise morale, leading to improved battlefield performance for the 367th and 368th in the final days of the war. The 365th and 366th did not have the time or opportunity to improve under Bullard, who was only slightly better as a commander of black soldiers, and subsequently performed road-building and labor. To cover his embarrassment regarding the deficient level of improvement, Bullard tried to get the entire division transferred back to the States, brazenly claiming that black soldiers could not be trusted among French civilians. All American divisions, black and white, were to remain in Europe until the end of the war. The Ninety-Second finished the war with a tarnished reputation that haunted them long after the war ended.

The Ninety-Third Infantry Division (Colored) escaped most of the American racism during the war and performed very well. The Ninety-Third was the first division to arrive in Europe, and they immediately received orders for labor detail. By February 1918, no decision had yet been made regarding any combat assignment of the Ninety-Third. The Fifteenth New York arrived in France on December 27, 1917, in snow and bitter cold. As they left their ship on January 1, they learned they were now the 369th Infantry Regiment. This news did not serve as a pleasant welcome to Europe because the number designated them as a draft regiment rather than a volunteer regiment. It also denied them the proud designation they enjoyed before their arrival. They traveled from Brest to Camp Coetquidan at St. Nazaire for labor duty with the Service of Supply. They labored for two months, with morale plummeting. Luckily, General John J. Pershing had promised the French he would provide some American troops to bolster depleted French manpower. He loaned the Ninety-Third to the French, which was the best thing that happened to them during the entire war. They became attached to the French Fourth Army for the duration of the war. By war's end, three regiments of the Ninety-Third, the 369th, 371st, and 372nd, received the French Croix de Guerre for their battlefield performance.[2] The 369th spent 191 days at the front, longer than any other American regiment. Of the original two thousand men of the 369th, more than thirteen hundred had been killed or wounded, including fifty-five officers, the highest casualty rate of any American regiment, with none taken prisoner.

This division was organized at Camp Stuart, Newport News, Virginia, in December 1917. The Ninety-Third was not fully organized, had only four infantry regiments and no support units, and could not really function as a division. Unlike the Ninety-Second, however, the Ninety-Third was comprised of mostly National Guard units and had better officers. The 1903 National Guard Act authorized exclusion of blacks. However, black National Guard units did exist, with nearly five thousand members in various units. The Eighth Illinois National Guard in Chicago included men who had fought against the Spanish and in the punitive expedition. The Eighth's officer corps and commanding colonel, Franklin A. Dennison, were black, making it the only black regiment in the American Expeditionary Force with nearly all black officers. New York Republican governor Charles Whitman signed the order to form the Fifteenth New York National Guard regiment on June 16, 1916, the first black National Guard unit in New York history. Some of the men of the Fifteenth spoke French, having moved north from Louisiana to join the regiment. Their white commanders included Colonel William Hayward, Lieutenant Colonel Woodell Pickering, Major Lorillard Spencer Jr., Captain Arthur W. Little, and Hamilton Stuyvesant Fish III. They all knew that leading a black unit would not help their careers as much as leading a white one would, a fact dating from the Civil War era, but most of them preferred this command over a white unit. Little, at forty-two years of age, believed he was too old to get a command at all and that his chances were better if he offered to serve in a black unit. Others, such as Hayward and Fish, supported the efforts of black Americans for the opportunity to serve. Hayward knew he should appoint blacks as field officers for good regiment relations. Black officers included George C. Lacy, fifty-two-year-old Charles Fillmore, Virgil Parks, who had served with A Troop of the Tenth Cavalry and had charged San Juan Hill with the Rough Riders, and Napoleon B. Marshall, who had defended the Buffalo Soldiers in the Brownsville Affair. Sergeant Gillard Thompson, originally from Shelbyville, Tennessee, had been a Buffalo Soldier, serving with F Troop of the Ninth from 1905–1908. He spent three years with the Twenty-Fourth Infantry, then another three, until 1914, at West Point as a cavalryman. He then moved to New York and, three years after leaving West Point, enlisted with the Fifteenth. Hayward also recruited noted jazz musician James Reese Europe and assigned him the task of assembling a top-notch regimental band. By July 1917, the regiment had the two thousand men necessary to qualify for federal service. They hoped to be assigned to the Forty-Second Division, known as the Rainbow Division because it contained units from twenty-seven states, not because of color. On Sunday, July 15, 1917, the Fifteenth was mustered into federal service, but while the all-white 167th Alabama received their hoped-for assignment in the Rainbow Division, the Fifteenth was informed that "black is not a color of the rainbow."[3]

At about that time, it was decided that the Fifteenth would go for more training at Camp Wadsworth near Spartanburg, South Carolina, a hotbed of racism and Jim Crowism. Spartanburg citizens had been assured no black soldiers would be sent to Camp Wadsworth for training. When news that the two thousand men of the Fifteenth would indeed be sent there, South Carolina readied itself to teach them their place. The Fifteenth reached Spartanburg on October 10 and 11, 1917, for combat training. Trouble began immediately. Europe's band played a role in maintaining a temporary peace, but in less than a month racial strains were extreme. Hayward returned to Washington to request the Fifteenth be taken out of the south. They left Spartanburg on October 24 for Camp Mills, near Garden City, Long Island, to complete their training. This move did not end their suffering from racism; they were billeted next to the 167th Alabama National Guard, who had already physically attacked the black soldiers. Two weeks after their arrival, they were ordered to move again … to France! The date to depart for France was November 11 aboard the *Pocahontas*, a ship in deteriorated condition. The ship broke piston rods at sea and had to return to New York. The Fifteenth was sent to Camp Merritt in New Jersey to await new orders. Once again, southern soldiers made trouble. The Fifteenth was kept in isolation to avoid trouble until it could board for Europe.

While the Fifteenth awaited transportation, on November 23, the War Department ordered the creation of the Ninety-Third U.S. Infantry Division, a black division with National Guard units from New York, Connecticut, Massachusetts, Illinois, Ohio, Maryland, Tennessee, and the District of Columbia. This Division never really panned out, though the Fifteenth was added to the 185th Brigade and was changed to the 369th Infantry, under the command of Brigadier General Albert H. Blanding. They were not informed of the designation change until they arrived in Europe. On December 15, the Fifteenth left Camp Merritt for another attempt to reach France on the *Pocahontas*, which, this time, had a fire in the coal bunkers. Repairs took ten days, during which the Fifteenth remained on the cramped ship. During their trip to Europe, ironically, thirteen soldiers of the Twenty-Fourth Infantry were hanged for participation in the Houston mutiny. During the trip, a British oil tanker kept ramming their ship because of high seas, tearing a hole in their ship. The men had to hang over the side of the ship in freezing weather to repair the huge gash.

They reached France on December 27 and had to stay on board until January 1, 1918, but when they left the ship, they were the first African American regiment to ever land on French soil. The band played as they marched, amazing the French with a sophisticated jazz version of the "Marseillaise." They boarded cattle cars in a howling snowstorm at Brest for the next leg of the journey to St. Nazaire, a coastal town about two hundred miles from the front, where, to their disappointment, the 1,949 men and fifty-one officers were slated to do labor as part of the Service of Supply, not fight, on orders from Pershing himself, as a way to keep them away from white soldiers and away from the battlefield. They built railroad tracks and a dam. They lived in horrid conditions with poor housing. They received racist treatment from white soldiers.

Hayward wrote to Pershing for help. Finally, on March 10, Pershing ordered the Fifteenth, the 369th, to join the French army at Connantre, east of Paris. The French gave them another name, the Trois Cent Soixante Neuvieme RIUS, part of the Sixteenth Division, under General Le Gallais, of the French Fourth Army, under the command of General Henri Gouraud, the Lion of France, and now commander of the Fifteenth. The Fifteenth was a combat unit! The band rejoined the regiment on March 21. The regiment went to Heirpont for final training. The French accepted them and treated them with respect.

They attached to the French just in time for the largest battle of the war, the German spring 1918 offensive. On April 13, the 369th headed to the front, to the trenches, to combat. On May 27, the 369th was part of the Third Battle of the Aisne. On July 15, they performed camouflage duty for a large German offensive, the Bastille Day offensive. On July 18, they went on the offensive for the first time, suffering fifty-one wounded and fourteen killed. By the first week of August, the regiment had been under fire every day for 130 days. On August 19, the regiment was pulled from the line and sent to join the all-black Ninety-Third U.S. Division. However, three weeks later, they were moved back to the French 161st Division. Pershing restructured in mid-July, with orders that black units would either have all-white officers or all-black. The 369th officers went to all white, unhappily, meaning Fillmore, Lacey, Reid, Napoleon, and initially Europe all transferred to other black units. Europe was finally returned to the 369th because of the band.

French Commander-in-Chief Ferdinand Foch was planning a series of attacks over four days in September to end the war before winter, on the 26th, 27th, 28th, 29th. On the 26th, the 369th, with Gouraud's French Fourth Army, would attack between the Aisne and Suippe Rivers. Specifically, the 369th was to move the Germans out of the villages of Ripont, Sechault, and Challerange and force them west of the Meuse. After a six-hour, twenty-five-minute bombardment from French artillery, the 369th left their trenches and moved forward toward the Germans. The going was easy at first, but then the Germans opened up with machine guns. Unfortunately, draftees recently placed with the regiment deserted under fire. The Germans then added artillery. The fight lasted until the regiment stopped for the night. They resumed their attack again in the morning, with mounting casualties. They continued the attack on the 28th and 29th. On the 30th, they had to cross a long stretch of open land to the town of Challerange. First Lieutenant George S. Robb, though wounded several times, refused to leave his men, and for his conduct received the only Medal of Honor of the entire regiment. The 369th was relieved by a French regiment on October 1.

The 369th had entered the campaign on September 25 with twenty-four hundred men. They lost 135 men and nine officers dead. Wounded numbered nearly a thousand. Fighting for the regiment was virtually over by October 6. The French had also started calling the regiment "Hell-fighters." They had been in combat for 191 straight days, longer than any other American regiment and with casualties from the Champagne

Province from April 8 to October 1 adding up to some of the highest of any American regiment. On November 20, 1918, they were the first American combat troops to reach the Rhine.

The 369th received 170 individual Croix de Guerre and a unit citation. They were released from French command on December 17, sailed from Brest on Jan 31, and arrived in New York on February 12. They received a parade in their honor on February 17 and were returned to a National Guard unit as the Fifteenth New York, the Harlem Hellfighters. Their dreams of full citizenship in return for service to their country did not come true. Many encountered racial violence and discrimination when they returned to their civilian lives. Some returning soldiers were even lynched while still wearing their uniforms. Henry Johnson was paid to share his wartime experiences on a speaking tour, until he mentioned the racism and abuse black soldiers suffered at the hands of white soldiers and officers. His speaking tour was cancelled. He died in 1929, alone and broke. Belatedly in 2014, Henry Johnson cleared the final hurdle to receiving the Medal of Honor for his bravery and sacrifice in World War I.[4] Some encountered other postwar adjustment problems. James Reese Europe planned a ten-week tour for the Hellfighters' Band from mid-March to mid-May, 1919. Drummer Herbert Wright had been acting strangely since his return from the war. At the last tour stop in Boston's Mechanics Hall, Wright stabbed Europe in the jugular, killing him. Europe was thirty-nine years old.

Like the Fifteenth New York, the Eighth Illinois (the Ninety-Third's 370th) also suffered tremendous racism and Jim Crowism when they were sent to Camp Logan in the South for training. They, too, were rushed to France. Another setback for the 370thwas the loss of their beloved black commander, Colonel Franklin A. Dennison, replaced by white commander, Colonel T. A. Roberts, for health reasons. The 370th boarded the SS *Finland* April 30, 1918, arriving at St. Nazaire May 12, 1918. A few days later, they went to Grandvillars, a town near the French-Swiss border. The 370th joined the French Tenth Division and fought at St. Mihiel, the Argonne Forest, and finally in the Soissons sector, where they captured German fortifications at Mont des Signes. They captured a German stronghold called the Hindenburg Cave, killed 275 Germans, and held their position for three difficult days. Jenkins received the Croix de Guerre and the American Distinguished Service Cross. Captain Leonard W. Lewis, an officer and recruiter for the 370th, called the black soldiers "Torch Bearers," who would make the world safe for democracy.[5]

The 371st and 372nd arrived in France in the summer of 1918 and served with the French 157th Red Hand Division. Though their service was not as spectacular as that of the 369th and 370th, they served admirably throughout the war. The Ninety-Third was the only American division fully incorporated into the French army, with action on the western front. Attachment to French forces was a blessing in disguise for the Ninety-Third for a number of reasons, mainly because the French treated them as equals. Americans did not approve of this equal treatment and tried to undermine it. In August 1918, the head of the French Military Mission to the AEF, Colonel Linard, distributed a document entitled "Secret Information Concerning Black American Troops." It advised the French not to offend the American people by treating the black troops as equals in any way. They were not to socialize with them off the battlefield or allow them near French women, and they were not to award them for battlefield actions. The French were disgusted with the requests and desired to ignore the document and its directives, but they had to maintain a balance in their treatment of black American troops and not offend their American allies by disregarding the directive. Americans needed blacks in the military but insisted on keeping them in a subservient role, even if they had to encourage their allies to be racist as well. The French continued to treat the men of the Ninety-Third in the same way they had before the document's circulation.

Four hundred thousand black soldiers served during World War I. Of the 200,000 who served in Europe, 160,000 were assigned to labor units of the Service of Supply (SOS) and to the Pioneer Infantry. The remaining 40,000 were the Ninety-Second and Ninety-Third. The military excluded blacks from flying planes in the war and from enlisting in the Marines. The Navy had nearly all white soldiers, allowing only 1 percent of their troops to be black, and they restricted those few to service roles. The Ninety-Second and Ninety-Third received the worst of the labor duties at the end of the war and immediately after the war. They loaded ships, searched for mines, and reburied the dead. They were among the first divisions scheduled to return to the States, simply because their officers thought they would behave badly in postwar Europe. Not only did they experience that racist insult but white divisions persistently boarded ships home before they did. Once they were finally aboard, these men who had served their country for the freedom of others were relegated to segregated and inferior areas of the ship. They received the same treatment when they returned home. Racism and Jim Crow were in full force after the war. White America wanted to be sure black America understood that service in the war did not change their circumstances at home. Violence increased upon their return home, so much so that the summer of 1919 was called "Red Summer." In 1918, eleven black veterans were lynched. In 1919, seventy-eight black veterans were lynched, with fourteen of those burned alive and several killed while still wearing their uniform. Race riots broke out in twenty-eight cities across the nation.[6] The military destroyed all progress implemented during the war and reverted back to pre-war thinking and treatment for black Americans, with calls for dismissal of all blacks from the military or at least the minimum numbers remaining to be assigned to labor battalions. The Ninth and Tenth Cavalry and Twenty-Fourth and Twenty-Fifth Infantry Regiments barely escaped the postwar downsize and return to pre-war practices. Conveniently for Congress and the military, they would still fulfill the obligations of the post–Civil War Army Act, but they were sent to the Philippines and kept out of the way, once again performing labor and occupation. These practices and conditions persisted through the interwar years, but by the mid-1930s, it was becoming clear that once again the black soldier would be needed to serve his country.

Epilogue

World War II and the Korean War

At the close of World War I, black soldiers were once again shunned, unappreciated, and the targets of racial violence. Some Americans, the German enemy, and many French had praised them for their actions during the war. Many Americans, however, resented their presence as part of the U.S. military, even if that presence provided labor and freed white men to serve in combat roles. After the war, that resentment deepened. Some Americans feared that, as a result of their service, these men would expect equality at home, and they vowed to put them in their place, so to speak, at every opportunity. Between the wars, Jim Crow laws kept black Americans in a world of increasing violence, discrimination, and struggle, even after their valorous service in Europe. World events would force change in American thinking and attitudes toward black Americans in the military, but that change would be interminably slow. Old ideas would die hard, but they would die. Black Americans struggled to gain more significant roles in the military, to gain the right to fight and to lead, and to take their rightful place in society. World War II meant another chance to serve. They fought for what they called the Double V, victory in Europe and victory at home. The struggle for Double V is evident in every war in which they served, from the days when Colonel Tye led his Black Brigade in the Revolution until the Korean War. This epilogue examines the service and struggles of black American soldiers in World War II and in the Korean War and places that service into the larger context of the Buffalo Soldiers. President Harry S. Truman desegregated the military in 1948, but that desegregation did not happen overnight. It did not happen in time for the troops serving in the Korean War, but it eventually did happen.

As early as the mid-1930s, and certainly by 1937, in the face of upcoming conflict in Europe, America's black community redoubled their pleas for complete integration of the military. As in the past, the response was disappointingly negative. Also as in the past, in the coming conflict, black officers would only fill lower ranks and would not command white troops. Black soldiers would receive labor assignments as much as possible. These decisions and plans were in place by the mid-1930s but were not widely shared. Once the coming war became a fact, war needs provided clear evidence that whites would not be able to provide the manpower needed and that increased black enlistments would be necessary, so the army created the all-black 47th and 48th Quartermaster Regiments in 1939 and, in 1940, a number of other all-black units, one artillery regiment, an engineering regiment, a coastal artillery unit, a transportation unit, and chemical units. As in World War I, white Americans believed black citizens should be required to serve, to take some of the burden off the white population, but white sentiment was still overwhelmingly against any use of blacks beyond labor, and they were adamantly against blacks in combat.

As past presidents, politicians, and military personnel had done, President Franklin D. Roosevelt practiced the language of equality when it benefitted him politically. He made lots of promises to black America in the election campaign for his third presidential term, but he kept few of those promises, and only token ones at that. In late October 1940, Roosevelt promoted a black American, Colonel Benjamin O. Davis Sr., to Brigadier General. Many considered this an empty gesture, politically motivated, and they were right. Promises kept coming. The September 16, 1940, Selective Service and Training Act was the first peacetime draft in the country's history and called for registration of all men, not exclusively white men, from the ages of twenty-one to thirty-five with a quota of eight hundred thousand draftees. Section 4 called for no discrimination based on race or color. While the administration planned to use blacks in proportion to population numbers, include blacks in combat and noncombat units, and admit blacks to officer training school, they made it clear they would not integrate the military. They would maintain separate, segregated units, partly to be sure that black officers would not command white soldiers. The black community was appalled. By November 1941, the reality was that blacks comprised only 5.9 percent of the military, not the promised 10 percent. That same month, the American Red Cross announced it would no longer accept black blood donations, since those donations might make their way to white patients. The black community was aghast and searching for a solution. They planned a peaceful protest in Washington, DC, in July 1941. The administration feared this would make the United States appear weak to its enemies and offered concessions in return for cancellation of the protest. One of the concessions was Executive Order No. 8802, the Fair Employment Act, signed on June 28, 1941, which, on paper at least, made racial discrimination in the government and in the defense industry illegal. The Japanese attack at Pearl Harbor on December 7, 1941, and subsequent American entry into the war put the debate over black service on the back burner. As Americans scrambled to send troops to Europe and the Pacific, they continued the discriminatory practices of the past, and black Americans stepped forward to serve as they always had.

Black soldiers faced racial discrimination at every step, from enlistment to training to deployment and beyond, with the South's Jim Crow laws still strongly in force. Private Felix Hall, stationed at Fort Benning, was lynched, with the perpetrators never found or punished. Upon deployment, black troops still received labor and construction assignments, with only about 15 percent assigned to combat roles. It felt like World War I all over again. Blacks adopted the Double V symbol.

In response to outcries from the black community that combat forces were still all white, in 1942, the Ninety-Second and Ninety-Third Infantry Divisions were reactivated. The Ninety-Third contained the Twenty-Fourth and Twenty-Fifth Infantry Regiments, the regular, all-black Buffalo Soldier regiments, with decades of experience. The army created a new Second Cavalry Division. The Ninth and Tenth Cavalry Regiments, the all-black Buffalo Soldier regiments with decades of service, were part of this division. The training for these units dragged out, while white units were quickly trained and deployed. It looked like the black regiments would not be deployed at all. At the last moment, perhaps as a political move at election time, Roosevelt called for the military to deploy the black units. They would head to the Pacific, beginning in early 1944. The Ninety-Third was split up and sent to places in the Pacific where the fighting had already concluded, with the Twenty-Fifth on Guadalcanal, the 368th on Banika, and the 369th on New Georgia. They received security, occupation, and labor duty only. In response to the uproar that followed the use of these troops in such ways, the Twenty-Fourth Infantry was sent to fight the Japanese on Bougainville in March 1944, where they did a satisfactory job in combat against the Japanese, an enemy that all American forces were discovering was fierce and dedicated. In late March, the Twenty-Fifth arrived at Bougainville. Company K experienced a mauling at the hands of the Japanese soon after their arrival. Despite the fact that white troops performed similarly to the Twenty-Fifth on this occasion, rumors of cowardice and company failure abounded and were directed only at the Twenty-Fifth, though the overall performance of the Twenty-Fifth in the campaign was satisfactory. The white units received a pass on such judgment of failure and cowardice, with arguments that the guerrilla warfare of the Japanese and the tropical climate of the Pacific Theater were understandable obstacles that excused their performance. After Bougainville, the Twenty-Fifth was relegated to fatigue duty and occupation of conquered territory. The Twenty-Fourth saw more combat than the rest of the Ninety-Third, on Saipan and Tinian, from May 1945 until the war's end. No matter how well they did, or how well they did in comparison to white counterparts, they were continual targets for accusations of cowardice. As a result, a reputation of cowardly and poor performance on the battlefield left a stain on their history that they never overcame.

Another disappointing and insulting event for black soldiers in World War II was the treatment of the Ninth and Tenth Cavalry Regiments, with an outstanding service history spanning seventy-five years. They were added to the newly formed Second Cavalry Division. For a while, it seemed they would not be deployed, but in the spring of 1944, they were deployed to the Mediterranean. In May 1944, with little warning, the division was disbanded and the black soldiers sent as support units to North Africa, where they were immediately stripped of their weapons and ordered to unload ships while white soldiers headed to combat units. The War Department claimed they were obsolete for modern warfare. The War Department did not explain why white cavalry units were transitioned to mechanized units or transferred to infantry.

The black soldiers faced racist treatment and discrimination at every turn, from white soldiers, from officers, and from medical staff. Before they stopped accepting blood donations from black soldiers, the Red Cross kept donations separated by race to prevent black blood going to white soldiers.

Perhaps the worst event was a slaughter resulting from the decisions of an apparently racist commander of the Buffalos of the Ninety-Second during the Italian Campaign in 1944. Major General Edward M. Almond believed blacks naturally lacked the skills necessary for combat duty and that they should never get battlefield opportunity. He resented being given command of black troops. He told his black soldiers of his resentment. "I did not send for you. Your Negro newspapers, Negro politicians and white friends have insisted on you seeing combat and I shall see that you get combat and your share of the casualties."[1] In

Ninety-Second Infantry Division escorting German prisoner, Lucca, Italy, World War II. (National Archives)

1945, he placed them in repeated frontal assaults straight into heavy German defenses along the Gothic Line, clearly intending lots of casualties. Almond accused them of cowardice when they took cover under intense enemy fire. President William J. Clinton posthumously awarded four of the Ninety-Second the Medal of Honor in 1997.

As had so often been the case with the use of blacks in wartime, critical manpower shortages led to the desperate measure of placing blacks on the battlefield and of placing blacks and whites together against the Germans in the Battle of the Bulge, the German counteroffensive through the Ardennes from December 16, 1944, to January 25, 1945. Outnumbered and undersupplied American forces faced two hundred thousand German soldiers and at least one thousand German tanks during one of the worst winters on record. The weather made conditions miserable for the more than half a million Americans. The snow was deep and temperatures frigid. Cloud cover made air support impossible. After initial German success, the determined Americans regrouped, gained the upper hand, and pushed the Germans back. Some commanders had used black troops grudgingly or refused to use them at all, but after their performance under fire at the Battle of the Bulge and other places, more commanders accepted and used them side by side with white units from March until the German surrender in May. The black soldiers performed

well and received the respect of the white soldiers. As soon as the manpower crisis ended, however, conditions reverted to pre-crisis conditions.
Black troops were taken off the front lines and sent back to labor detail.

Other branches of the military did little better than the army in answer-
ing the call to use black Americans. Some did worse. The marines upheld
their traditional ban on black soldiers. The five thousand black sailors
were all assigned to labor and service. Under pressure from Roosevelt,
the navy reluctantly allowed black enlistment for service other than mess
attendants in April 1942. Though trained as clerks, radio operators, gun-
ners and signalmen, the navy posted these men at ammunition facilities
and on construction battalions. In February 1943, the War Manpower
Commission mandated that all services had to take more draftees, black
and white. Again, the navy protested, but Roosevelt pressured Secretary
of Navy Knox to comply. Continued pressure from the black community
led to two ships manned with black crews and white officers, the USS
Mason, launched in March 1944, and the USS *PC-1264*, launched in
April of the same year. The men on both vessels performed exemplary
service during the war, but the navy denied them credit for their accomplishments and selected these vessels to be among the first ones decom-
missioned after the war.

While the navy only reluctantly made way for blacks beyond the role
of mess men, they did make some important accomplishments. Sixteen
black cadets graduated in 1944 from the navy's officer training and
education program, the V-12. One of these graduates, Ensign Samuel L.
Gravely, became an officer on the *1264* in May 1945 and became the
first black man in American naval history served a meal in the officers'
mess. In June, the navy ended segregated basic training. Later that year,
Wesley A Brown became the first black appointee at Annapolis and the
first black officer to graduate from the academy. The marines, too, had
to comply with the April 1942 requirement that all branches accept both
white and black draftees. The marines were more successful in limiting
blacks to labor and service roles. Black marines did deploy to the Pacific
in 1944 but only unloaded ships and guarded supplies. Some, however,
did come under fire while performing these duties and handled the situation well. While denied combat roles, they lost nine killed and seventy-
eight wounded from enemy fire.

Even with discrimination and disappointing assignments to labor service, examples abound to demonstrate that black soldiers served with
valor when they did reach the battlefield, and those who did not performed beyond expectations, no matter what the assignment. When possible, black units were deployed to remote locations, and they received

mostly negative attention, but some completed feats that the white press could not ignore.

One of the most dramatic examples of black Americans stepping up in time of need was the Red Ball Express, an emergency system designed to get supplies to American forces at the front. The term Red Ball Express was not exclusive to this operation, but the men of this operation made their part in it noteworthy. After the Allies gained ownership of the beaches at Normandy, their hard fighting made impressive progress. This progress presented its own problems, the main one being the inability of supply lines to keep the army moving forward. When armies move quickly, they need not only ammunition and medical supplies but also gasoline, without which the progress grinds to a halt. The solution came in the form of the Red Ball Express, a round-the-clock truck convoy that operated from August 25 to November 16, 1944. Seventy-five percent of the drivers were black Americans, who took this risky and demanding task in stride, knowing that without the supplies they delivered, the army would stall. Worse, without the supplies, they might fall to the enemy. The Red Ball Express drove for many hours at a time, sometimes under fire, and with no lights at night. They averaged over five thousand tons of supplies a day for much of their three-month operation. American success depended on these men, and they delivered.

No less dramatic was a response to the continuing critical manpower shortages. By the summer and fall of 1944, the campaigns in Italy and North Africa and the war in the Pacific Theater were taking an extreme toll. Most American units were far short of full-strength manpower. Shortages were so bad that the Americans risked losing or prolonging the war. General Dwight D. Eisenhower urgently needed riflemen and turned to black soldiers for volunteers. He planned to integrate platoons individually into white units in the European Theater where needed. Nearly three thousand volunteers were formed into fifty-three platoons. They moved into their new assignments in March 1945. White units were mostly glad to see help of any color arrive to continue the fight. With little training, they provided Americans units the strength to continue the fight and continue to gain victories.

Black Americans also served in tank battalions, and World War II boasts the first all-black tank battalion, the 761st Tank Battalion, also known as Patton's Black Panthers. They saw combat against German Panzers in November 1944. The American tanks were stalling in thick mud, and the Panzers threatened to make quick work of them. First Sergeant Samuel J. Turley gave his life while providing covering fire that gave other soldiers time to escape. He continued to man a machine gun until German fire literally cut him in half. The next day, Sergeant Warren G. H. Crecy placed himself in danger to protect his fellow soldiers. Staff Sergeant Ruben Rivers died in a similar sacrifice to save others. When American forces faced at least one thousand German tanks in the Battle of the Bulge in late 1944, the Black Panthers pushed the Germans back. They went on as part of the assault that broke through the Siegfried Line in March 1945. In 1978, the unit received a presidential unit citation. In 1997, Ruben Rivers posthumously received the Medal of Honor.[2]

Perhaps the most famous all-black unit of World War II was the 332nd Fighter Group, the Tuskegee Airmen, with the 99th, 100th, 301st, and 302nd Squadrons. The 332nd first saw action on June 2, 1943, and fought until October 19, 1945. The 332nd had nearly one thousand men and flew more than fifteen thousand sorties. Their wartime record is astounding. White pilots requested them because of their accomplishments. Most of the time, their units were hard pressed to cover all the assignments because they were in such demand. A myth persists that they never lost a bomber. Recent scholarship revealed that they actually lost twenty-five, but that does not diminish the outstanding service record and their sacrifices to be one of the best units of the war. The war might have ended without black pilots having the opportunity to serve.

Only after intense pressure did the U.S. Air Corps make provision for a single black pilot-training school. They diligently tried to maintain their traditional exclusion of black pilots from service, but the Selective Training and Service Act of September 1940 made this difficult. Their plan was to accept blacks but use them only in labor battalions. The War Department formed the 99th Pursuit Squadron in January 1941, a black unit that would operate separately from white units. They trained at the Tuskegee Airfield in Alabama as the Tuskegee Experiment. Thirteen cadets entered the school on August 25, 1941, with five completing in March of 1942, one of whom was Benjamin O. Davis Jr., who had served with the Twenty-Fourth Infantry Regiment. Upon graduation, he assumed command of the 99th, re-designated the 99th Fighter Squadron. They had to fight for deployment, but they arrived in French Morocco in April 1943, based in the town of Fez. In June, they joined the 324th Fighter Group. Colonel Davis assumed command of the all-black 332nd Fighter Group in October 1943. They deployed to Italy in February 1944, where the 99th joined them. The 332nd had the tails of their planes painted red and became known as the "Red Tails." Henry Johnson's son Herman served with the 332nd Fighter Group. The Tuskegee Airmen flew 1,578 missions, 15,533 combat sorties, destroying 261 enemy aircraft and damaging 148. This record did not protect them from racism, which, once again, had a crippling effect. Davis and forty officers of the 332nd took command of the 477th, slated for eventual service in Japan. Racism demoralized them beyond recovery. In April 1945, at Freeman Field in Indiana, one hundred and one black officers were arrested and imprisoned for trying to enter an officers' club. The charges were dismissed, but the damage was done. The 477th could not be ready for service in Japan.[3]

The men in these units, the Tuskegee Airmen, Patton's Black Panthers, and the Red Ball Express drivers, owed a debt of gratitude to the Buffalo Soldiers, some of whom were sent to Europe during the war. Black Americans played a significant role in World War II, helping the United States to gain victory in Europe. The service and performance of black Americans in the war did little to change their circumstances. Black officers were still not allowed to command whites. The percentage of black officers remained miniscule, with only one general out of 776 and seven colonels out of 5,220. Their hope of Double V did not come to fruition as a result of their service. They returned home to discrimination, segregation, Jim Crow, violence, and continued lynching, some beaten and lynched while still in the uniform representing their service to their country. Many of the service advantages they had gained during the war disappeared in peacetime. Blacks and whites struggled during the years after the war for their ideas to prevail. Finally, on July 26, 1948, President Truman struck a blow against decades of racism and oppression when he ended segregation in the armed forces with Order No. 9981:

> It is essential that there be maintained in the armed service of the United States the highest standards of democracy, with equality of treatment and opportunity for all those who serve in our country's defense. It is hereby declared to be the policy of the President that there shall be equality of treatment and opportunity for all persons in the armed forces without regard to race, color, religion, or national origin. This policy shall be put into effect as rapidly as possible, having due regard to the time required to effectuate any necessary changes without impairing efficiency or morale.[4]

Needless to say, Order No. 9981 met stiff opposition. Kenneth Royall, Secretary of the Army, was to implement desegregation in the army, but he refused, citing to Truman the old argument that blacks, while qualified for labor, had proven their inability to perform well in combat roles in both world wars. Royall retired soon after this confrontation with Truman. His replacement, Gordon Gray, did not refuse to implement desegregation, but he simply did not get the job done. Frank Pace took his place in less than a year. The difficulty did not fall completely on the reluctance or inability of these men, though they contributed. The bigger difficulty was the reluctance or even refusal of senior military personnel to comply with the order. The Fahy Committee, the President's Committee on Equality and Opportunity in the Armed Forces, assigned to oversee transition and implementation of 9981, struggled over the next two years, working with each branch to reach the order's requirements. The Fahy Committee announced in early June 1950 that all the branches were making satisfactory progress. That satisfactory progress, however, was still slow. As part of an executive order, the Fahy Committee did not carry the power to implement 9981 effectively. Later that month, results of integration would face the test of war in Korea, a conflict that caught the United States with a focus on the Soviet Union and stopping the spread of communism and with an overall lack of preparedness otherwise. The United States was vastly underprepared for the war, with shortages in manpower and training. The U.S. started the war with all white units, but enlistment apathy and high casualties soon created need for the U.S. to once again call on its black citizens to serve in time of need. This war increased the pace of the implementation of Order No. 9981.[5]

The Twenty-Fourth Infantry, still segregated, left occupation duty in Japan to fight the tenacious North Koreans in late June. They joined with white units in the Twenty-Fifth Infantry. They did not perform well, becoming known as the "bug-out Twenty-Fourth." White units performed just as poorly, but the Twenty-Fourth received the brunt of negative attention for their battlefield behavior. Additionally, the Twenty-Fourth had the worst officers because whites still did not want to serve in black units. When white units performed poorly, officers could be replaced to improve leadership and thereby improve performance. This was not the case with the Twenty-Fourth. Racism in Korea led to black soldiers once again performing fatigue duty instead of fighting on the battlefield. Officers such as General Douglas MacArthur and his chief of staff, Lieutenant General Edward M. Almond, whose racism had already cost the lives of black soldiers in World War II, refused to integrate, even if it meant units were fighting far below the authorized strength. When General Matthew B. Ridgway replaced MacArthur on April 11, 1951, he immediately pushed for integration of all units.

By 1953, with 90 percent of black servicemen integrated, the men of the four black regiments were serving their last days together. The Ninth and Tenth Cavalry Regiments became the 509th and 510th Tank Battalions. Parts of the Twenty-Fifth Infantry became part of the Ninety-Fourth and Ninety-Fifth Infantry before they were deactivated on December 20 and 22, 1952. Other units of the Twenty-Fifth went to the First Armored Division in November 1952. Sadly, the Twenty-Fourth Infantry had to live with the reputation of cowardice it unfairly received in Korea. Men from the Twenty-Fourth transferred into the Thirty-Seventh Infantry or the Twenty-Fifth before the Twenty-Fourth was completely disbanded in October 1951. The Department of the Army later reviewed the performance of the Twenty-Fourth in Korea and cleared them of all accusations of cowardice in 1995, again, too little, too late.

One other all-black unit that served in Korea deserves mention. They are the Buffalo Rangers, who served as part of the Second Ranger Infantry Company (Airborne). Their service marked a first in United States military because it was the first time black Americans had the opportunity to attend ranger training, as part of Truman's Executive Order 9981. Even though the order called for complete integration, the Buffalo Rangers were still an all-black unit, and even though they were elite soldiers, they still experienced racist treatment. The order was signed into law in July 1948, but the military was slow to implement it, and units in Korea were still segregated. As in the past, manpower shortages, more than anything else, prompted use of blacks in combat roles in Korea. The Buffalo Rangers trained at Fort Benning, Georgia, in November 1950, and in California in December. They shipped first to Pearl Harbor and then to Korea in December. They were in the combat zone for seven months, where they engaged the enemy in several significant actions. They were part of the first ranger combat jump, in March 1951. They seized key locations, such as Hill 151, Hill 258, Hill 545, and Hill 581. They served gallantly and received individual citations and a company citation. Members such as Master Sergeant Edward L. Posey were inducted into the Ranger Hall of Fame. They deactivated in August 1951.[6]

The end of the Korean War brought the end of segregation in the military—and the end of the Buffalo Soldiers. The army reported complete desegregation in October 1954, but the legacy of the Buffalo Soldiers continued. In 1870, the Cheyenne dubbed the Tenth Cavalry the Buffalo Soldiers. Though evidence suggests they did not refer to themselves as Buffalo Soldiers, the Tenth incorporated the buffalo as part of their regimental crest. Not long after, the Ninth Cavalry, the Twenty-Fifth Infantry, and the Twenty-Fourth Infantry adopted the emblem of the Buffalo Soldier. Eventually, all black soldiers from the Indian Wars through the Korean War were known as Buffalo Soldiers. The Ninety-Second Division in World War I was called the Buffalo Division. Their uniform shoulder patch included a black buffalo. During World War II, the Ninety-Second Division were still called the Buffalo Division and even had a live buffalo for a mascot. In Korea, the men of the Second Ranger Infantry Company (Airborne) were called the Buffalo Rangers. The name represented honest and faithful service, from men who showed toughness and endurance both on and off the battlefield. All of these men looked back to the first all-black regiments formed and organized in 1866 and 1869 as part of their proud heritage and tradition. They looked back to the first black American soldiers, to Colonel Tye, and Americans who fought for the British in the hope of gaining freedom from slavery. They looked back to Andre Cailloux of the Louisiana Native Guards, who gallantly led his men at Port Hudson. They had much in common. They served their country in almost every war. They fought the enemy and their fellow Americans. Through it all, they served with distinction. The 150th anniversary of the organization of the post–Civil War all-black regiments calls for renewed attention and memorialization of their courageous service and sacrifice.

Appendix A

Medal of Honor Recipients

The recipients are listed by last name, first name, rank, regiment, and the year of the action for which they earned the award.

Stance, Emanuel: Sergeant, Ninth Cavalry, 1870

Paine, Adam: Private, Twenty-Fourth Infantry, Black Seminole Scout, 1874

Factor, Pompey: Private, Twenty-Fourth, Black Seminole Scout, 1875

Payne, Isaac: Trumpeter, Twenty-Fourth, Black Seminole Scout, 1875

Ward, John: Sergeant, Twenty-Fourth, Black Seminole Scout, 1875

Greaves, Clinton: Corporal, Ninth Cavalry, 1877

Boyne, Thomas: Sergeant, Ninth Cavalry, 1879

Denny, John: Sergeant, Ninth Cavalry, 1879

Johnson, Henry: Sergeant, Ninth Cavalry, 1879

Jordan, George: Sergeant, Ninth Cavalry, 1879

Shaw, Thomas: Sergeant, Ninth Cavalry, 1881

Walley, Augustus: Private, Ninth Cavalry, 1881

Williams, Moses: First Sergeant, Ninth Cavalry, 1881

Woods, Brent: Sergeant, Ninth Cavalry, 1881

Brown, Benjamin: Sergeant, Twenty-Fourth Infantry, 1889

Mays, Isaiah: Corporal, Twenty-Fourth Infantry, 1889

McBryar, William: Sergeant, Tenth Cavalry, 1889

Wilson, William O.: Corporal, Ninth Cavalry, 1890

Baker, Edward L., Jr.: Sergeant Major, Tenth Cavalry, 1898

Bell, Dennis: Private, Tenth Cavalry, 1898

Lee, Fitz: Private, Tenth Cavalry, 1898

Thompkins, William H.: Private, Tenth Cavalry, 1898

Wanton, George H.: Private, Tenth Cavalry, 1898

Appendix B

Executive Order 9981

Establishing the President's Committee on Equality of Treatment and Opportunity In the Armed Forces.

WHEREAS it is essential that there be maintained in the armed services of the United States the highest standards of democracy, with equality of treatment and opportunity for all those who serve in our country's defense:

NOW THEREFORE, by virtue of the authority vested in me as President of the United States, by the Constitution and the statutes of the United States, and as Commander in Chief of the armed services, it is hereby ordered as follows:

1. It is hereby declared to be the policy of the President that there shall be equality of treatment and opportunity for all persons in the armed services without regard to race, color, religion or national origin. This policy shall be put into effect as rapidly as possible, having due regard to the time required to effectuate any necessary changes without impairing efficiency or morale.
2. There shall be created in the National Military Establishment an advisory committee to be known as the President's Committee on Equality of Treatment and Opportunity in the Armed Services, which shall be composed of seven members to be designated by the President.
3. The Committee is authorized on behalf of the President to examine into the rules, procedures and practices of the Armed Services in order to determine in what respect such rules, procedures and practices

may be altered or improved with a view to carrying out the policy of this order. The Committee shall confer and advise the Secretary of Defense, the Secretary of the Army, the Secretary of the Navy, and the Secretary of the Air Force, and shall make such recommendations to the President and to said Secretaries as in the judgment of the Committee will effectuate the policy hereof.

4. All executive departments and agencies of the Federal Government are authorized and directed to cooperate with the Committee in its work, and to furnish the Committee such information or the services of such persons as the Committee may require in the performance of its duties.

5. When requested by the Committee to do so, persons in the armed services or in any of the executive departments and agencies of the Federal Government shall testify before the Committee and shall make available for use of the Committee such documents and other information as the Committee may require.

6. The Committee shall continue to exist until such time as the President shall terminate its existence by Executive order.

Harry Truman
The White House
July 26, 1948

Notes

Chapter 1

1. Douglas R. Egerton, *Death or Liberty: African Americans and Revolutionary America* (Oxford: Oxford University Press, 2009).

2. Graham Russell Hodge, "Black Revolt in New York City," in *New York in the Age of the Constitution, 1775–1780*, ed. Paul L. Gilje and William Pencak (London: Associated University Presses, 1992).

3. Verner W. Crane, *The Southern Frontier, 1670–1732* (Ann Arbor: University of Michigan Press, 1956), 187–189.

4. Sidney Kaplan and Emma Nogrady Kaplan, *The Black Presence in the Era of the American Revolution*, rev. ed. (Amherst: University of Massachusetts Press, 1989), 64.

5. Bernard C. Nalty, *Strength for the Fight: A History of Black Americans in the Military* (New York: The Free Press, 1986), 22–23.

6. Alexander Slidell Mackenzie, *Life of Commodore Hazard Perry*, vol. 1 Washington, DC: Library of Congress, 1843. (Nabu Press, 2013), 166.

7. Kenneth W. Porter, *The Black Seminoles: History of a Freedom-Seeking People*, rev. and ed. Alcione M. Amos and Thomas P. Senter (Gainesville: University Press of Florida, 1996), 106.

Chapter 2

1. Union General George H. Thomas, the "Rock of Chickamauga," after the December 15–16, 1864, Battle of Nashville. Joseph A. Altsheler, *The Rock of Chickamauga* (Middlesex: Echo Library, 2007), 154.

2. Stephen J. Ochs, *A Black Patriot and a White Priest: Andre Cailloux and Claude Paschal Maistre in Civil War New Orleans* (Baton Rouge: Louisiana State University Press, 2000).

3. James G. Hollandsworth Jr., *The Louisiana Native Guards: The Black Military Experience during the Civil War* (Baton Rouge: Louisiana State University Press, 1998).

4. U.S. War Department, *The War of the Rebellion: Official Records of the Union and Confederate Armies*, 128 vols. (Washington, DC: Government Printing Office, 1880–1901), ser. 3, vol. 3: 252.

5. Quoted in Forrest G. Wood, *Black Scare: The Racist Response to Emancipation and Reconstruction* (Berkeley: University of California Press, 1970), 43. Original quotation in *The Congressional Globe*, 37 Congress, 3 Session (February, 2-5, 1863), 680–690, and Appendix (February 2, 1863), 93; White, "Speech."

6. *Official Records*, 1 Ser., VIII, 369.

7. *Official Records*, 1 Ser., VIII, 370.

8. *Official Records*, 1 Ser., VI, 177.

9. *Official Records*, 1, Ser., III, 467.

10. *Official Records*, 1 Series, XIV, 377, Aug. 25, 1862.

11. *Official Records*, 1 Series, XIV, 191–92, Nov. 10, 1862.

12. James R. Arnold and Robert Weiner, eds., *American Civil War: Essential Reference Guide* (Santa Barbara, CA: ABC-CLIO, 2011), 5.

13. U.S. War Department, *The War of the Rebellion: Official Records of the Union and Confederate Armies*, 128 vols. (Washington, DC: Government Printing Office, 1880–1901), ser. 4, vol. 3: 1161–162.

14. U.S. War Department, *The War of the Rebellion: A Compilation of the Official Records of the Union and Confederate Armies* (Washington, DC: Government Printing Office, 2006).

15. *Journals of the Congress of the Confederate States of America* (Charleston, SC: Nabu Press, 2007), 3: 386–387.

16. Hollandsworth, *Louisiana Native Guards*, 57.

17. Noah Andre Trudeau, *Like Men of War: Black Troops in the Civil War, 1862–1865* (Boston: Little, Brown, 1998), 464.

18. W. E. Woodward, *Meet General Grant* (New York: Horace Liveright, 1928), 237.

19. James M. McPherson, *The Negro's Civil War: How American Negroes Felt and Acted during the War for the Union* (New York: Pantheon Books, 1965), viii.

Chapter 3

1. William A. Dobak and Thomas D. Phillips, *The Black Regulars, 1866–1898* (Norman: University of Oklahoma Press, 2001), xiii.

2. John F. Marszalek Jr., *Court Martial: The Army vs. Johnson Whittaker, an Account of the Ordeal of a Black Cadet at West Point* (New York: Charles Scribner's Sons, 1972).

3. Arlen Fowler, *The Black Infantry in the West, 1869–1891* (Norman: University of Oklahoma Press, 1996), 92–108. Alan K. Lamm, "Buffalo Soldier Chaplains of the Old West," in *Buffalo Soldiers in the West: A Black Soldiers Anthology*, Bruce A. Glasrud and Michael N. Searles, eds. (College Station:

Texas A&M Press, 2007), 68–83. Frank N. Schubert, *Voices of the Buffalo Soldier: Records, Reports, and Recollections of Military Life and Service in the West* (Albuquerque: University of New Mexico Press, 2003), 173.

4. William H. Leckie, *The Buffalo Soldiers: A Narrative of the Negro Cavalry in the West* (Norman: University of Oklahoma Press, 1967). William A. Dobak and Thomas D. Phillips, *The Black Regulars, 1866–1898* (Norman: University of Oklahoma Press, 2001).

5. Schubert, *Voices*, 31.

6. Leckie, *The Buffalo Soldiers*, 163–64. Fowler, *Black Infantry*, 57–62.

7. Louise W. Knight. *Citizen: Jane Addams and the Struggle for Democracy* (Chicago: University of Chicago Press, 2006), 309.

8. Paul J. Scheips, "Darkness and Light: The Interwar Years, 1865–1898," in *American Military History: Army Historical Series* (Washington, DC: Center of Military History, United States Army, 1989), 281–300.

9. Fowler, *Black Infantry*, 57–62.

10. Jane Landers, *Black Society in Spanish Florida* (Chicago: University of Illinois Press, 1999).

11. Kenneth W. Porter, *The Black Seminoles: History of a Freedom-Seeking People*, rev. and ed. Alcione M. Amos and Thomas P. Senter, foreword by Rosalyn Howard (Gainesville: University of Florida Press, 2013), x.

12. Porter, *Black Seminoles*, 178.

13. Charles W. Hanna, *African American Recipients of the Medal of Honor: A Biographical Dictionary, Civil War Through Vietnam War* (Jefferson, NC: McFarland, 2002), 3. Selecting a few representative stories of the deeds of Medal of Honor recipients is difficult because all the men deserve their story told. See also, James H. Willbanks, ed., *America's Heroes: Medal of Honor Recipients from the Civil War to Afghanistan* (Santa Barbara, CA: ABC-CLIO, 2011); Frank N. Schubert, *Black Valor: Buffalo Soldiers and the Medal of Honor, 1870–1898* (Lanham, MD: Rowman & Littlefield, 1997).

14. Congressional Medal of Honor Society, entry for Corporal Freddie Stowers, accessed July 31, 2014, http://www.cmohs.org/recipient-detail/2595/stowers-freddie.php.

15. Paul Grohdahl, "Sgt. Henry Johnson clears key Medal of Honor hurdle." http://www.timesunion.com/local/article/Sgt-Henry-Johnson-clears-key-Medal-of-Honor-5482160.php, retrieved May 20, 2014.

Chapter 4

1. Mirabeau Buonaparte Lamar, Harriet Smither, and Charles Adams Gulick, *The Papers of Mirabeau Buonaparte Lamar* (Austin, TX: A. C. Baldwin Printers, 1922), 2: 152.

2. Quoted in Dan L. Thrapp, *Victorio and the Mimbres Apaches* (Norman: University of Oklahoma Press, 1974), 22, 60, 78, 81.

3. Thrapp, *Victorio and the Mimbres Apaches*, 133.

4. Harold McCracken, ed., *Frederic Remington's Own West* (New York: Dial, 1960), 28–29.

5. Kathleen P. Chamberlain, *Victorio: Apache Warrior and Chief* (Norman: University of Oklahoma Press, 2007), 140–41.

6. Randolph B. Marcy, *Thirty Years of Army Life on the Border* (New York: Harper, 1866), 169.

7. William Tecumseh Sherman, from John L. Kessel, "General Sherman and the Navajo Treaty of 1868: A Basic and Expedient Misunderstanding," *Western Historical Quarterly* 12 (1981): 251–272.

8. Ibid.

9. Quoted in Thrapp, *Victorio and the Mimbres Apaches*, 311.

Chapter 5

1. Robert Wooster, *Frontier Crossroads: Fort Davis and the West*, Canseco-Keck History Series 7 (College Station: Texas A&M University Press, 2006), 6.

2. Marcos E. Kinevan, *Frontier Cavalryman: Lieutenant John Bigelow with the Buffalo Soldiers in Texas* (El Paso: Texas Western Press, 1998). Kathleen P. Chamberlain, *Victorio: Apache Warrior and Chief* (Norman: University of Oklahoma Press, 2007). Dan L. Thrapp, *Victorio and the Mimbres Apaches* (Norman: University of Oklahoma Press, 1974). Edward L. N. Glass, *The History of the Tenth Cavalry, 1866–1921* (Tucson, AZ: Acme, 1921). Frank N. Schubert, *Voices of the Buffalo Soldier: Records, Reports, and Recollections of Military Life and Service in the West* (Albuquerque: University of New Mexico Press, 2003).

3. William H. Leckie and Shirley A. Leckie, *Unlikely Warriors: General Benjamin Grierson and His Family* (Norman: University of Oklahoma Press, 1984), 78.

4. Schubert, *Voices of the Buffalo Soldier*, 12–20. Col. George Augustus Armes, *Ups and Downs of an Army Officer* (Washington, DC: Government Printing Office, Library of Congress, 1900), 236–248.

5. Schubert, 24–28.

6. Robert K. DeArment, *Bat Masterson, The Man and the Legend* (Norman: University of Oklahoma Press, 1989), 15–25.

7. Herman Lehmann, *9 Years Among the Indians, 1870–1879: The Story of the Captivity and Life of a Texan Among the Indians*, ed. J. Marvin Hunter (Albuquerque: University of New Mexico Press, 1993), 171.

8. Paul H. Carlson, *The Buffalo Soldier Tragedy of 1877* (College Station: Texas A&M University Press, 2003), 82–90.

9. Douglas C. McChristian, ed., *Garrison Tangles in the Friendless Tenth: The Journal of First Lieutenant John Bigelow, Jr., Fort Davis, Texas* (Bryan, TX: J. M. Carroll, 1984), 52.

10. William H. Leckie, *Buffalo Soldiers* (Norman: University of Oklahoma Press, 1967), 163–70, 230–39. Schubert, *Voices*, 114–122.

11. Glass, *History of the Tenth Cavalry*, 28.

12. Ibid., 29–30.

13. Ibid., 31.

Chapter 6

1. From a poem by Ada Iddings Gale, June 23, 1899, quoted in William G. Muller, *The Twenty-fourth Infantry Past and Present: A brief history of the regiment compiled from official records, under the direction of the Regimental Commander*, introduction by John M. Carroll (Fort Collins, CO: The Old Army Press), 1972.

2. Paul H. Carlson, *"Pecos Bill": A Military Biography of William R. Shafter* (College Station: Texas A&M University Press, 1989), 39.

3. Arlen L. Fowler, *The Black Infantry in the West, 1869–1891* (Norman: University of Oklahoma Press, 1996).

4. Michael A. Eggleston, *The Tenth Minnesota Volunteers, 1862–1865. A History of Action in the Sioux Uprising and the Civil War with a Regimental Roster* (Jefferson, NC: McFarland, 2012), 14.

5. Ernest Wallace and E. Adamson Hoebel, *The Comanches: Lord of the South Plains*, The Civilization of the American Indian Series (Norman: University of Oklahoma Press, 1986), 55.

6. Randolph B. Marcy, *Explorations of the Red River of Louisiana in the Year 1852, by Randolph B. Marcy; assisted by George B. McClellan. With reports on the natural history of the country, and numerous illustrations*. Reprint. (Ann Arbor: University of Michigan Library, October 2004): 85.

7. Alfred Barnaby Thomas, *After Coronado: Spanish Exploration Northeast of New Mexico, 1696–1727*, 2nd ed. (Norman: University of Oklahoma Press, 1966).

8. Wallace and Hoebel, *The Comanches*, 45.

9. Rachel Plummer and James W. Parker, *Rachel Plummer Narrative* (New Delhi: Gyan Books, 2013).

10. Randolph B. Marcy, *Exploration of the Red River of Louisiana in 1852*, 32nd Cong., 2nd sess., Executive Document 54 (Washington, DC, 1854), 85.

11. Carlson, *"Pecos Bill,"* 3.

12. Loyd M. Uglow, *Standing in the Gap: Army Outposts, Picket Stations, and the Pacification of the Texas Frontier, 1866–1886* (Fort Worth: Texas Christian University Press, 2001), 8.

13. William G. Muller, *The Twenty-fourth Infantry Past and Present* (Fort Collins, CO: The Old Army Press, 1972), 11. Muller was Captain and Adjutant to the Twenty-Fourth.

14. Ibid., 12–16.

15. Fowler, *Black Infantry in the West*, 77.

16. Muller, *The Twenty-fourth Infantry*, 17.

17. Ibid., 31.

Chapter 7

1. *Senate Documents, December 2, 1907–May 30, 1908, 60th Cong., 1st Sess., in Congressional Edition* (Washington, DC: Government Printing Office, 1908), 5252: 7.

2. Ibid., 280–82.

3. Mary Church Terrell, "A Sketch of Mingo Saunders," from Frank N. Schubert, *Voices of the Buffalo Soldier: Records, Reports, and Recollections of Military Life and Service in the West* (Albuquerque: University of New Mexico Press, 2003), 243. Schubert notes that Terrell always spelled Sanders's name Saunders, but his military records record his name as Sanders.

4. Irene Schubert and Frank N. Schubert, *On the Trail of the Buffalo Soldier II: New and Revised Biographies of African Americans in the U.S. Army, 1866–1917* (Lanham, MD: Scarecrow Press, 2004), 254.

5. *Senate Documents*, 5252: 9.

6. Congressional Edition, Volume 5252, United States Congress. Senate Documents of 60th Congress, 1st Session, December 2, 1907—May 30, 1908, volume 19 of 36 volumes. Washington: Government Printing Office, 1908.

7. Irene Schubert and Frank N. Schubert, *On the Trail of the Buffalo Soldier: New and Revised Biographies of African Americans in the U.S. Army, 1866–1917* (Lanham, MD: Scarecrow Press, 2004), 254–55.

8. James D. Weaver, *The Senator and the Sharecropper: Exoneration of the Brownsville Soldiers* (College Station: Texas A&M University Press, 1997).

9. Quintard Taylor Jr. quoted in John J. Nankivell, *Buffalo Soldier Regiment: History of the Twenty-fifth United States Infantry, 1869–1926*, introduction by Quintard Taylor Jr. (Lincoln: University of Nebraska Press, 2001), ix.

10. Nankivell, *Buffalo Soldier Regiment*, 24–25.

11. Arlen L. Fowler. *The Black Infantry in the West, 1869–1891* (Westport, CT: Greenwood Publishing, 1971), 48.

Chapter 8

1. Robert Leckie, *The Wars of America* (Edison NJ: Castle Books, 1992), 550.

2. William B. Gatewood Jr., *Smoked Yankees and the Struggle for Empire: Letters from Negro Soldiers, 1898–1902* (Urbana: University of Illinois Press, 1971), 240.

3. Leckie, *Wars of America*, 572.

4. Ibid., 569.

5. United States War Department, *Five Years of War Department Following War with Spain, 1899–1903, As Shown in Annual Reports of Secretary of War*, Primary Source Edition Paperback (Nabu Press: October, 22, 2013; original printed in Washington, DC: Government Printing Office, 1904), 320.

6. James W. Hurst, *Pancho Villa and Black Jack Pershing: The Punitive Expedition in Mexico* (Westport, CT: Praeger, 2008), 90.

7. Ibid., 94.

Chapter 9

1. Chad Williams, *Torchbearers of Democracy: African American Soldiers in the World War I Era*, John Hope Franklin Series in African American History and Culture (Chapel Hill: University of North Carolina Press, 2010), 52.

2. Jennifer D. Keene, *World War I: The American Soldier Experience* (Lincoln: University of Nebraska Press, 2006), 104.

3. Arthur W. Little, *From Harlem to the Rhine: The Story of New York's Colored Volunteers* (New York: Covici Friede, 1936), 9.

4. Paul Grondahl, "Sergeant Henry Johnson Clears Key Medal of Honor Hurdle." http://www.timesunion.com/local/article/Sgt-Henry-Johnson-clears-key-Medal-of-Honor-5482160.php, retrieved May 20, 2014.

5. Williams, *Torchbearers of Democracy*, 2.

6. James Rawn Jr., *The Double V: How Wars, Protest, and Harry Truman Desegregated America's Military* (New York: Bloomsbury, 2013), 79.

Epilogue

1. Robert B. Edgerton, *Hidden Heroism: Black Soldiers in America's Wars* (Boulder, CO: Westview Press, 2002), 151, 155–157.

2. Charles W. Sasser, *Patton's Panthers: The African-American 761st Tank Battalion in World War II* (New York: Pocket Books, 2005).

3. Joseph Caver, Jerome Ennels, and Daniel Haulman, *The Tuskegee Airmen: An Illustrated History: 1939–1949* (Montgomery, AL: NewSouth Books, 2011). Daniel Haulman, *The Tuskegee Airmen and the "Never Lost a Bomber" Myth (*Montgomery, AL: NewSouth Books, 2011).

4. Executive Order No. 9981: Desegregation of the Armed Forced (1948). The President's Committee on Equality of Treatment and Opportunity in the Armed Services was established by Executive Order 9981, on July 26, 1948, to recommend revisions in military regulations in order to implement the government's policy of desegregation of the armed services. The Government's policy, announced in the same order, was that there was to be equality of treatment and opportunity for all members of the armed forces, regardless of race, color, religion, or national origin. The seven-member advisory committee, which was chaired by Charles Fahy, was more commonly known as the Fahy Committee. The Fahy Committee terminated upon submission of its final report on May 22, 1950. The final report of the committee was published as an eighty-two-page document entitled Freedom to Serve.

The Fahy Committee was created within the National Military Establishment and had the following members: Charles Fahy, Charles Luckman, Lester Granger, John H. Sengstacke, William E. Stevenson, Dwight Palmer, and Alphonsus J. Donahue. All departments and agencies of the Federal Government were instructed to cooperate with the committee and furnish it with information or services as required. The committee conducted an inquiry; examined the rules and practice of the armed services; and made recommendations for policy improvements to carry out the mandate of Executive Order No. 9981. All of the committee's recommendations were approved and accepted by the president, the secretary of defense, and the service secretaries. Retrieved May 26, 2014. http://www.trumanlibrary.org/9981.htm

5. Edgerton, *Hidden Heroism*, 165–169.

6. Edward L. Posey, *The U.S. Army's First, Last, and Only All-Black Rangers: The 2nd Ranger Infantry Company (Airborne) in the Korean War, 1950–1951* (New York: Savas Beattie, 2009).

Bibliography

Altsheler, Joseph A. *The Rock of Chickamauga*. Middlesex: Echo Library, 2007.

Armes, Col. George Augustus. *Ups and Downs of an Army Officer*. 1900. Reprinted from the collections of the University of California Libraries. Washington, DC: Library of Congress. 1900. Reprint London: Forgotten Books, 2012.

Arnold, James R., and Roberta Wiener. *American Civil War: The Essential Reference Guide*. Santa Barbara, CA: ABC-CLIO, 2011.

Astor, Gerald. *The Right to Fight: A History of African Americans in the Military*. Novato, CA: Presidio, 1998.

Barbeau, Arthur E., and Florette Henri. *The Unknown Soldiers: African-American Troops in World War I*. Philadelphia: Da Capo, 1996.

Bigelow, Lt. John, Jr. *The Tenth Regiment of Cavalry, from the Army of the United States Historical Sketches of Staff and Line with Portraits of Generals-in-Chief*. Edited by Theophilus F. Rodenbough and William L. Haskins. New York: Maynard, Merrill, 1896.

Billington, Monroe Lee. *New Mexico's Buffalo Soldiers, 1866–1900*. Niwot: University Press of Colorado, 1991.

Burns, W. F. *The Pullman Boycott: A Complete History of the Great R.R. Strike*. St. Paul, MN: McGill, 1894.

Carlson, Paul H. *"Pecos Bill": A Military Biography of William R. Shafter*. College Station: Texas A&M University Press, 1989.

Carlson, Paul H. *The Buffalo Soldier Tragedy of 1877*. College Station: Texas A&M University Press, 2003.

Cashin, Herschel V. *Under Fire with the Tenth U.S. Cavalry*. Niwot: University Press of Colorado, 1993.

Caver, Joseph, Jerome Ennels, and Daniel Haulman. *The Tuskegee Airmen: An Illustrated History: 1939–1949*. Montgomery, AL: NewSouth Books, 2011.

Chamberlain, Kathleen P. *Victorio: Apache Warrior and Chief*. Norman: University of Oklahoma Press, 2007.

Cornish, Dudley Taylor. *The Sable Arm: Black Troops in the Union Army, 1861–1865*. Lawrence: University of Kansas Press, 1987.

Crane, Verner W. *The Southern Frontier, 1670–1732*. Ann Arbor: University of Michigan Press, 1956.

Crenshaw, Douglas. *Fort Harrison and the Battle of Chaffin's Farm*. Charleston, SC: The History Press, 2013.

DeArment, Robert K. *Bat Masterson, The Man and the Legend*. Norman: University of Oklahoma Press, 1989.

Dobak, William A., and Thomas D. Phillips. *The Black Regulars, 1866–1898*. Norman: University of Oklahoma Press, 2001.

Edgerton, Robert B. *Hidden Heroism: Black Soldiers in America's Wars*. Boulder, CO: Westview Press, 2002.

Egerton, Douglas R. "Black Independence Struggles and the Tale of Two Revolutions." *Journal of Southern History* 64 no. 1 (1998), 95–116.

Egerton, Douglas R. *Death or Liberty: African Americans and Revolutionary America*. Oxford: Oxford University Press, 2009.

Eggleston, Michael A. *The Tenth Minnesota Volunteers, 1862–1865. A History of Action in the Sioux Uprising and the Civil War with a Regimental Roster*. Jefferson, NC: McFarland, 2012.

Fowler, Arlen L. *The Black Infantry in the West, 1869–1891*. Westport, CT: Greenwood Publishing Corporation, 1971.

Glasrud, Bruce A., and Michael N. Searles, eds. *Buffalo Soldiers in the West: A Black Soldiers Anthology*. College Station: Texas A&M Press, 2007.

Glass, Edward L. N. *The History of the Tenth Cavalry, 1866–1921*. Tucson, AZ: Acme, 1921.

Glatthaar, Joseph T. *Forged in Battle: The Civil War Alliance of Black Soldiers and White Officers*. New York: The Free Press, 1990.

Hanna, Charles W. *African American Recipients of the Medal of Honor: A Biographical Dictionary, Civil War through Vietnam War*. Jefferson, NC: McFarland, 2002.

Harris, Stephen L. *Harlem's Hell Fighters: The African-American 369th Infantry in World War I*. Washington, DC: Brassey's, 2003.

Haulman, Daniel. *The Tuskegee Airmen and the "Never Lost a Bomber" Myth*. Montgomery, AL: NewSouth Books, 2011.

Hodge, Graham Russell. "Black Revolt in New York City," in *New York in the Age of the Constitution, 1775–1800*. Paul A. Gilje and William Pencak, editors. London: Associated University Presses, 1992.

Hollandsworth, James G., Jr. *The Louisiana Native Guards: The Black Military Experience During the Civil War*. Baton Rouge: Louisiana State University Press, 1998.

Hurst, James W. *Pancho Villa and Black Jack Pershing: The Punitive Expedition in Mexico*. Westport, CT: Praeger, 2008.

Jackson, Luther P. "Virginia Negro Soldiers and Seamen in the American Revolution." *Journal of Negro History* 27, no. 3 (July 1942): 247–287.

Journal of the Congress of the Confederate States of America. Charleston, SC: Nabu Press, 2007.

Kaplan, Sidney, and Emma Nogrady Kaplan. *The Black Presence in the Era of the American Revolution.* Rev. ed. Amherst: University of Massachusetts Press, 1989.

Keene, Jennifer D. *World War I: The American Soldier Experience.* Lincoln: University of Nebraska Press, 2011.

Kessel, John L. "General Sherman and the Navajo Treaty of 1868: A Basic and Expedient Misunderstanding." *Western Historical Quarterly* 12 (1981): 251–272.

Kinevan, Marcos E. *Frontier Cavalryman: Lieutenant John Bigelow with the Buffalo Soldiers in Texas.* El Paso: Texas Western Press, 1998.

Knight, Louise W. *Citizen: Jane Addams and the Struggle for Democracy.* Chicago: University of Chicago Press, 2006.

Lamar, Mirabeau Buonaparte, Harriet Smither, and Charles Adams Gulick. *The Papers of Mirabeau Buonaparte Lamar.* Vol. 2. Austin, TX: A. C. Baldwin Printers, 1922.

Landers, Jane. *Black Society in Spanish Florida.* Chicago: University of Illinois Press, 1999.

Leckie, Robert. *The Wars of America.* Edison, NJ: Castle Books, 1992.

Leckie, William H. *The Buffalo Soldiers: A Narrative of the Negro Cavalry in the West.* Norman: University of Oklahoma Press, 1967.

Leckie, William H., and Shirley A. Leckie. *Unlikely Warriors: General Benjamin Grierson and His Family.* Norman: University of Oklahoma Press, 1984.

Lehmann, Herman. *9 Years Among the Indians, 1870–1879.* Austin, TX: Von-Beockmann-Jones, 1927.

Little, Arthur W. *From Harlem to the Rhine: The Story of New York's Colored Volunteers.* New York: Covici Friede, 1936.

Marcy, Randolph B. *Thirty Years of Army Life on the Border.* New York: Harper, 1866.

Marszalek, John F., Jr. *Court Martial: The Army vs. Johnson Whittaker, an Account of the Ordeal of a Black Cadet at West Point.* New York: Charles Scribner's Sons, 1972.

Maslowski, Pete. "National Policy toward Use of Black Troops in the Revolution." *South Carolina Historical Magazine* 73, no. 1 (1972): 1–17.

McChristian, Douglas. *Garrison Tangles, in the Friendless Tenth: The Journal of Lieutenant John Bigelo, Jr., Fort Davis, Texas.* Charleston, SC: J.M. Carroll, 1985.

McCracken, Harold, ed. *Frederic Remington's Own West.* New York: Dial, 1960.

McPherson, James M. *The Negro's Civil War: How American Blacks Felt and Acted during the War for the Union.* New York: Pantheon Books, 1965.

Muller, William G. *The Twenth-fourth Infantry Past and Present.* Fort Collins, CO: The Old Army Press, 1972.

Nalty, Bernard C. *Strength for the Fight: A History of Black Americans in the Military.* New York: The Free Press, 1986.

Nelson, Peter N. *A More Unbending Battle: The Harlem Hellfighters' Struggle for Freedom in WWI and Equality at Home.* New York: Basic Civitas Books, 2009.

Nankivell, John J. *Buffalo Soldier Regiment: History of the Twenty-fifth United States Infantry, 1869–1926.* Lincoln: University of Nebraska Press, 2001.

Ochs, Stephen J. *A Black Patriot and a White Priest: Andre Cailloux and Claude Paschal Maistre in Civil War New Orleans.* Baton Rouge: Louisiana State University Press, 2000.

Plummer, Rachel, and James W. Parker. *Rachel Plummer narrative a stirring narrative of adventure hardship and privation in the early days of Texas, depicting struggles with the Indians and otherwise.* Isha Books, Darya Ganj, New Dehli: Gyan Books, 2013.

Porter, Kenneth W. *The Black Seminoles: History of a Freedom-Seeking People.* Revised and edited by Alcione M. Amos and Thomas P. Senter. Foreword by Rosalyn Howard. Gainesville: University of Florida Press, 2013.

Posey, Edward L. *The U.S. Army's First, Last, and Only All-Black Rangers: The 2nd Ranger Infantry Company (Airborne) in the Korean War, 1950–1951.* New York: Savas Beattie, 2009.

Quarles, Benjamin. *The Negro in the Making of America.* New York: Collier, 1987.

Rawn, James, Jr. *The Double V: How Wars, Protest, and Harry Truman Desegregated America's Military.* New York: Bloomsbury, 2013.

Sasser, Charles W. *Patton's Panthers: The African-American 761st Tank Battalion in World War II.* New York: Pocket Books, 2005.

Scheips, Paul J. *"Darkness and Light: The Interwar Years, 1865–1898."* Chapter 13 in American Military History: Army Historical Series. Washington, DC: Center of Military History, United States Army, 1989, 281–299.

Schubert, Frank N. *Black Valor: Buffalo Soldiers and the Medal of Honor, 1870–1898.* Lanham, MD: Rowman & Littlefield, 1997.

Schubert, Frank N. *Voices of the Buffalo Soldier: Records, Reports, and Recollections of Military Life and Service in the West.* Albuquerque: University of New Mexico Press, 2003.

Schubert, Irene, and Frank N. Schubert. *On the Trail of the Buffalo Soldier: New and Revised Biographies of African Americans in the U.S. Army, 1866–1917* (vol 2). Lanham, MD: The Scarecrow Press, 2004.

Sgt. Henry Johnson clears key Medal of Honor hurdle. Accessed May 20, 2014. http://www.timesunion.com/local/article/Sgt-Henry-Johnson-clears-key-Medal-of-Honor-5482160.php. www.timesunion.com. Published May 15, 2014.

Slotkin, Richard. *Lost Battalions: The Great War and the Crisis of American Nationality.* New York: Henry Holt, 2005.

Tate, Michael L. *The Frontier Army in the Settlement of the West.* Norman: University of Oklahoma Press, 1999.

The War of the Rebellion, *A Compilation of the Official Records of the Union and Confederate Armies, Volumes I and II.* U.S. War Department. Washington DC: Government Printing Office, 2006.

Thomas, Aflred Barnaby. *After Coronado: Spanish Exploration Northeast of New Mexico, 1696–1727.* Norman: University of Oklahoma Press, 1935.

Thrapp, Dan L. *Victorio and the Mimbres Apaches.* Norman: University of Oklahoma Press, 1974.

Trudeau, Noah Andre. *Like Men of War: Black Troops in the Civil War, 1862–1865.* Boston: Little, Brown, 1998.

Uglow, Loyd M. *Standing in the Gap: Army Outposts, Picket Stations, and the Pacification of the Texas Frontier, 1866–1886.* Fort Worth: Texas Christian University Press, 2001.

United States Congress. *Congressional Edition, Volume 5252, Senate Documents, 60th Congress, 1st Session, December 2, 1907–May 30, 1908.* Washington: Government Printing Office, 1908.

United States Senate. *Hearings before the Committee on Military Affairs, United States Senate concerning the affray at Brownsville, Tex., on the night of August 13 and 14, 1906.* Washington, DC: Government Printing Office, 1908.

United States War Department. *Five Years of War Department Documents Following War with Spain, 1899–1903, As Shown in Annual Reports of Secretary of War.* Nabu, 2013. Originally printed Washington, DC: Government Printing Office, 1904.

United States War Department. *The War of the Rebellion: A Compendium of the Official Records of the Union and Confederate Armies, 128 volumes, Series 4, vol. 3.* Washington, DC: Government Printing Office, 1880–1901.

Wallace, Ernest, and E. Adamson Hoebel. *The Comanches: Lord of the South Plains.* Norman: University of Oklahoma Press, 1986.

Weaver, James D. *The Senator and the Sharecropper: Exoneration of the Brownsville Soldiers.* College Station: Texas A&M University Press, 1997.

Willbanks, James H., ed. *America's Heroes: Medal of Honor Recipients from the Civil War to Afghanistan.* Santa Barbara, CA: ABC-CLIO, 2011.

Williams, Chad L. *Torchbearers of Democracy: African American Soldiers in the World War I Era.* John Hope Franklin Series in African American History and Culture. Chapel Hill: University of North Carolina Press, 2010.

Wilson, Joseph Thomas. *The Black Phalanx: African American Soldiers in the War of Independence, the War of 1812, and the Civil War.* New York: Da Capo, 1994.

Wood, Forrest G. *Black Scare: The Racist Response to Emancipation and Reconstruction.* Berkeley: University of California Press, 1970.

Woodward, W. E. *Meet General Grant.* New York: Horace Liveright, 1928.

Wooster, Robert. *Frontier Crossroads: Fort Davis and the West.* Canseco-Keck History Series 7. College Station: Texas A&M University Press, 2006.

Wright, Donald R. *African Americans in the Colonial Era: From African Origins through the American Revolution.* 3rd ed. The American History Series. Wheeling, IL: Harlan Davidson, 2010.

Suggested Readings

Barbeau, Arthur E., and Florette Henri. *The Unknown Soldiers: African-American Troops In World War I.* Philadelphia: Da Capo, 1996.

Berlin, Ira, and Ronald Hoffman, eds. *Slavery and Freedom in the Age of the American Revolution.* Charlottesville: The University Press of Virginia, 1983.

Burkhardt, George S. *Confederate Rage, Yankee Wrath: No Qurter in the Civil War.* Carbondale: Southern Illinois University Press, 2007.

Carter, Robert G. *On the Border with Mackenzie, or Winning West Texas from the Comanches.* Austin: Texas State Historical Association, 2007.

Christian, Garna L. *Black Soldiers in Jim Crow Texas, 1899–1917.* College Station: Texas A&M University Press, 1995.

Claxton, Melvin, and Mark Puls. *Uncommon Valor: A Story of Race, Patriotism, and Glory in the Final Battles of the Civil War.* Hoboken, NJ: John Wiley & Sons, 2006.

Clendenen, Clarence C. *Blood on the Border: The United States Army and the Mexican Irregulars.* London: Macmillan, 1969.

Gilje, Paul A., and William Pencak, eds. *New York in the Age of the Constitution, 1775–1800.* London: Associated University Presses, 1992.

Glatthaar, Joseph T. *Forged in Battle: The Civil War Alliance of Black Soldiers and White Officers.* New York: The Free Press, 1990.

Hamilton, Allen Lee. *Sentinal of the Southern Plains: Fort Richardson and the Northwest Texas Frontier, 1866–1878.* Fort Worth: Texas Christian University Press, 1988.

Hutton, Paul Andrew. *Phil Sheridan & His Army.* Norman: University of Oklahoma Press, 1999.

Katz, William Loren. *The Black West: A Documentary and Pictorial History of the African American Role in the Westward Expansion of the United States.* New York: Simon & Schuster, 1996.

Kenner, Charles L. *Buffalo Soldiers and Officers of the Ninth Cavalry, 1867–1898.* Norman: University of Oklahoma Press, 1999.

Kly, Y. N., ed. *The Invisible War: The African American Anti-Slavery Resistance from the Stono Rebellion through the Seminole Wars.* Atlanta, GA: Clarity Press, 2008.

Leckie, William H. *The Military Conquest of the Southern Plains.* Norman: University of Oklahoma Press, 1963.

Logan, Rayford W. *The Betrayal of the Negro, from Rutherford B. Hayes to Woodrow Wilson.* New York: Da Capo, 1997.

Longacre, Edward G. *A Regiment of Slaves: The 4th United States Colored Infantry, 1863–1866.* Mechanicsburg, PA: Stackpole Books, 2003.

McConnell, Roland C. *Negro Troops of Antebellum Louisiana: A History of the Battalion of Free Men of Color.* Baton Rouge: Louisiana State University Press, 1968.

Mershon, Sherie, and Steven Schlossman. *Foxholes & Color Lines: Desegregating the U.S. Armed Forces.* Baltimore: Johns Hopkins University Press, 1998.

Moskos, Charles C, and John Sibley Butler. *All That We Can Be: Black Leadership and Racial Integration the Army Way.* New York: Basic Books, 1996.

Mulroy, Kevin. *Freedom on the Border: The Seminole Maroons in Florida, the Indian Territory, and Texas.* Lubbock: Texas Tech University Press, 1993.

Nevins, Allan, ed. *A Diary of Battle: The Personal Journals of Colonel Charles S. Wainwright, 1861–1865.* Gettysburg, PA: Stan Clark Military Books, 1962.

Quarles, Benjamin. *The Negro in the American Revolution.* Chapel Hill: University of North Carolina Press, 1996.

Rister, Carl Coke. *Land Hunger: David L. Payne and the Oklahoma Boomers— Primary Source Edition.* Norman: University of Oklahoma Press, 1942.

Robinson, Charles III. *Bad Hand: A Biography of General Ranald S. Mackenzie.* Abilene, TX: State House Press, 2005.

Sammons, Jeffrey T., and John H. Morrow Jr. *Harlem's Rattlers and the Great War: The Undaunted 369th Regiment and the African American Quest for Equality.* Lawrence: University Press of Kansas, 2014.

Schama, Simon. *Rough Crossings: Britain, the Slaves, and the American Revolution.* New York: HarperCollins, 2006.

Schubert, Frank N. *Out post of the Sioux Wars: A History of Fort Robinson.* Lincoln and London: University of Nebraska Press, 1995.

Sonnichsen, C. L. *The Mescalero Apaches.* Norman: University of Oklahoma Press, 1973.

Steward, T. G. *Buffalo Soldiers: The Colored Regulars in the United States Army.* Amherst, NY: Humanity Books, 2003.

Taylor, Quintard. *In Search of the Racial Frontier: African Americans in the American West, 1528–1990.* New York: W. W. Norton & Company, 1998.

Urwin, Gregory J. W., ed. *Black Flag Over Dixie: Racial Atrocities and Reprisals in the Civil War.* Carbondale: Southern Illinois University Press, 2004.

Ward, Andrew. *The Slaves' War: The Civil War in the Words of Former Slaves.* Boston: Houghton Mifflin, 2008.

Washington, Versalle F. *Eagles on Their Buttons: A Black Infantry Regiment in the Civil War.* Columbia: University of Missouri Press, 1999.

Williams, George Washington. *A History of the Negro Troops in the War of the Rebellion, 1861–1865.* New York: Fordham University Press, 2012.

Young, Alfred F., ed. *Beyond the American Revolution: Explorations in the History of American Radicalism.* DeKalb: Northern Illinois University Press, 1993.

Index

About the Author

DEBRA J. SHEFFER is Professor of History at Park University in Parkville, Missouri. She was a 2007 Fellow at the West Point Summer Seminar in Military History. Her published works include "Lincoln's Wartime Diplomacy and the Emancipation Proclamation" in *The Routledge Handbook of Military and Diplomatic History: The Colonial Period to 1877* and "The Convergence" in *A Companion to Custer and the Little Big Horn Campaign* from Wiley-Blackwell. Sheffer holds a PhD in Military History, United States History, and the History of Indigenous Peoples from the University of Kansas.